Counter-Terrorism

Counter-Terrorism

Community-Based Approaches to Preventing Terror Crime

Edited by

Basia Spalek
University of Derby, UK

COUNTER-TERRORISM: COMMUNITY-BASED APPROACHES TO PREVENTING TERROR CRIME
Introduction, selection and editorial matter © Basia Spalek 2012, 2016
Individual chapters © Contributors 2012, 2016
Softcover reprint of the hardcover 1st edition 2016 978-0-230-24213-5
Corrected Printing 2012

First published 2012
Published in paperback 2016 by
PALGRAVE MACMILLAN

Palgrave Macmillan in the UK is an imprint of Macmillan Publishers Limited, registered in England, company number 785998, of Houndmills, Basingstoke, Hampshire, RG21 6XS.

Palgrave Macmillan in the US is a division of Nature America, Inc., One New York Plaza, Suite 4500 New York, NY 10004–1562.

Palgrave Macmillan is the global academic imprint of the above companies and has companies and representatives throughout the world.

ISBN 978-1-349-31782-0   ISBN 978-1-137-00952-4 (eBook)
DOI 10.1057/9781137009524
Paperback ISBN: 978–1–137–59283–5
E-PUB ISBN: 978–1–137–00950–0

Distribution in the UK, Europe and the rest of the world is by Palgrave Macmillan®, a division of Macmillan Publishers Limited, registered in England, company number 785998, of Houndmills, Basingstoke, Hampshire, RG21 6XS.

Library of Congress Cataloging-in-Publication Data is available from the Library of Congress.

A catalog record for this book is available from the Library of Congress.

A catalogue record for the book is available from the British Library.

Typeset by MPS Limited, Chennai, India.

Contents

List of Figures

Preface

This book presents a series of chapters by leading authors in relation to community-based approaches to counter-terrorism. Whilst the majority of the contributions have come from academics who have undertaken research in relation to communities defeating Al-Qaeda-linked or influenced terrorism, the lessons learned and the key messages that are featured here are relevant when thinking about the role of communities in helping to counter other forms of ideologically or politically motivated violence. This book presents a unique set of approaches to preventing and responding to terrorism, which can be applied across different international contexts, albeit in different ways. Key issues that are addressed include: an analysis of community-focused and community-targeted approaches to counter-terrorism; the role of trust and community empowerment; the ways in which communities and police engage and can even enter into partnership with each other; the role of community policing; responses to terrorism in relation to questions of governance; the role of gender, youth and religion; and the ways in which socio-political contexts can create particular challenges for both communities and practitioners. As such, this book provides real insights into community-based approaches to counter-terrorism—insights which can help communities and practitioners, including police officers, who are involved in co-producing security within wide-ranging social, political and cultural locations. Importantly, implicit in this book is the notion of connectors being individuals who may experience community memberships in highly complex ways and are able to negotiate forms of frame alignment so that groups with very different positionalities are able to work with each other towards common goals.

Notes on Contributors

Jonathon Byrne is a lecturer in criminology and a member of the Institute for Research in the Social Sciences (IRiSS) at the University of Ulster. He has nearly 15 years' experience of working with the community and the voluntary sector in Northern Ireland in relation to policing. His current research focuses upon the peace divides of Northern Ireland, along with sectarian division and policy making. He has published numerous reports relating to Northern Ireland through the Institute for Conflict Research. He is also on the Board of Directors for the Community Relations Council for Northern Ireland.

Salwa El-Awa is a lecturer at Ain Shams University, Cairo, Egypt. Her expertise lies in researching international programmes of de-radicalization. She was also the co-investigator for two high-profile AHRC/ESRC-funded projects focusing upon exploring partnership approaches to challenging religiously endorsed violence involving Muslim groups and the police.

Abdul Haqq Baker is Lecturer in Terrorism Studies at the Centre for Studies in Terrorism and Political Violence (CSTPV) at the University of St Andrews and is a research associate at the European Muslim Research Centre (EMRC) at the University of Exeter. The focus of his PhD research at the University of Exeter was the phenomenon of violent extremism in the UK amongst Muslim converts, the subject of his paper being: 'Countering Extremism Locally: A Convert Community Perspective'. His book *Extremists in Our Midst: Confronting Terror* (Palgrave Macmillan) was published in July 2011. In 2010 he co-authored a report titled 'Muslim Communities Perspectives on Radicalisation in Leicester, UK' for the Centre for Studies in Islamism and Radicalisation (CIR), Department of Political Science, Aarhus University, Denmark. He has also co-authored a chapter with Basia Spalek and Robert Lambert, 'Minority Muslim Communities and Criminal Justice: Stigmatised UK Faith Identities Post-9/11 and 7/7', in H. Bhui (ed.), *Race and Criminal Justice*.

Laura Zahra McDonald is a research fellow within the Institute of Applied Social Studies at the University of Birmingham. Her research interests include Islam, gender and activism, Muslim experiences and critical perspectives of 'new terror', and the politics of diversity and identity. She is keen to develop the links between academic research, grassroots activism and public policy, particularly with regard to their impact on minority groups in Britain.

Basia Spalek is Reader in Communities & Justice within the Institute of Applied Social Studies at the University of Birmingham. Her research interests lie in community-based approaches to counter-terrorism, criminal and social justice in relation to minorities, and faith/ethnicity and diversity in relation to victimization. Along with with Salwa El-Awa, Laura McDonald and Robert Lambert, she has led two high-profile AHRC/ESRC-funded projects focusing upon exploring partnership approaches to challenging religiously-endorsed violence involving Muslim groups and police. She has written and edited a number of publications including: *Counter-Terrorism: Community-Based Approaches to Preventing Terror Crime* (Palgrave Macmillan, 2010); *Ethnicity and Crime: A Reader* (2008); *Communities, Identities and Crime* (2008); and *Crime Victims: Theory, Policy and Practice* (Palgrave Macmillan, 2006).

John Topping is a lecturer in criminology and a member of Institute for Research in the Social Sciences (IRiSS) at the University of Ulster. His research interests include policing, police reform and officer training. He has published widely on policing and has experience of engaging with policing organizations and acting as a consultant for the PSNI designing community policing training, as well as working with the Police Ombudsman for Northern Ireland on informal resolutions to officer complaints. He is also on the Board of Directors for Community Restorative Justice Ireland.

1
Introducing Counter-Terrorism Studies

Basia Spalek

Introduction

Traditionally, terrorism and counter-terrorism studies have been highly specialized fields, confined predominantly to the subject areas of political science, international relations and terrorism studies. Astonishingly perhaps, over the last ten years or so, there has been an enormous increase in the number of academics writing about terrorism and counter-terrorism from a wide range of different subject disciplines, including the arts, humanities and social science fields, such as policing studies, sociology, history, criminology, psychology, Islamic studies, religious studies, theology, law, anthropology and philosophy, alongside terrorism, critical terrorism studies, international relations and political science. Added to this, engineering, computer science and other 'hard' sciences have also increasingly focused upon questions of national security through developing and testing various new technologies that can be used for surveillance, risk identification and detection among other purposes.

There are a number of underpinning dynamics that have led to the rapid expansion of research into terrorism and counter-terrorism. For one thing, security is now a key research theme within research calls made by major research councils in the UK as well as in European and other international bodies funding research. Security is of course a broad concept, incorporating issues relating to poverty, exclusion, violence and racism, and perhaps is indicative of a wider malaise affecting the world, with issues like climate change, war and financial instability becoming more prevalent in recent years. Within security research strands, terrorism and countering terrorism are key and expanding areas, leading researchers increasingly to grapple with issues that for a long time have been marginalized in most mainstream academic disciplines. At the same time, the high-profile terrorist attacks on the World Trade Center on 11 September 2001, with the subsequent Bush administration-led 'War on Terror', underpinned by an increasingly accepted notion within policy circles of 'new terrorism', have stimulated academic and policy interest in terrorism and counter-terrorism. Moreover, alongside the maxim that 'communities can defeat terrorism' (Briggs *et al.*, 2006), communities have increasingly been expected to take part in counter-terrorism measures, which has helped to stimulate further academic and community-generated research and debate. There has also been a whole series of terror-related incidents around the world, some of which have been linked to or influenced by Al-Qaeda networks or groupings.

The growing variety of different academic perspectives on and different theoretical traditions in relation to terrorism and counter-terrorism is to be welcomed as this enables terrorism and counter-terrorism to become richly debated and hotly contested arenas, which can greatly benefit from a wealth of different voices and experiences. Nonetheless, it is important to highlight that, as with other academic and policy fields, some perspectives have become more dominant and commonly accepted than others, and that some researchers have cultivated better links with policy makers than others and so have been able to influence national and international responses to a greater degree. It may be that academic approaches that are policy-led and that tend to support government policy, rather than acting as a critical friend, are those best supported by governments and other elites, receiving large amounts of research funding. Other, more critical voices struggle for funding and for their work to be published, and are often marginalized from key arenas where policy is discussed and implemented.

Another interesting dynamic is the way in which counter-terrorism in the UK has been mainstreamed into the policies and practices of many statutory and non-statutory organizations across a wide range of sectors including education, children and youth services, criminal justice and local government. The work of practitioners within schools, universities, policing, prisons, probation and youth work is being influenced by counter-terrorism strategies largely developed by central governments keen to develop and impose top-down security policies through the involvement of individuals. Although communities are viewed as key to countering terrorism, at times there can be conflicts between community-led, 'bottom-up' approaches and state-driven agendas. Practitioners working with communities can on occasion find themselves having to negotiate their way through conflicting values or discourses – those arising from their work cultures, from government policy documents and approaches, their own personal values and perspectives as well as the values of community members that individuals are working with. Counter-terrorism is an incredibly complex and rich field, requiring considerable skill and expertise, and there is a concern that counter-terrorism policies and practices have been mainstreamed into society too quickly and far too broadly – potentially encompassing everybody – and yet there is much to be said of real expertise in this arena, expertise that is underpinned by a sound ethical basis in relation to a broader human rights framework. The unfortunate thing is that the detention centre at Guantanamo Bay in Cuba, the killing of Jean Charles de Menezes and other inappropriate counter-terrorism responses have tended to place the media spotlight onto poor professional practice rather than highlighting the positive practices of ethical counter-terrorism practitioners, those who often have had to resist the 'War on Terror' and the 'new terrorism' discourse for their unsound rationale and unethical bases.

Terrorism and counter-terrorism: some key terms

Terrorism

It is important to highlight and explain some key terms when looking at research, policy and practice in relation to terrorism and counter-terrorism. Terrorism itself is a deeply problematic and highly contested notion with multiple meanings (Wilkinson, 2006; Silke, 2008). For Wilkinson (2006: 6), terrorism 'is not a synonym for violence or insurgency in general, but it is a very broad concept. Terrorism is a weapon-system, which can be used by an enormous variety of groups and regimes with rapidly differing aims, ideologies and motivations'. Therefore, using this definition, both state and non-state actors can carry out acts of terrorism. According to the terminology used by the EU, which all EU Member States have agreed to use, 'terrorism is not an ideology but is a set of criminal tactics which deny the fundamental principles of democratic societies. Terrorist acts are those which aim to intimidate populations, compel states to comply with the perpetrators' demands, and/or destabilise or destroy the fundamental political, constitutional, economic or social structures of a country or an international organisation' (Europol TeSat, 2010: 5). A further important dimension to terrorism is its use as a means of communication; thus, for Schmid (2004), terrorism is not only about violence but is also a means of communication as propaganda. Schmid (2004: 205–6) argues that 'terrorism, by using violence against one victim, seeks to coerce and persuade others. The immediate victim is merely instrumental, the skin on a drum beaten to achieve a calculated impact on a wider audience'. Terrorism may also involve the tactic of provoking a particular response from the perceived enemy. For example, according to Al-Qaeda propagandist Saif al-Adl, 9/11 was intended to provoke the USA to 'lash out militarily against the ummah'[1] in the manner of, if not the scale of, the 'War on Terror' (Gerges, 2005: 270). 'The Americans took the bait', he continues, 'and fell into our trap', doubtless using hindsight to describe Al-Qaeda's ability to predict the massive scale and range of the response to 9/11 (Spalek *et al.*, 2008: 50). It is also important to note that strategies put forward by terrorists are not necessarily always implemented. Thus, according to Clarke and Soria (2010: 26):

> What terrorist groups would like to do, what they plan to do, and what they actually do in mounting attacks against a society are three completely different things. So much in the incidence of terrorism: the new wave terrorism is contingent on other factors: the quality of terrorist cells and their tradecraft, the effectiveness of counterterrorist measures, the competition between terrorists' reconnaissance and government intelligence, and the shares of good and bad luck in the circumstances of an active plot or attack.

Within terrorism studies, there has been significant discussion of 'old' and 'new' types of terrorism, with Neumann (2009) arguing that nowadays there is a new kind of terrorism due to factors associated with globalization and, importantly, Al-Qaeda terrorism may or may not constitute a 'new' form of terrorism. Nonetheless, it is important to stress that since 9/11, the notion of 'new terrorism' has gained increasing ascendancy across numerous policy, security, policing, media and other contexts, both nationally and internationally, particularly in relation to Al-Qaeda. 'New terrorism' constitutes a set of rationalities and technologies in relation to a so-called new form of terrorism that is global and indiscriminate, linked to groups associated with or influenced by Al-Qaeda. Importantly, this new form of terrorism, as constructed by 'new terrorism' discourses and technologies, is linked to Islam as a religion, thereby setting it largely outside understandings of terror crime as being a feature of national- and ethnic-based struggles around the globe; rather, the 'new terrorism' is said to be unbounded and uses indiscriminate targeting, while interpretations of Islamic texts and concepts are said to be used not only as a moral foundation but as sacred motivators and legitimizers. Jackson (2005: 10) has argued that Islam is viewed in a number of normative discourses, including academic discussions, to be the source of the 'threat'.

According to the *Oxford English Dictionary*, to counter something is to oppose it; therefore, to counter terrorism is to oppose terrorism. This is not to necessarily suggest, however, that terrorism precedes counter-terrorism, for counter-terrorism strategies may be in place as a result of a perceived rather than a real threat. Counter-terrorism strategies may also be part of a wider system of hegemonic control by the state, and so it may be that in some cases they play a significant role in producing terrorism.

Violent extremism

Within government counter-terrorism strategies, the notion of extremism, as well as violent extremism, is often mentioned, although rarely defined. Strands within counter-terrorism strategies aim to prevent people from being drawn towards violent and/or extremist positions. The difficulty with official discourse is that it tends to use extremism and violent extremism interchangeably, so it is unclear whether the target of government policy and practice is to prevent individuals from being extremists or whether it is to prevent individuals from being violent extremists. Being extreme itself should not be an issue, for extreme positions can be benign and indeed beneficial for society and for communities. According to the *Oxford English Dictionary*, 'extreme' can be defined as reaching a high or highest degree, as severe, stringent, lacking restraint or moderation. Interestingly, 'extremism' is defined by the *Oxford English Dictionary* as holding extreme or fanatical political or religious views and especially resorting to or advocating extreme action. Within this definition there is no clarity over what is meant by extreme action. According to Davies (2008), extremism is not about doing something extreme, as in the case of extreme sport, but, rather, extremism is thought of as the denial of other realities. Part of this may involve expressing hatred and violence towards others; however, because government policy and practice is not clear about whether extremism per se should be targeted or whether only violent extremism should be the focus, it is not clear what the goals of counter-terrorism are. Thus, does preventing terrorism within a counter-terrorism strategy involve reducing the propensity of individuals to commit acts of violence whilst holding their extremist positions intact, is the focus upon changing individuals at a more fundamental level, at the level of personal identity, so that they no longer hold extremist views, or is it a combination of the two? Moreover, what are the implications of the pursuit of these strategies in terms of people's civil liberties within Western democratic states? In addition, there is debate over the perceived and actual dangerousness of individuals holding extremist views. The Cantle Report (2001) on community cohesion, written in the aftermath of a series of disturbances in northern towns in the UK, has been hugely influential on counter-terrorism policy. According to the Cantle Report, ignorance about each others' communities can easily grow into fear, especially where this is exploited by extremist groups determined to undermine community harmony and foster divisions. The Report's authors further observed that although the physical segregation of housing estates and inner cities came as no surprise, they had been repeatedly struck by the degree to which the existence of 'separate educational arrangements, community and voluntary bodies, employment, places of worship, language, social and cultural networks means that many communities operate on the basis of a series of parallel lives'. For the authors of the Report, there needs to be a greater collective and individual effort on the part of all sections of the community to improve their knowledge and understanding of each other, and also for the largely non-white community to develop a greater acceptance of, and engagement with, the principal national institutions. However, this position is open to criticism as it seems to link a lack of community cohesion directly to extremism without offering any evidence of this tentative link. Additionally, are all individuals who hold extremist views a potential threat to nation-state security as they are all at risk of becoming violent extremists? According to the Quilliam Foundation, a heavily criticized think-tank on countering terrorism, four types of behaviours may be distinguished in Islamic extremism:

- *Political ideology*: the use of political propaganda that describes political systems and countries as Kufr or anti-Islamic.
- *Suspended morality*: the development of a mindset that distorts Islam and focuses on scripture alone without external guidance as to correct behaviour, leading to a position where violence can be justified.
- *Conspiratorial mindset and 'Westophobia'*: the tendency to view the West in general as the source of all evil.
- *Ultra-conservative outlook*: a literalist reading of Muslim texts (Teachernet, 2008).

Clearly, if individuals identified as holding any of the above positions are viewed as dangerous and requiring state surveillance and control, then it may be that large swathes of people are affected by counter-terrorism policies and practices, even though the notion of violence only features in one of the above positions. This issue takes us to another ill-defined notion – that of radicalization.

Radicalization

Radicalization is a notion that has been increasingly problematized in the aftermath of the terror attacks in London on 7 July 2005 and the attempted attacks on 21 July 2005, when considerable discussion was generated within the media and political arenas about the possible pathways to 'radicalization' that young men in particular may take, and the sites at which radicalization or extremist recruitment may occur (such as bookshops, mosques and community centres). Within these discussions, populations deemed 'at risk' from radicalization have been identified, including North African male immigrants; second- or third-generation Muslims, particularly Pakistani males; and those (predominantly Black Caribbean and East African)[2] males who have converted to Islam, whilst places that have been recognized as 'at risk' include universities, mosques, Islamic bookshops, youth centres and prisons. Nonetheless, sustained and detailed research exploring potential pathways to 'radicalization' is rare, as is public information about jihadist terrorists (Pargeter, 2006).

In the latest British counter-terrorism strategy, CONTEST 2, there appears to be a policy of the identification of clear-cut binaries and assumptions: moderate Muslim groups/individuals/communities have a duty and an ability to identify and isolate radicals – those with illegitimate beliefs, politics, values, grievances, expression and dissent – in order to prevent terrorism. Factors such as political activism, narrow interpretations of the Qur'an, travelling abroad and the glorification of martyrdom and martyrs have been propagated by state agencies as indicators of the potential movement of individuals towards violent extremism, requiring active intervention and monitoring and, in some cases, reporting and referral. Nonetheless, the theoretical and empirical bases of such analyses are suspect and, moreover, it is potentially possible to cast suspicion over any individual as the range of factors is so broad and encompasses majority rather than minority Muslim and other populations (Spalek and McDonald, 2009). It appears that the problematization of radicalization has deeper origins in US policy discourse, with the RAND Corporation's testimony 'Moderate and Radical Islam' (Rabasa, 2005) having become mainstreamed into British government counter-terrorism strategy. Echoing the aforementioned wording of CONTEST 2 (HM Government, 2009: 13) some four years earlier, Rabasa asserts:

> In some cases, the term radical or militant is defined in terms of support for terrorism or other forms of violence. We believe that this is too narrow a focus, that there is, in fact, a much larger universe of fundamentalist or Salafi groups who may not themselves practice violence, but that propagate an ideology that creates the conditions for violence and that is subversive of the values of democratic societies. (Spalek and McDonald, 2009: 127)

Further evidence of the notion of radicalization being viewed as problematic can be seen in a report published for the New York Police Department, where it is stated that:

> It is useful to think of the radicalization process in terms of a funnel. Entering the process does not mean one will progress through all four stages and become a terrorist. However, it also does not

mean that if one doesn't become a terrorist, he or she is no longer a threat. Individuals who have been radicalized but are not jihadists may serve as mentors and agents of influence to those who might become the terrorists of tomorrow. (Silber *et al.*, 2007: 10)

The question of what we mean by radicalization and whether there is a link with terrorism needs further exploration. Indeed, to what extent is radicalization different from radicalism? According to Dutch intelligence in 2007, radicalism is problematic, defined as 'the active pursuit of and/or support for fundamental change in society that may endanger the continued existence of the democratic order (aims), which may involve the use of undemocratic methods (means) that may harm the functioning of the democratic order'. But there is insufficient clarity here and an automatic assumption that radicalism is something negative, as something that threatens rather than enhances democratic society. Indeed, Dr Marcus Garvey, a Black Jamaican spiritual leader, once referred to radicalism as 'a label that is always applied to people who are endeavouring to get freedom' (Wilmore, 1999: 197). In the *Oxford English Dictionary*, the word 'radical' is defined in the following ways: far-reaching; thorough; advocating thorough reform; holding extreme political views, revolutionary; a fundamental principle, a basis. Therefore, there is much dispute around the notion of radicalization. It should be noted that practitioners are not necessarily passively receiving and responding to policies and practices that have been inspired by the problematization of the notion of radicalization, as many argue that this essentially means government policy attempting to depoliticize individuals, particularly Muslim minorities. As such, it is important to consider how and the ways in which practitioners and community members can resist rhetoric in order to put together far more inclusive, less value-orientated approaches in the successful prevention of terrorism, an issue that is returned to later on in this book.

Securitization

There is a danger that counter-terrorism policies and practices become too broad, encompassing wide sections of society, and so it is to another term that we now turn – the notion of securitization. First of all, it is important to briefly discuss the word 'security', for it is a complex and contested term. Within the discipline of international relations, which is the academic field that has traditionally dealt with security issues, security has tended to be viewed in military and state terms. This focus upon the state and the military has attracted considerable criticism, so security as a notion has been broadened out to include other dimensions such as migration, transnational crime and intrastate conflict (Wilkinson, 2007). Whilst issues of migration are being increasingly linked to questions of national security, it is also important to consider the ways in which migrant communities themselves understand and experience questions in relation to human security. The notion of security can therefore also encompass social issues within communities, including violence, poverty, exclusion, racism, mental and physical health, etc. Securitization, on the other hand, might be thought of as the instigation of emergency politics in that a particular social issue that becomes securitized is responded to above and beyond established rules and frameworks that exist within what might be termed 'normal politics' (Jutila, 2006).

Much has been written about the instigation and implementation of wide-ranging new laws and state powers in relation to the perceived new threat from 'new terrorism' post-9/11 (Pantazis and Pemberton, 2008; Zedner, 2008; McGovern, 2010). Powers and policies that have particularly been criticized include the Terrorism Act 2006, which extended the power to detain suspects without charge from 7 to 28 days because of the supposedly qualitatively different threat now posed; the use of the asylum system to detain Muslim foreign nationals and the extended powers of the Special Immigration Appeals Commission (SIAC) by the Anti-Terrorism, Crime and Security Act 2001 (McGovern, 2010); the recently rescinded power to designate places where people can be stopped and searched without reasonable grounds for suspicion under s. 44 of the Terrorism Act 2000; stop and searches under Schedule 7 to the Terrorism Act 2000; and the use of 'extraordinary rendition', with allegations of torture having taken place in detention facilities in Afghanistan and Guantanamo Bay. According to Lord Dear, the former Chief Inspector of Constabulary, 'the best course for a terrorist is to provoke a government into over-reacting to a security threat by eroding civil liberties, increasing executive powers and diminishing due process by the denial of justice' (*The Independent*, 2008). According to Pantazis and Pemberton (2009), recent experience of the political violence in connection with Northern Ireland suggests that the perceived and lived injustices of 'suspect' communities targeted by draconian counter-terrorism legislation does little to ensure greater public safety and may even serve to escalate conflict. Longstaff and Graham (2008) have argued that care must be taken to ensure that legislation introduced in response to the very real threat of terrorism does not lead, over time, to largely imperceptible but potentially irreversible changes in the freedoms taken for granted in advanced democracies. For Vincenzo (2008), the use of extraordinary rendition might be thought of as constituting a post-Fordist model of penal production where in the political and judicial vacuum that is created, there is space for a 'flexible' treatment of inmates, which means the denial of the rights of individuals. Thus, there is a danger that counter-terrorism policies and practices deny individuals their human rights and, in doing so, play into the hands of terrorist strategists, who not only recruit, inspire and promote terrorist movements, opening up and maintaining strategic presences within and across countries, but who also exploit local grievances for recruitment and propaganda purposes (Spalek *et al.*, 2008).

Rehabilitation

Rehabilitation is another key term when thinking about counter-terrorism. Rehabilitation in the context of preventing violent extremism might mean de-radicalization – 'the social and psychological process whereby an individual's commitment to, and involvement in, violent radicalisation is reduced to the extent that they are no longer at risk of involvement and engagement in violent activity' (Horgan, 2009: 141). Rehabilitation may also include an element of empowerment, where empowerment might be thought of as 'achieving reasonable control over one's destiny, learning to cope constructively with debilitating forces in society, and acquiring the competence to initiate change at the individual and systems levels' (Pinderhughes, 1983: 336). Within counter-terrorism practice, there are individuals who mentor those individuals deemed to be actual or potential violent extremists in order to reduce the likelihood that these individuals will engage in violent activities. Mentors build trusting relationships with their clients in order to try and reduce their set of vulnerabilities, where vulnerability might be defined as 'a feeling of insecurity, lack of self-confidence, low self-esteem, lack of trust in self and others, fear of the unknown, a sense of social injustice, feeling of being socially excluded and marginalised'. Vulnerability can be triggered by numerous factors, including a painful childhood, dysfunctional family life, racism, discrimination, a traumatic event (such as war), abuse by others, relationship breakdown, bullying, loss of job, unemployment, poverty, homelessness and poor education (Spalek *et al.*, 2010: 20). Therefore, mentors will work with a series of vulnerabilities, including political or religious ideological frameworks of understanding. Currently, it is not known whether the aim of mentoring is to reduce the propensity of individuals to commit acts of violence or whether it is about helping individuals to undergo personal transformations. Whilst desistance from acts of violence is measurable, changes in identity may not be or may require the specialist skills of mentors to assess accurately. Whilst primary desistance is a temporary state, secondary desistance is more long-lasting and may be possible to measure in terms of changes at the level of personal identity (Farrall and Maruna, 2004).

Counter-terrorism policy: national and international

The British government's main counter-terrorism strategy, CONTEST, and more recently CONTEST 2, contains four main strands of countering terrorism: protect, prevent, prepare and pursue. Protect involves strengthening defences against terrorist attacks; prevent involves stopping people becoming terrorists or violent extremists; prepare involves lessening the impact of terrorist attacks; and pursue involves disrupting plots and bringing terrorists to justice (Home Office, 2010).

The Prevent strategy was reviewed by the Conservative/Liberal Democrat government of the UK and this led to a publication of the Prevent Review in June 2011. The Prevent Review was long awaited by those working for public sector agencies within wide-ranging sectors such as criminal justice, health and education, and also by a broad array of community groups whose work has directly or indirectly been impacted by Prevent. The Review has raised questions such as which community groups who work towards preventing terrorism will have their funding cut or completely abolished and for what reasons? How much space will the Prevent Review give to bottom-up, locally-driven initiatives that draw upon the skills and knowledge of local community members? What implications does the Review have for police–community engagement and partnership in order to prevent terrorism? There appear to be a number of mixed messages in the Review. There is an acknowledgement of the government being committed to a fundamental shift of power away from central government to communities, families and individuals (through the 'Big Society') so that the knowledge, access and influence of people and communities to challenge extremist and terrorist ideology is valued. But there is also a further clear message in the Review: that the government will not fund or work with extremist groups where extremism is understood as meaning to be in active opposition to fundamental British values, including democracy, the rule of law, individual liberty and the mutual respect and tolerance of different faiths and beliefs. The Prevent Review is clear in positioning Al-Qaeda-linked or influenced terrorism as the most significant terrorist threat. This means that it is Muslim communities that will be the focus of attention, specifically regarding questions of who is or is not 'extremist'. It is concerning that all-encompassing labels like 'Salafi' and 'Islamist' will be used to judge individuals and groups as 'extremist', thereby denying access to government resources. The validity of government assessments according to which group is or is not 'extremist' is questionable, partly because within overarching categories there are important nuances and multiple positionings of individuals. At the same time, Islamic practices and identities that are religiously conservative and have a real or a perceived opposition to established secular values may be construed as 'extreme', particularly when considering that the broader socio-political context whereby neo-conservative politics have influenced counter-terrorism agendas so that Muslims' religious beliefs and practices have been characterized as 'moderate' or 'radical' and given that the settlement of Muslims in Europe and their claims for public recognition can be viewed as a threat by Western secular states which separate politics from religion. In local areas where there are currently community-focused interventions aimed at preventing terrorism, which include individuals and groups who could be labelled as 'extremist' under the Prevent Review, funding is being taken away from community organizations where the interventions are based. This may leave a vacuum for terrorist propagandists to exploit, particularly if those individuals and groups labelled as 'extremist' by the Prevent Review are precisely those that are able to pull individuals away from committing acts of violence. At the same time, it is important to consider that some areas where important preventative work is taking place are areas where there is significant poverty and violence. As part of a recent research study undertaken by Spalek *et al.* (2011), young people were interviewed from within deprived contexts who were the subjects of wide-ranging community-based initiatives alongside a focus upon preventing terrorism. Many of those interviewed spoke about the normalization of violence in their lives and some of the difficult encounters they had had with police officers. These young people came to these community centres not only because these centres provided them with something to do but also because they provided them with a safe space away from violence, whilst at the same time providing them with access to adults who are able to intervene in local, street-based disputes in order to make the environment safer for them (Spalek, 2011). It is therefore rather concerning that some of these community centres might stop receiving government funding because of a perceived label of 'extremist' being attached to them. It would appear that the Prevent Review is a top-down rather than bottom-up approach. It is underpinned by the speech given by the British Prime Minister David Cameron at a security conference in Munich in February 2011, where he referred to 'muscular liberalism', whereby those community groups deemed to hold ideologies and religious positionings not in line with values associated with integration would no longer receive state funding, and this includes counter-terrorism funding.

Similarly, since 9/11 and in the aftermath of a series of other terror attacks, in particular the terrorist attacks in Madrid and London in 2005, the EU has developed a counter-terrorism strategy built around four main strands. These strands are similar to those within the UK's CONTEST 2 strategy. The first is Prevent – to prevent people from turning to terrorism; the second is Protect – to protect citizens and critical infrastructure by reducing vulnerabilities; the third is Pursue – to pursue and investigate terrorists, impede planning, travel and communications, cut off funding and access to attack materials, and bring terrorists to justice; and the fourth is Respond – to respond in a coordinated way by preparing to manage and minimize the consequences of a terrorist attack by improving the capabilities to deal with the aftermath and by taking into account the needs of victims.[3] The synergies between the EU's counter-terrorism policy and that of the UK reflect how preventing and responding to terrorism increasingly involves efforts at an international as well as at a national level. Thus, the prevention of terrorism is being viewed as comprising national efforts as well as efforts involving international cooperation, as exemplified by the Council of Europe's Convention on the Prevention of Terrorism (2007). The Council of Europe has adopted this new Convention to increase the effectiveness of existing international texts on the fight against terrorism. It aims to strengthen the efforts of Member States to prevent terrorism and sets out two ways to achieve this objective:

– by establishing as criminal offences certain acts that may lead to the commission of terrorist offences, namely, public provocation, recruitment and training;
– by reinforcing co-operation on prevention both internally (national prevention policies) and internationally (modification of existing extradition and mutual assistance arrangements and additional means).

The Convention also contains a provision on the protection and compensation of victims of terrorism.[4] The United Nations (UN) has also put together a Global Counter-Terrorism Strategy, which was adopted by Member States on 8 September 2006. The Strategy aims to enhance national, regional and international efforts to counter terrorism. This was the first time that all Member States agreed to a common strategic approach to fight terrorism. This includes strengthening the state capacity to counter terrorist threats in order to better coordinate the counter-terrorism activities of the UN system.[5]

Interestingly, the Prevent Review in the UK stresses that whilst Al-Qaeda-linked or influenced terrorism continues to be a focus for government-led and other interventions, a broader set of extremisms will be targeted, including far-right extremism. This is because a common criticism of Prevent has been the almost exclusive targeting of Muslim communities. It is therefore likely that in the UK and across the EU a broader range of communities will be the subject of focus in the prevention of terrorism, particularly in light of the terrorism perpetrated by Anders Breivik on Utoya Island, 20 miles from Oslo in Norway, on 22 July 2011.

Indeed, the author is aware of mentoring schemes that exist for those deemed at risk of committing acts of violence influenced by far-right extremism. This reflects deeper historical, political, cultural and other roots in relation to hate crimes that are committed across the

EU, motivated by individuals with racial/religious/political and other prejudices or hatreds. For many years, non-governmental organizations (NGOs), as well as statutory agencies, have been working with hate crime offenders in order to try to reduce their propensity to engage in acts of violence (Goodey, 2008). Increasingly, within policy and practice contexts, overlaps between responding to the perpetrators of terrorism and responding to the perpetrators of hate crime are being acknowledged. For example, conferences are being held and partnership work and research are taking place, which involve statutory and non-statutory organizations and community groups, including a focus upon responding to both terrorism and hate crimes (Middlesex University, 2010). In addition, the use of the notion of violent extremism suggests increasing links between researching and responding to terrorism and hate crime, for the notion of violent extremism can capture both. Therefore, there are links between hate crime and terrorism that are clearly worth exploring, although these are beyond the scope of this book.

It is important to stress that although most of the work in this book is based upon research regarding community-based approaches, specifically in relation to Muslim communities (because of the almost exclusive focus upon Al-Qaeda terrorism), it is not only Muslim communities that may experience community-based counter-terrorism initiatives. Whilst raising questions specifically for Muslim communities, this book also examines broader issues in relation to community-based approaches to counter terrorism. These issues relate to questions of citizenship, social cohesion and governance, and form the subject matter of Chapters 2 and 9. Furthermore, Chapter 8 examines community-based approaches to counter-terrorism in Northern Ireland as a way of extending the discussions in this book to the communities there.

Assessing terrorist threats

Within the UK there exists a threat assessment system which assesses the risk from terrorist attacks according to the following five levels of threat:

- critical – an attack is expected imminently;
- severe – an attack is highly likely;

- substantial – an attack is a strong possibility;
- moderate – an attack is possible but not likely;
- low – an attack is unlikely.

This system of threat levels has been designed in order to keep members of the public informed about the risk of terrorism at any given time. It is also designed to assist police and other law enforcement agencies in terms of deciding how to allocate staff. Whilst MI5, the internal security service within the UK, is responsible for setting the risk level for Irish-related terrorism, the Joint Terrorism Analysis Centre (JTAC) is responsible for assessing and setting the threat from international terrorism. In September 2010, for example, the UK domestic terrorist threat was raised by MI5 from moderate to substantial, meaning that an Irish-related terrorist attack was a strong possibility. This was the first time an Irish-related threat assessment had been published.[6]

What kind of terrorist attacks are committed in the EU?

A good source of data in relation to the amount and kinds of terrorist attacks being committed within the EU are the TE-SAT reports, which are public documents that are published every year and can be downloaded from Europol's website.[7] The TE-SAT reports aim to provide law enforcement officials, policy makers and the general public with facts and figures regarding terrorism in the EU, while also seeking to identify trends in the development of this phenomenon. The data reported in the document comes from information provided and verified by law enforcement authorities in the EU Member States. TE-SAT stands for the EU Terrorism Situation and Trend Report. This was established in the aftermath of the 9/11 attacks in the USA as a reporting mechanism from the Terrorism Working Party of the Council of the EU to the European Parliament. The latest report of TE-SAT, which was published in 2010, highlights that EU Member States continue to be exposed to a serious threat from Islamist, ethno-nationalist and separatist terrorism, as well as from left-wing and anarchist terrorism. However, the overall number of terrorist attacks in all Member States in 2009, excluding the UK, decreased by 33 per cent compared to 2008 and is almost half that of the number of attacks reported in 2007. Data from the UK has been excluded from the 2010 report as a result of differences in the statistical criteria applied.

According to the 2010 TE-SAT report, in 2009, six Member States reported a total of 294 failed, foiled or successfully perpetrated terrorist attacks, while an additional 124 attacks in Northern Ireland were reported by the UK. Thirteen Member States, excluding the UK, arrested a total of 587 individuals on suspicion of offences related to terrorism, a figure which marks a decrease of 22 per cent in comparison to 2008 and of about 30 per cent in comparison to 2007. The majority of arrests were carried out on the basis of suspicion of membership of a terrorist organization. Other arrests were made for attack-related offences, which include the preparation of attacks, propaganda, the financing of terrorism and its facilitation. The financing of terrorism is a significant issue, and indeed, according to the 2010 TE-SAT report, substantial amounts of money are transferred from Europe to conflict areas using a variety of means. In relation to Islamist terrorism, the financing of terrorism and membership of a terrorist organization remain the most common reasons for arrests. Although much has been written about Al-Qaeda-linked and influenced 'new terrorism', statistics from the 2010 TE-SAT report suggest that this is only one type of terrorism that EU Member States face. For example, in 2009 France experienced the following set of failed, foiled or successfully executed attacks: 89 separatist, 0 left-wing, 0 right-wing, 0 Islamist, 1 single issue and 5 not specified. Italy experienced the following: 0 separatist, 2 left-wing, 0 right-wing, 1 Islamist, 0 single issue and 0 not specified (TE-SAT, 2010: 12). In relation to the issue of gender, it appears that terrorism is an act predominantly committed by men. In 2009 in the EU, women accounted for only 15 per cent of suspects arrested, compared to 10 per cent in 2007, and the majority of these arrests were for separatist terrorism. In the UK since 2000 there have been 20 significant jihadist terror plots. Such activities have resulted in the imprisonment of 235 people, with another 22 awaiting trial as of December 2009 (Clarke and Soria: 2010: 24). The difficulty with quantitative-based analyses of terrorism is that they often fail to take into consideration local complexities, an issue that will be discussed below.

Counter-terrorism studies: macro-, micro-, global, international and local dynamics

Prevalent within approaches to understanding terrorism are macro-level analyses that seek to plot transnational networks operating between actors that might generally be linked to particular movements or groupings of people that instigate or help support terror-related crime. These approaches often fail to take into consideration local contexts and dynamics. Nikolic-Ristanovic (2008) argues that it is important to have a real understanding of local conflicts and the real scope of human suffering in them, and there is a need to know the impacts of humanitarian interventions and international government in local contexts, which may at times exacerbate local violence and set the ground for fuelling the hatred of future generations. Nikolic-Ristanovic suggests that local conflicts usually have long and complex histories of different (ethnic, religious, political) group relationships, attacks and victimization, and are often accompanied by structural violence, have biased historical records and lack mutual confidence-building and reconciliation efforts. Zones of conflict may also have a history of denial and of the creation of multiple truths, with each group passing on its own truth from generation to generation, as well as a history of the exploitation of its own people's victimization (Nikolic-Ristanovic, 2008). Indeed, according to Findlay (2007), in contexts of deep conflict, disputes regarding 'truth' in relation to crime and victimization issues are often the factors that underpin violence, both locally and globally. Thus, what counts as 'real knowl-edge', whose voices are listened to and why, and how that listening is constructed are all particularly pertinent questions for localities which are characterized by violent and non-violent conflict.

In the post-9/11 era, Al-Qaeda-linked or influenced terrorism has been of particular research and policy interest. Al-Qaeda terrorism has been characterized as a form of 'new terrorism', as a recently evolved form of terrorism that is unique for its apparent lack of focused, bounded aims, the use of indiscriminate targeting and its drawing upon interpre-tations of Islamic texts and concepts not only as a moral foundation but as sacred motivators and legitimizers (Spalek and McDonald, 2009). The 'new terrorism' has been linked by neo-conservative strands in the USA and the UK to Salafi and Islamist movements, movements which have been viewed from an all-encompassing and homogenized approach that labels all Salafis and Islamists as dangerous and potential terrorists (Lambert, 2010). This approach has stigmatized these Muslim minorities, for it fails to acknowledge the diversity of identities, politi-cal affiliations, Islamic strands and positionings, etc. of the individuals identified within the broad and generalized labels of 'Salafi' and/or

'Islamist'. It may be that some Salafi and Islamist groups have the experience and credentials to help prevent terrorism and so, rather than being deemed as part of some kind of Al-Qaeda-type network, they should be viewed as citizens who can help the state prevent terrorism (Lambert, 2010). This implies that macro-level analyses of terrorism and counter-terrorism are insufficient, that there needs to be a greater emphasis upon micro-level analyses that explore individuals and their motivations in depth and the extent to which they have the requisite skills to counter terrorist propaganda.

An underlying theme within this book is that counter-terrorism research, policy and practice would benefit greatly from a focus upon local spaces and the actions undertaken by local actors to prevent terrorism. Terrorist strategists take advantage of local contexts in order to create new frameworks of grievance as a way of opening emotional and psychological spaces – so-called cognitive and emotional openings – within which they can influence individuals. As a result, it is of prime importance that local resilience is built through engaging with local actors in order to counter the narratives that terrorist strategists create. Of course, what is meant by 'local' is itself problematic and requires further exploration and analysis. For instance, a 'local' approach to countering terrorism includes a focus upon local spaces and contexts, a focus upon inter- and intra-community dynamics, as well as a focus upon individuals and inter- and intra-personal dynamics. Furthermore, engaging with local actors is not unproblematic, given the distrust generated by the 'War on Terror' as a result of state-led practices that have abused individuals' human rights across the globe. Therefore, engagement and partnership work within a counter-terrorism context is an emerging specialist area in itself, pioneered by the work of Briggs et al. (2006), Haqq Baker (2010), Lambert (2010) and Spalek (2010). As highlighted in the next chapter, where community-based approaches to counter-terrorism are discussed at length, traditionally countering terrorism has not been viewed as requiring the support of communities. Nonetheless, increasingly, community support is being sought and, indeed, communities are viewed as being an important ally in helping to prevent terrorism. The involvement of communities in counter-terrorism initiatives raises many questions, some of which this book aims to answer. These questions include the following:

- What empirical evidence exists of engagement and partnership between state actors and communities in preventing terrorism? In particular, how do the police work with Muslim communities to in order to prevent religio-political extremism amongst Muslim youth? To what extent is such work characterized by partnership? To what extent is trust an important element in partnership work? How, in what ways and to what extent are state actors, including police officers, and Muslim community members involved in trust-building activities when engaging with each other? How does this work when involving youth? What are the components of trust within partnership work? What factors serve to help undermine trust (for example, British foreign policy)? To what extent is a multi-agency environment helping to shape counter-terrorism policy and practice?

Overview of the coverage of this book

This book consists of an edited collection of nine chapters. The main theme underpinning all of the chapters is that of the notion of community, how counter-terrorism policies and strategies might increasingly engage with, and incorporate, the notion of community. Chapter 2 considers the significance of the notion of community for counter-terrorism policy and practice. It highlights the complexity of the notion of community, but it is stressed here that although community is a fluid and difficult to define term, this does not mean that it is not relevant for countering terrorism. The chapter makes an important distinction between community-focused and community-targeted approaches to counter-terrorism and stresses that policy makers and practitioners need to reflect upon the strategies they are engaged with in relation to how community-targeted or how community-focused they are. This chapter also argues that key characteristics of a community-focused approach appear to be the existence of partnerships between communities and state officials, the existence of community consent and participation in the actual governance of the various strategies and approaches that are applied, and the existence of trust between state officials and security practitioners and community members. It is a challenge for counter-terrorism policy and practice to develop community-focused approaches. Chapter 3 focuses on examining policing in relation to counter-terrorism, particularly community policing models. It highlights the important role that community policing can play in a counter-terrorism context. Within a context of fear and distrust generated by 'hard' policing strategies, it seems that community policing has an important role to play in building trust between communities and the police. However, the chapter highlights that the utilization of community policing within a counter-terrorism context is not without its difficulties. In order for community-based policing not to be viewed as little more than a public relations exercise or as a form of 'soft power' whereby communities are viewed primarily as informants, it is important for police officers to engage with communities so as to empower communities and support independent community interests. This work is itself difficult, however, given that the values associated with community policing may clash with the values more commonly associated with intelligence-led models of policing, and so effective police practitioners within this field need to be able to negotiate conflicting values. Chapter 4 examines and discusses the effectiveness of partnership approaches between statutory agencies and Muslim communities, particularly insofar as they precede the more recent former government's Prevent strategy, which was aimed at empowering and facilitating the very same communities. It also highlights a few strategies being implemented by the 2009 award-winning STREET programme in relation to its methodology of engagement with its target audiences. The work described perhaps supports arguments in favour of the grassroots, bottom-up approach to countering not only violent radicalization but also social issues which continue to affect the 'Big Society' at its core insofar as it relates to the disconnection and disaffection of some second- and third-generation Muslims and converts. The chapter concludes by raising the issue that although there is a general consensus on the inclusion and necessity of grassroots, community-led organizations in successful counter-radicalization initiatives, there is disagreement regarding the type or ideological profile of communities and organizations that should be involved or receive public funding. It is likely that these debates will continue for the foreseeable future. Chapter 5 focuses on gender issues in relation to community-based approaches to counter-terrorism. It highlights that the most hard-edged community work – with violent extremist groups, gangs and prisoners, for example – has been male-dominated. However, Muslim women are involved in community-led approaches to countering terror crime and are thus contributing significantly. Women are engaging individuals with violent extremist ideas, supporting community members affected in various ways by terror crime and counter-terrorism practices, and building trusting relationships between different community groups and state actors. As members of Muslim communities, as women and as British citizens, they are contributing to the building of a more holistic approach to security, one which highlights the need for human and community security as well as state security, and in which women are acknowledged as actors who must be recognized and engaged with. Chapter 6 looks at youth in relation to counter-terrorism. It notes that young Muslims have felt the impact of counter-terrorism policies and practices most acutely. In particular, those considered vulnerable to violent extremism have become a focal point for the security agenda. Yet, despite this difficult context, grassroots initiatives are succeeding in engaging young people not in order to neutralize or suppress, but to empower and support. This chapter explores this in more detail. Chapter 7 examines religion, theology and counter-terrorism. It looks at the role of religion and religious knowledge in counter-terrorism work between the police and communities, and focuses on whether religion comes into counter-terrorism work; whether religion and religious belief help or hinder counter-terrorism; whether partnerships with individuals and groups who have particular religious affiliations are useful to the police in counter-terrorism work or whether religion has been a cause of tension in these cases; and the nature and role of the religiosity of individuals in relation to motivating Muslim community members in the field of counter-terrorism. The chapter concludes by suggesting that counter-terrorism increasingly involves engaging with Muslim minorities and that engagement between police and Muslim communities is complex and in constant flux. A further issue that this chapter focuses on is the work of Muslim police officers working in counter-terrorism. It may be that for Muslim police officers to become involved in counter-terrorism policing, they first need to trust the aims and objectives of the counter-terrorism operations that they are being asked to engage in. Chapter 8 explores the reform of policing and the introduction of community policing in Northern Ireland since the peace process. It proposes that there is little evidence to suggest that 'softer' styles of policing by the Police Service of Northern Ireland (PSNI) will have any discernable effect upon the terrorist threat posed by dissident Republican factions. Although there are some examples of good practice at a local level, these are small in scale given the complex, dynamic and deep-rooted 'Northern

Ireland problem', which simultaneously demands 'normal' policing yet the operationalization of which is tainted by the political legacy of counter-terrorism measures of the past. Chapter 9 comprises a conclusion, asking wider questions about community-based approaches to counter-terrorism and raising some key issues for future research, policy and practice.

Notes

1. The community of believers.
2. The would-be suicide bombers of 21 July 2005 were predominantly of Somali and Ethiopian origin, none of whom was born in the UK, although most attended school here. Almost all were converts. For example, Hamdi Isaac and his wife converted from being Orthodox Copts to Wahabi Muslims. Mukhtar Ibrahim converted to the same strand after a brief criminal career and five years in prison.
3. http://ec.europa.eu/home-affairs/policies/terrorism/terrorism_intro_en.htm (date accessed 4 December 2011).
4. http://conventions.coe.int/Treaty/EN/Summaries/Html/196.htm (date accessed 4 December 2011).
5. www.un.org/terrorism/strategy-counter-terrorism.shtml (date accessed 4 December 2011).
6. www.homeoffice.gov.uk/media-centre/news/terrorist-threat (date accessed 4 December 2011).
7. www.europol.europa.eu (date accessed 4 December 2011).

References

Briggs, R., Fieschi, C. and Lownsbrough, H (2006) 'Bringing It Home. Community-based Approaches to Counter-terrorism'. Demos, www.demos.co.uk/files/Bringing%20it%20Home%20-%20web.pdf (date accessed 4 December 2011).
Cantle Report (2001) *Community Cohesion: A Report of the Independent Review Team*, chaired by Ted Cantle. London: Home Office, http://resources.cohesioninstitute.org.uk/Publications/Documents/Document/DownloadDocumentsFile.aspx?recordId=96&file=PDFversion (date accessed 4 December 2011).
Clarke, M. and Soria, V. (2010) 'Terrorism: The New Wave', *RUSI Journal* 155(4): 24–31.
Davies, L. (2008) *Educating Against Extremism*. Stoke-on-Trent: Trentham.
Europol TeSat (2010) 'EU Terrorism Situation and Trend Report', www.consilium.europa.eu/uedocs/cmsUpload/TE-SAT%202010.pdf (date accessed 4 December 2011).
Farrall, S. and Maruna, S. (2004) 'Desistance-Focussed Criminal Justice: Introduction to a Special Issue on Desistance from Crime and Public Policy', *Howard Journal of Criminal Justice* 43(4): 358–67.

Findlay, M. (2007) 'Terrorism and Relative Justice', *Crime, Law and Social Change* 47: 57–68.

Gerges, F.A. (2005) *The Far Enemy: Why Jihad Went Global*. Cambridge University Press.

Goodey, J. (2008) 'Racist Violence in Europe: Challenges for Official Data Collection', in B. Spalek (ed.), *Ethnicity and Crime: A Reader* (Maidenhead: McGraw-Hill), pp. 185–203.

Haqq Baker, A. (2010) 'Countering Extremism Locally: A Convert Muslim Perspective', PhD thesis, University of Exeter.

HM Government (2006) *Countering International Terrorism: The United Kingdom's Strategy*, Cm 6888. London: The Stationery Office.

——. (2009) *Pursue, Prevent, Protect, Prepare: The United Kingdom's Strategy for Countering International Terrorism*, Cm 7547. London: Home Office.

Home Office (2010) 'What We're Doing', www.homeoffice.gov.uk/counter-terrorism/what-we-are-doing (date accessed 4 December 2011).

Horgan, J. (2009) *Walking Away from Terrorism*. London: Routledge.

The Independent (2008) 'Government Abandons 42-Day Detention Plan', 13 October, www.independent.co.uk/news/uk/politics/government-abandons-42day-detention-plan-960075.html (date accessed 6 January 2012).

Jackson, R. (2005) *Writing the War on Terrorism: Language, Politics and Counter-Terrorism*. Manchester University Press.

Jutila, M. (2006) 'Desecuritizing Minority Rights: Against Determinism', *Security Dialogue* 37(2): 167–85.

Lambert, R. 2010. 'The London Partnerships: An Insider's Analysis of Legitimacy and Effectiveness', unpublished dissertation in partial fulfilment of PhD degree, University of Exeter.

Longstaff, A. and Graham, J. (2008) 'Anti-Terrorism and Police Powers: Should We Be Concerned?', *Criminal Justice Matters* 73: 15–16.

McGovern, M. (2010) 'Countering Terror or Counter-Productive? Comparing Irish and British Muslim Experiences of Counter-Insurgency Law and Policy', report of a Symposium held in Cultúrlann McAdam Ó Fiaich, Falls Road, Belfast, 23–24 June 2009, www.edgehill.ac.uk/documents/news/CounteringTerror.pdf (date accessed 6 January 2012).

Middlesex University (2010) 'Tackling Hatred Head On: Working with Hate Crime Offenders', Symposium, 21 September.

Neumann, P. (2009) *Old and New Terrorism*. Cambridge: Polity Press.

Nikolic-Ristanovic, V. (2008) 'Local Conflicts and International Interventions: Victimisation of Civilians and Possibilities for Restorative Global Responses', *Contemporary Justice Review* 11(2): 101–15.

Pantazis, C. and Pemberton, S. (2008) 'Trading Civil Liberties for Greater Security?: The Impact on Minority Communities', *Criminal Justice Matters* 73: 12–14.

Pargeter, A. (2006) 'North African Immigrants in Europe and Political Violence', *Studies in Conflict and Terrorism* 29(8): 731–47.

Pinderhughes, E.B. (1983) 'Empowerment for our Clients and for Ourselves: Social Casework', *Journal of Contemporary Social Work* 64(6): 331–8.

Rabasa, A. (2005) 'Moderate and Radical Islam', CT-251, testimony presented before the House Armed Services Committee Defense Review Terrorism and Radical Islam Gap Panel on 3 November 2005, RAND Corporation testimony series, www.rand.org/content/dam/rand/pubs/testimonies/2005/RAND_CT251.pdf (date accessed 4 December 2011).

Schmid, A. (2004) 'Frameworks for Conceptualising Terrorism', *Terrorism and Political Violence* 16(2): 197–221.

Silber, M.D. and Bhatt, A. (2007) *NYPD Intelligence Division Radicalization in the West: The Homegrown Threat.* New York Police Department.

Silke, A. (2008) 'Holy Warriors: Exploring the Psychological Processes of Jihadi Radicalization', *European Journal of Criminology* 5(1): 99–123.

Spalek, B. (2010) 'Community Policing, Trust and Muslim Communities in Relation to "New Terrorism"', *Politics & Policy* 38(4): 789–815.

——. (2011) '"New Terrorism" and Crime Prevention Initiatives Involving Muslim Young People in the UK: Research and Policy Contexts', *Religion, State and Society* 39: 2–3.

Spalek, B. and Davies, L. (2010) *Key Evaluation Findings of West Midlands 1-2-1 Mentoring Project,* University of Birmingham.

Spalek, B., Davies, L. and McDonald, L.Z. (2010) 'Key Evaluation Findings of the West Midlands 1-2-1 Mentoring Project', University of Birmingham.

Spalek, B., Lambert, R. and El-Awa, S. (2008) 'Preventing Violent Extremism in Prison: Key Policy and Practice Issues', *Prison Service Journal*: 45–54.

Spalek, B. and McDonald, L.Z. (2010) 'Anti-Social Behaviour Powers and the Policing of Security', *Social Policy and Society* 9(1): 123–33.

Spalek, B., McDonald, L.Z. and El-Awa, S. (2011) 'Preventing Religio-Political Violent Extremism Amongst Muslim Youth: A Study Exploring Police–Community Partnerships', University of Birmingham.

Vincenzo, S. (2008) 'The Sweatshops of Penality: Guantanamo, the Renditions and Post-Fordist Penality', *Criminal Justice Matters* 73: 31–2.

Wilkinson, P. (2006) 'Terrorism', in M. Gill (ed.), *The Security Handbook.* Basingstoke: Palgrave Macmillan.

Wilkinson, C. (2007) 'The Copenhagen School on Tour in Kyrgyzstan: Is Securitization Theory Useable Outside Europe?', *Security Dialogue* 38(5): 5–25.

Wilmore, G. (1999) *Black Religion and Black Radicalism,* third edn. New York: Orbis Books.

Zedner, L. (2008) 'Terrorism, the Ticking Bomb, and Criminal Justice Values', *Criminal Justice Matters* 73: 18–19.

2
Community-Based Approaches to Counter-Terrorism

Basia Spalek

Introduction

Community itself is a complex and contested notion; however, in this chapter the significance of community for counter-terrorism policy and practice is discussed. The relevance of the notion of community in relation to countering terrorism has generated some discussion, particularly in relation to communities actively and/or passively supporting terrorism and the relevance of this for counter-terrorism initiatives. This chapter first explores the notion of community in relation to terrorism and counter-terrorism. Community-focused and community-targeted counter-terrorism is then conceptualized and discussed, before the coverage turns more specifically to community-based approaches and Muslim communities.

This chapter aims to illustrate that as a result of mass migration, globalization and shifting national and international borders, alongside the significant presence of international ethnic and faith diasporas whose loyalties are not necessarily given to the nation state in which individuals reside, security policies and strategies should increasingly focus upon the notion of community, for it is within communities that individual and collective identities are expressed and contested. It is within communities that the legitimacy of terror and counter-terror tactics, acts and ideological and other justifications are debated, experienced and challenged. Thus, community should be a key notion in terrorism studies and in counter-terrorism research, policy and practice. Currently in the UK, within counter-terrorism policy, the notion of community features as both object and subject; as object because the (Muslim) community is problematized and targeted by state policies and practices that place nation-state security over community concerns; and as subject because within counter-terrorism there is space for community members to be active participants in the delivery of outcomes and to actively question and scrutinize counter-terrorism policies and practices. These aspects to communities and counter-terrorism can at times conflict, creating tensions, especially between counter-terrorism practitioners and community members. Indeed, there are often struggles within and between communities, and indeed between communities and the state, over issues relating to the governance of counter-terrorism strategies, the actual implementation of these and how effectiveness is to be conceptualized and examined. This chapter examines some of these tensions, illustrating how community is a site at which the social world is experienced, acted upon and understood, even though these sites may be temporary, in constant flux and underpinned by power relations. A key tension that is focused upon is that of what may be thought of as comprising a community-targeted approach as opposed to a community-focused approach. It is suggested that whilst some counter-terrorism policy officials, practitioners and communities actively promote a community-targeted approach, others involved in counter-terrorism promote a community-focused approach. It is likely that tensions between the two approaches will be ongoing for the foreseeable future.

'Community': a neglected concept in terrorism and counter-terrorism research, policy and practice

Community and counter-terrorism

Whilst the notion of community features within peace-building literature, there remains a level of contestation over the relevance of the notion of community to counter-terrorism. For example, terrorism may be thought of as the actions of a network of individuals who lie outside of communities. Furthermore, studies of counter-terrorism policing show uncertainty if community involvement indeed prevents extremism; nonetheless, according to Gregory (2009), it is still important to investigate these processes. The relevance of community to counter-terrorism might be thought of as complex and sensitive, relying on the careful construction of certain forms of community engagement rather than an all-encompassing claim that 'communities defeat terrorism', with the quality of the engagement depending on the delicate design of the cooperation. Several policy documents in the UK relate the view of the centrality of community to the prevention or support of violent extremisms. Rooted within the Northern Ireland experience, 'communities defeat terrorism' has become an accepted counter-terrorism maxim (Briggs et al., 2006: 83; Lambert, 2010a: 4), as evidenced by the Prevent strategy. This features the notion that effective community engagement and the winning of 'hearts and minds' stems from a local, 'bottom-up' approach (Briggs *et al.*, 2006: 1). There is thus a major onus on community ability and responsibility for counter-terrorism, with the need for faith-based approaches and openness about engagement with faith and faith communities (Briggs *et al.*, 2006: 15–16, 59). The notion that communities can defeat terrorism includes engagement and partnership work between communities and police officers, through a number of different mechanisms, both nationally and locally. According to Demos (Briggs *et al.*, 2006), there is a need to get away from 'the community' and respond to diversity; police and other state agencies must engage more openly with faith groups and those on the periphery, such as Salafis. Morevoer, this needs to be more transparent – state agencies should respond openly to grievances and make room for discussion on topics that may provoke grievances, for example, foreign policy.

Discussions have featured the extent to which community support for terrorism should be viewed as an issue for counter-terrorism. Some perspectives seem to support the notion that generalized support for terrorism is a real issue and that counter-terrorism should seek to challenge this wider support. For example, according to the West Midlands Police Authority:

> Beyond the small core of active or potentially active extremists, and the members of the radical political movements that surround them, there appears to be a much larger group of British Muslims who are morally ambivalent and who are unwilling to explicitly condemn the violent extremists. Polls carried out by a number of respected survey organisations indicate that this figure may amount to between 10 and 20% of the total Muslim population in Britain. (WMPA, 2008: 9)

According to Anderson (2011), violence committed for or in the name of communities – at local, national and transnational levels – is an important dynamic to consider, as popular support is necessary for social change. Community perceptions of the legitimacy or not of violence should also be considered (Anderson, 2011), as should the theological influence in relation to such perceptions, for example, in the case of martyrdom. Social and political factors should also feature when trying to understand community support for terrorism. Social factors like poverty or disenfranchisement can play a role (Schmid, 2007) and, according to Alden:

> the social nature of suicide terrorism makes societal support a necessary ingredient for its continued occurrence. (Alden, 2009)

It is important to stress that support within communities may fluctuate. According to Crenshaw:

> Lack of popular support at the outset of a conflict does not mean that the terrorists' aims lack general appeal. Even though they cannot immediately mobilize widespread and active support, over the course of the conflict they may acquire the allegiance of the population. (Crenshaw 1981: 388)

Furthermore, passive support by communities may comprise the 'backbone' of terrorist action; thus, according to Galam (2002: 269), only one passive supporter is needed to aid/allow a terrorist at any one time. Thus, counter-terrorism policy and practice should aim towards reducing community support:

> The strategic center of gravity for militant Islamic terrorist groups is the popular support of the Muslim world. Popular support provides the terrorists [with] invaluable sources of funding, manpower, legitimacy, and the real potential to threaten entrenched governments in Muslim countries. Without this popular support, Osama bin Laden and other violent global Muslims will not be able to achieve their desired end-state. (Kohn, 2002: 4)

Furthermore, there appear to be a number of factors that affect popular and/or community support for terrorism. It is important to consider the social programmes that some terrorist groups may provide, for example, the charitable work supported by Hamas. The IRA responded to law and order issues in Northern Ireland when police were distrusted by the majority of Catholics. The suffering of the collective may also influence public support in that if the atrocities committed by terrorists are deemed disproportionate and have created significant suffering within a community, then support for the terrorist group(s) may decline (Bloom, 2004). State repression may also influence popular support:

> Rather than closing the gap between the Asian-Muslim population and wider British society, in the 2007 policy the DCLG have singled out a specific group and like the PTA, this group is treated differently to the rest of British society. Additionally, by coupling attempts to treat community-based alienation but not state-based alienation with hardline legislation such as the PTA and ATCSA, British policy-makers create a situation whereby state forces have to maintain their vigilance against 'at risk' communities and respond forcefully to attempted attacks. With this heightened sense of an existing threat from a specific community, British counterterrorist policies can contribute to the distancing of state actors from that community and the radicalisation process. Such hardline tactics serve to construct a dangerous other, distance state forces from communities and legitimise the use of radical action. (Duffy, 2009: 140)

Understanding 'community'

Added to the above discussions, the notion of 'community' is problematic and highly contested. In a previous book, for example, I have argued that the term 'community' can be a catch-all phrase used by the government as a way of simplifying, merging and combining complex social identities and groupings for the purposes of policy development and implementation. Furthermore, although the term 'community' gives the outward impression of neutrality, the ways in which the term tends to be used and operationalized by the government suggests that it is loaded with assumptions about the kinds of social identities that are included, as well as fostered, for the purposes of community participation, engagement and scrutiny of performance. I further argued that it seems to be the case that those sections of the community that help the state to legitimize its power are often encouraged and approached by statutory agencies, though not necessarily in a conspiratorial way (Spalek, 2008).

Although the notion of community is problematic and can only ever be partially understood in relation to micro- and macro-level fluctuations in relation to wide-ranging factors like history, politics, geography, religion, culture, etc., it is important to stress here that communities constitute sites at which the social world is experienced, acted upon and understood, even though these sites may be temporary, in constant flux and underpinned by power relations. Many communities might be thought of being both local and geographically specific, as well as containing both a local, geographical dimension and consisting of connections between individuals across wider spaces in relation to factors like ethnicity, culture, politics, etc. Some communities have been conceptualized as consisting of 'diasporas', which are both local and global in character, with the development of new technologies having enabled dispersed populations to interact and link together important parts of their social and cultural lives (Gilroy, 2002). In diasporas individual members gain a sense of belonging, devising narratives about themselves and their origins, about how they are linked to broader global religions, nationalities and/or ethnicities as well as to localities that are 'simultaneously home and a place of exile' (Rew and Campbell, 1999: 167). Significant heterogeneity is to be found within international diasporas with respect to factors like class, education and generational cohort, and so whilst claiming a broader group identity, individuals may also live with the fragmented and plural nature of the particular diaspora(s) with which they associate themselves (Kennedy and Roudometof, 2004).

Community as a concept encompasses both individual and group identities and dynamics, both influencing and being influenced by these. Community might be thought of as a space of belonging, consisting of one or more of a combination of geographical, imaginative, emotional, political and other ties. Importantly, it is the contours of the space called community and how these contours link with wider social structural dynamics that both shape and are shaped by individual and group actions. For example, the conflict between Palestine and Israel may cause a small group of young British Muslims to paint a mural showing their support for the Palestinians on a wall outside a community centre in inner-city Birmingham and filming this to post on YouTube. Community comes in here because not only might these young people have a sense of belonging to a small geographical neighbourhood within Birmingham, as well as to a wider, international Muslim community, but the community (whether consisting of geographical, familial, religious, ethnic, emotional or political ties) will also shape, and be shaped by, this action, and will determine, as well as be determined by, the nature and extent of any impacts here, whether these impacts are political, religious and so forth. The impacts that this action might generate may include discussions within communities about what these young people have done and whether this is to be viewed positively or negatively, and may include future similar activities being performed by other groups or individuals belonging to the same or other communities of belonging, as well as anti-Muslim activities and sentiments by individuals and groups supporting Israel. As such, the actions of any one individual or group of individuals, it is being suggested here, will reverberate within and between wide-ranging and overlapping communities, shaping as well as being shaped by communities.

Whilst key thinkers have conceptualized community as consisting of shared meanings between individuals and groups (Lash, 1994) – for example, according to Kennedy and Roudometof (2004: 6), 'communities are units of belonging whose members perceive that they share moral, aesthetic/expressive or cognitive meanings, thereby gaining a sense of personal as well as group identity' – there is insufficient exploration here of community as a dynamic process, as a space of engagement, dialogue and conflict, a space that is subject to both micro- and macro-level fluctuations that link to wider political, social, economic and other factors. As such, community might be thought of as a space undergoing constant transformation, as an organic process that matters as a site for social policy because it directly influences wide-ranging social issues whilst also being shaped by these. Nonetheless, community as a concept has often been largely omitted from analyses of terrorism and counter-terrorism. Whilst identity as a notion has generated substantial research and policy interest in relation to terrorism, the notion of community has often been omitted, even though community might be thought of as the space within which identities reside and operate, as a space that influences and is influenced by identities, the space where individual and group collective identities are expressed and contested, as will be further explained below.

As a result of mass migration, globalization and shifting national and international borders, alongside the significant presence of international ethnic and faith diasporas whose loyalties are not necessarily given to the nation state in which individuals reside, security policies and strategies, and indeed research, have increasingly focused upon the notion of identity. Moisi (2009) has argued that within an increasingly globalized world, where nation-state borders are increasingly questioned and changing, struggles over identity have replaced ideological struggles. The emergence of new legislation in relation to terrorism has increased the powers of the police, extended the limits of the laws which govern policing and has placed a burden on the police to assess and decide upon those thought to be at risk of committing acts of terrorism. The need for the police to assess risk has invariably led to sections of the population being subject to criminal law sanctions on the sole basis of possessing certain identity characteristics (Lambert, 2008; Walklate and Mythen, 2008). Identities viewed as being particularly 'at risk' from engaging in Al-Qaeda-linked or motivated terrorism within policing and security circles are religious and political identities in relation to Islam, notably Salafis and Islamists, as well as specific ethnic groupings that intersect with Islam – in particular, Black Caribbean and African Muslim converts, and Pakistani and Somali ethnic Muslims. Security policies and practices have increasingly turned towards a focus upon identity with respect to processes of radicalization and associated risks in relation to committing acts of terrorism. For example, according to Choudhury (2007), risk factors associated with radicalization include individual factors such as individuals' attitudes and their sense of identity, and interpersonal dynamics such as individuals' interactions with radicalized groups/individuals. There is also wider discussion about the long-term consequences of empowering certain groups to work with individuals deemed vulnerable to violent radicalization, as within some security circles these groups are considered to have 'extreme' identities that should not be encouraged within a liberal state democracy.

Within the focus of identity in relation to security research, policy and practice, community is often overlooked, yet it is within communities that individual and group identities are played out, contested and so forth. All communities are likely to contain a dimension of fantasy and imagination, whereby myths of commonality may be created. Colic-Peisker (2004) argues, for instance, that within diasporas, ideological mechanisms may be at play that create imagined communities through myths of common history, ancestry and interests. Castells (2004) suggests that all communities can be viewed as imagined if we take the position that all feelings of belongingness are culturally constructed. Thus, if all communities work through minds, attitudes and discourses, as well as through geographical locales or social, familial and other ties, then it is clear that terrorism and counter-terrorism strategists and actors aim to influence the very construction of communities, the particular forms of belongingness experienced and expressed within and through communities. They may do so through perpetrating acts of violence and intimidation, as well as through constructing and perpetuating narratives aimed at gaining communities' support for their causes, aims and methods through the various multimedia, social and political channels that operate within communities and across wider society. Community spaces can be and are penetrated by terrorists and those working in counter-terrorism in order to influence the kinds of individual and group collective identities that are tolerated, actively encouraged, expressed and contested within communities.

A feature that is rarely discussed within the literature on community is how communities can provide safe spaces in which extreme (meaning those lying outside of the mainstream) views and actions can be expressed and supported. It is likely to be the case that in mainstream society any views and non-violent acts deemed 'extreme' are not tolerated and discussion is closed down (Spalek *et al.*, 2010). Thus, it is within communities that space is afforded to views that are rarely openly discussed within mainstream society and where a shared sense of belongingness can be sustained through coalescing around certain shared views and values, some of which may be deemed unacceptable by wider, mainstream society. Communities will be ripe with dissenting viewpoints and alternative perspectives, for, as argued by Fricker (2000), different social identities constitute different social locations through which the world is experienced and viewed, so that at any given moment, the social world can be viewed rationally from more than one perspective. It is power relations within communities, and also between communities and the wider society, that can influence the legitimacy granted to the multitude of views held within communities. In particular, the perspectives of those individuals who lie in disempowered positions (due to social and economic deprivation, religious or political marginalization, etc.) within communities are likely to be granted less legitimacy, and this may generate grievances within these groupings of individuals. Moreover, there is a danger that counter-terrorism policy operates clandestinely to shut down those ideas and value systems viewed as 'extreme' by the state and/or by the wider communities within which these operate, which may have the outcome of pushing individuals into committing acts of violence. This is especially dangerous within a political climate where governments attempt to reinvent nationalistic identities around which a sense of belonging can be socially engineered because of deep-rooted anxiety over mass migration, diversity and terrorism within liberal state democracies. Indeed, it is important to highlight that if communities involve shared meanings, then it is likely to be the case that shared emotions underpin shared meanings and so communities can also share emotions, whether these are of hope, fear and/or humiliation (Moisi, 2009). Struggles take place globally over the emotional-political landscapes of communities, so that 'winning hearts and minds' is a strategy adopted not only by terrorists but also by those seeking to counter terrorism. Again, community is a key site for political and social intervention and manipulation by political, religious and other interests, and so the emotional landscapes of communities are also an important, and often neglected, dimension for counter-terrorism study, policy and practice. There is, perhaps, an important distinction to be made between a community-focused approach to understanding terrorism and to countering this and one that is community-targeted. The next section discusses this distinction.

Community-focused versus community-targeted counter-terrorism

Counter-terrorism policies and practices have been dominated by state-led approaches that have placed nation-state security above that of the security and other needs of communities, particularly those communities deemed to be suspect as a result of the kinds of individual and group identities being expressed within the spaces afforded by the notion of community. It is probably fair to say that counter-terrorism officials and practitioners, whether these practitioners are police officers or those working for the security services, have been traditionally working from a perspective of applying a community-targeted approach rather than a community-focused approach. It is important to stress that this is not necessarily about the specific tactics that are operationalized, but rather the values underpinning those tactics. A community-targeted approach might be characterized as one that ignores the issue of gaining the consent of those communities that are being targeted, with the well-being of targeted communities often being compromised by attempts to achieve the broader goal of maintaining nation-state security. At the same time, a community-targeted approach is characterized by distrust between communities and security officials and practitioners. Community-focused approaches, on the other hand, can perhaps be characterized by partnership between communities and state officials, by community consent and participation in the actual governance of the various strategies and approaches that are applied, and trust existing between state officials and security practitioners and community members (Spalek *et al.*, 2009). At the same time, a community-focused approach embraces communities for their complexities in relation to ethnicity, religion, politics, emotions, grievances, locales, histories, etc. This approach seeks to work with communities rather than to manipulate them.

The distinction between community-focused and community-targeted approaches is helpful in that it allows us to go beyond the rather simplistic binary that is often portrayed in research literature in relation to 'top-down' and 'bottom-up' approaches to counter-terrorism. This is because top-down approaches, whilst predominantly and traditionally community-targeted, might, with appropriate community consent, be community-focused. Thus, tactics such as stop and search and the use of surveillance technology can be community-focused where community consultation has taken place, where there are partnerships between security practitioners and community members and where trust has been developed. At the same time, 'bottom-up' approaches can be community-targeted rather than community-focused where community participation is not based on real partnerships but rather is used to instigate state-led agendas. For example, the use of informants draws upon the skills and networks of community members; however, these often operate in secrecy, with no wider community consent or involvement in the governance of these strategies. At the same time, 'top-down' approaches to counter-terrorism can draw upon communities as part of a strategy of counter-subversion, where this involves strategies which aim to target and stigmatize those groupings deemed to be subversive in the same way that terrorists would be targeted. This can potentially add to intra- and inter-community tensions. With respect to inter-community tensions, where community-targeted approaches to counter-terrorism involve the portrayal of Muslims as being at risk of committing acts of terrorism, this can lead to a fear of Muslims, resulting in violence against them (Mythen *et al.*, 2009; Lambert and Githens-Mazer, 2010). Community-targeted approaches can therefore potentially play into the hands of extreme right-wing groups like the British National Party (BNP), in whose interests it is to deem Muslim communities as communities of extremists. In Derby, for example, the Voice of British Resistance League use Islamist extremism as a way of gaining support for the BNP. Their website charts 'rising Islamic terrorism in Derbyshire' and includes slogans such as 'stop the Sharia clock'.[1] In Birmingham the English Defence League has exacerbated inter-community tensions between Muslim youths and white youths.

Although critics argue that a focus upon any particular community when countering terrorism can have the effect of labelling an entire community as suspect, thereby stigmatizing individuals and helping to perpetuate and maintain broader social structures that enable hate crimes to flourish, it might be argued that a community-focused approach that does not criminalize communities but rather seeks to work in partnership with community members will not have the effect of labelling people as suspect. This is also where community intelligence comes in, because maybe it is useful to distinguish between community intelligence that is supplied through community-focused approaches and that which is supplied by community-targeted approaches. Community intelligence might be thought of as comprising community sentiments and concerns, concerns that may be linked to more standard forms of intelligence that police gather in terms of information about criminal activities, but which may also go beyond this to include information about tensions between individuals and communities, tensions which may have cultural, geographical, religious, racial and other underpinnings. Community intelligence also includes citizens' stories about their lives, which may, in a counter-terrorism context, be particularly pertinent given that some individuals may have first-hand accounts of their interactions with terrorist suspects either in the UK or in other places around the world (see Baker, 2010). Trust has been identified as being a key component of community intelligence and so it would appear that security officials and practitioners should have a community-focused, trust-building approach towards communities rather than a community-targeted approach that precludes and often mitigates against trust (Spalek, 2010). Nonetheless, the nature of trust and trust-building in counter-terrorism is an area that seldom features in research and policy agendas.

Whilst some community-focused counter-terrorism initiatives existed before the 7 July 2005 attacks, as in the case of partnership work between the Muslim Contact Unit and Brixton and the Finsbury Park mosque communities (Baker, 2010; Lambert, 2010b), the Prevent strand has broadened out the focus of countering terrorism to wide-ranging state and non-state actors, including local authorities, educators, youth workers and community groups. The Prevent strategy perhaps exemplifies the kinds of tensions and controversies that community-based approaches to counter-terrorism generate because there is often insufficient clarity and distinction made between a community-focused and a community-targeted approach by policy makers and security practitioners. Community-based approaches have been experienced at times as a kind of Trojan horse for 'top-down' state security-led approaches that involve the penetration of communities to be used as spying networks (Goldsmith, 2005; Hewitt, 2010). Indeed, an accusation made against the Prevent strategy is that it may have alienated sections of Muslim communities because it may have encouraged community members to watch and share information on suspicious neighbours or friends with police (Kudnani, 2009). Openness, community participation and engagement can play a significant role in challenging community-targeted approaches and in developing and implementing community-focused initiatives. This links directly to the question of who it is that governs counter-terrorism policy and practice, and so the next section will focus upon the notion of community in relation to the governance of counter-terrorism.

Community and the governance of counter-terrorism

Communities can play an important role in helping to govern, as well as to implement, counter-terrorism initiatives. According to Brennan *et al.* (2007: 13), 'the world of governing has seen a revolution expressed in a shift from government to governance'. For them, the notion of governance is to be understood as that which includes both government and civil society, with the state and the civic engaging in decision making and other processes through the interaction of top-down, state-led imperatives and bottom-up approaches, which include networks, groups, communities and others that are part of what might be deemed civil society. The involvement of communities in relation to countering threats from Al-Qaeda-linked and/or influenced terrorism reflects the involvement of communities in tackling other social problems such as anti-social behaviour, unemployment and so forth. Like traditional forms of crime, the governance of 'new terrorism' reflects broader developments in governance, whereby responsibility and accountability for preventing terror crime is increasingly focused towards local levels, whilst at the same time centralized control in terms of resources and target setting is maintained. In addition, formal responsibilities for policy implementation and service delivery are progressively being shared across statutory, voluntary agencies and community groups in the form of partnership work. A further aspect to the governance of 'new terrorism' which might be linked to bottom-up approaches is reflectivity. Here, the greater visibility of security intelligence in the public domain has led to an increased awareness, scrutiny and critique by politicians, media commentators, non-governmental organizations (NGOs), communities and the general public (Youngs, 2010).

After 9/11, in responding to the perceived global threat from 'new terrorism', a 'War on Terror' was instigated globally, led by the Bush administration in the USA. The 'War on Terror' has been criticized for potentially being a war on Islam, as evidenced from the very early stages of post-9/11 strategy by George Bush's use of the word 'crusade'.[2] Indeed, in a survey carried out in 2006 by the 1990 Trust, based on a sample of 1,213 British Muslims, 91 per cent of British Muslims surveyed disagreed with UK government foreign policy, 93 per cent felt that UK government policy on terrorism was dictated by the USA and 81 per cent believed the 'War on Terror' to be a war on Muslims (Thiel, 2009: 27). The 'War on Terror' might be viewed from the perspective of global governance as being top-down, as comprising dominant political and economic actors and authorities determining the legitimacy of risk in relation to questions of security, being linked to wider geopolitical power plays between nation states in relation to the global world order (Findlay, 2007). The 'War on Terror' is thus a politicized global strategy, helping to reconfigure security issues at the level of the nation state and locale. Thus, international and nation-state-led approaches have prioritized the maintenance of international and nation-state security over individual and community security concerns.

Often, there are struggles within and between communities, and indeed between communities and the state, over issues to do with the governance of counter-terrorism strategies, the actual implementation of these and how effectiveness is to be conceptualized and examined. These struggles are, in part, a component of wider struggles that exist over whether counter-terrorism should be community-focused or community-targeted. Thus, despite the 'top-down' 'War on Terror' security-led policy, since 7/7 in the UK in particular, 'bottom-up', community-focused approaches to counter-terrorism have developed, particularly within the Prevent strand of CONTEST and CONTEST 2, with 'communities can defeat terrorism' having become a counter-terrorism maxim (Briggs *et al.*, 2006). Bottom-up approaches are also about the increasing involvement of civil society in government in terms of playing a role in decision-making processes and holding decision makers to account (Brennan *et al.*, 2007), and so communities are now increasingly involved in holding security and government officials to account in relation to counter-terrorism policies and practices. This shift from government to governance is perhaps indicative of broader socio-politico-cultural changes within liberal democratic societies, which many commentators have argued are reflexive societies. When conceptualizing the notion of reflexivity, Lash (1994: 200) draws upon the work of Beck (1992) to suggest that this might be viewed as consisting of the ways in which the side-effects, the dangers or 'bads' arising out of modernity's production of goods are dealt with in order to minimize insecurities associated with the social changes here. Importantly, reflexivity can include reflection, where reflection might be thought of in terms of individuals, collective groups and/or institutions intentionally and rationally reflecting upon the part that they play in the perpetuation of identified social problems, as well as reflecting upon ways in which they can intervene and act so as to minimize harms (Lash, 1994; McGhee, 2005). Reflection might also be thought of as comprising of a participative democracy, whereby state institutions open themselves up to the communities that they serve, with the lay public engaging with, as well as critiquing, rival forms of expertise (Spalek and Lambert, 2010b).

It would seem to be the case that the notion of community is the site at which particular struggles exist in relation to who governs the development and implementation of policies and practices aimed at countering terrorism. Within community-targeted approaches, not only is 'community' viewed as problematic but 'community' is also drawn upon to legitimate or help implement 'top-down' initiatives. At the same time, whilst community-based approaches stress the mantra that 'communities can defeat terrorism' (Briggs *et al.*, 2006), where community members are used as part of community-targeted approaches, this can create significant tensions for 'bottom-up' initiatives.

It is important to highlight that the involvement of wide-ranging state and non-state actors at a local level suggests that there may be 'space' for interpretation and that well-placed actors can mediate nationally driven policy agendas (Barnes *et al.*, 2007). There is therefore room for state-instigated policies and practices to be questioned by communities and other actors. Moreover, some counter-terrorism initiatives have grown directly out of a grassroots, 'street-based', community context which have at their core the aim of helping individuals deemed at risk of committing acts of terrorism rather than supplying the state with information. Such community-focused initiatives involve individuals who possess the knowledge about, and shared experience of, backgrounds and credibility of young people vulnerable to or already engaged in violent discourse and action. Such a 'street' approach is invaluable to this form of countering terrorism. A study by Spalek *et al.* (2009) focusing on community–police partnerships within counter-terrorism found that those Muslim community groups who are able to fully understand and communicate on a theological and political level with those deemed to have the potential to carry out extremist acts of violence are better placed to assist and advise counter-terrorism practitioners than Muslims who have no experience in this field. Moreover, partnership with such communities opens up the potential for gaining insider knowledge from those with experience of dealing with violent extremists. Some community leaders may have a long history of resisting and tackling violent extremist activities and may be willing to advise the state through the establishment of a trust-based, equal relationship that constitutes a partnership. Additionally, by opening up channels of communication with some of the most marginalized communities, confidence in state institutions may be built, increased and sustained, contributing to the cohesion which government strives for (Spalek and McDonald, 2010).

Community-focused approaches in local areas can help to subvert top-down government-led approaches that tend to target communities rather than enter into partnership with them. Locally, partnerships can develop between communities and state actors which could be deemed politically too sensitive to encourage at a national, highly visible level. Thus, although the Muslim Council of Britain (MCB) had developed a working relationship with the government, in 2006 it was attacked for taking its inspiration from political Islamism associated with reactionary movements in the Middle East and South Asia (Brighton, 2007), and, sensitive to these accusations, the government's response was to marginalize the MCB from engagement processes. However, this does not mean that at a local level state actors cannot engage with, or indeed partner, individuals and groups associated with, or part of, the MCB. Government-led, nation-state security policies and strategies can thus be reinterpreted and reworked at a local level. Rather than approaching particular communities as informants or subversives, it is possible to approach community actors as potential partners within any counter-terrorism initiatives that are developed. Evidence of this exists in the research carried out by Spalek *et al.* (2009), Baker (2010), Lambert (2010) and Spalek and Lambert (2010). At the same time, whilst the 'War on Terror' has problematized Islamic religious views and actions in particular (Spalek and McDonald, 2010), local initiatives can embrace Islamic religious beliefs and practices. Religion can be used directly in terror prevention strategies – to pull those deemed at risk away from vulnerability. At the same time, it can also be a motivating factor as to why communities partner the state to counter terrorism. The study by Spalek *et al.* (2009) found that openly stating a religious standpoint acted as a way to clarify what is often felt to be an essential ground rule for community members in developing relations with the police: that any relationship should not be built on misunderstandings or false pretences.

In the case of the Muslim Contact Unit (MCU) police officers participating in the research, the fact that their Muslim partners and, indeed, colleagues are happy to talk openly about how their faith will feature in their work is also a source of reassurance that they are realizing one of the MCU's principles: to develop open, respectful and equal relationships with their community partners without requiring them to make compromises against their will. In fact, one police participant stated that he saw this as an essential element of good working relations with Muslim community leaders, because compromises on religion undermine the credibility of such leaders, the trust their communities place in them and therefore their ability to successfully facilitate partnerships and positive engagement for countering violence. As such, the MCU's particular method and approach encouraged community members and leaders to cooperate with the police on what is viewed as a common aim – the protection of society at large from crime committed in the name of Islam (Spalek *et al.*, 2009).

The study found that individuals became involved in helping to counter terrorism primarily as part of a dedication to preventing violence underpinned by feelings of social justice, the protection and security of British society, diverse communities and future generations; as a religious duty, which includes factors such as a feeling of being able to affect social change, to help bring communities together and to improve the image of Muslims and Islam; to represent a particular ethnic, religious, gender, political or ideological perspective; and to contribute a community voice to debates (Spalek *et al.*, 2009). Therefore, local initiatives offer a real opportunity for the development and implementation of a community-focused approach to counter-terrorism. It is important to highlight, however, that developing and implementing a locally-based, community-focused initiative in relation to countering terrorism is fraught with difficulties because the dominance of community-targeted approaches within counter-terrorism can place significant strain on any partnerships developed between communities and state actors. As a result, those individuals wishing to create space for dialogue, interaction and partnership have to draw upon significant personal and professional resources in order to effectively negotiate their ways through the difficult terrain (see Spalek and Lambert, 2010).

Conclusion

Within the notion that communities can defeat terrorism lie struggles between those state and non-state actors working from a community-targeted approach and those working from a community-focused approach. This chapter makes the case for there being a more community-focused approach to countering terrorism, as this can encompass both 'hard' policing and intelligence perspectives like stop and search and surveillance as well as 'softer' approaches involving community initiatives aimed at working with individuals deemed at risk of committing terrorism. This chapter has argued that key characteristics of a community-focused approach appear to be there being existing partnerships between communities and state officials, community consent and participation in the actual governance of the various strategies and approaches that are applied, and trust existing between state officials and security practitioners and community members. Community-targeted approaches, on the other hand, might be characterized as those that ignore the issue of gaining the consent of those communities that are being targeted, with the well-being of targeted communities often being compromised in the efforts to achieve the broader goal of maintaining nation-state security. At the same time, community-targeted approaches can be characterized as there being distrust between communities and security officials and practitioners. Overall, this chapter illustrates that although the notion of community is complex and is often marginalized in research, policy and practice in relation to terrorism and counter-terrorism, communities as spaces of belonging, consisting of one or more of a combination of geographical, imaginative, emotional, political and other ties, are important for terrorism and counter-terrorism. Therefore, much more focus needs to be given in any future work here. The next chapter considers the notion of community in relation to counter-terrorism further, through a focus upon community policing.

Case study

In late 2007 West Midlands Police began to create Project Champion to enable the West Midlands Counter Terrorism Unit to create a vehicle movement 'net' around two distinct geographical areas within the city of Birmingham, namely Alum Rock and

Sparkhill. These areas were the focus of a large percentage of their counter-terrorist operations. The system was needed in order to carry out surveillance operations against identified suspects without having to follow them into and out of residential areas and therefore risk being compromised. The project began with a scoping exercise and a request to the Association of Chief Police Officers (ACPO) (Terrorism and Allied Matters: TAM) to advise the Home Office to support the funding of the project to the anticipated cost of £3 million. The funding was approved in March 2008 and more detailed analysis was undertaken to produce a specification for the system, which was intended to install a joint Automatic Number Plate Recognition (ANPR)/CCTV network that would support Counter Terrorist Unit (CTU) operations and provide benefits to general policing. The project team began to install the cameras in January 2010, but by April 2010 questions were beginning to emerge from the community around the positioning of the cameras. Following enquiries by members of the public and their local representatives into the reason for this work, it emerged that this was a counter-terrorism project and the cameras began to be spoken about as 'anti-terrorism spy cameras'. The subsequent interest and adverse comment that this generated led to a public meeting on 4 July 2010 at the Bordesley Centre in Sparkbrook. During this meeting, a commitment was given by West Midlands Police to halt the project and commission an independent review into the matter.

(Source: Project Champion Review, Thames Valley Police, September 2010, www.west-midlands.police.uk/latest-news/docs/Champion_Review_FINAL_30_09_10.pdf, date accessed 10 December 2011.)

Notes

1. http://derbypatriot.blogspot.com/2010/04/terrorism-crime-and-immigration-in.html (date accessed 15 December 2011).
2. George W. Bush, 'Remarks upon Arrival at the White House', *White House News Releases*, 16 September 2001, www.presidency.ucsb.edu/ws/index.php?pid=63346#axzz1gbEnBy2P (date accessed 10 December 2011); 'More than 1/3 of US Muslims see War on Islam', *Washington Times*, 19 October 2004, www.washingtontimes.com/news/2004/oct/19/20041019-115241-3792r/ (date accessed 10 December 2011); Leslie Evans, 'War on Terrorism Looks Too Much Like a War on Islam, Arab Scholar Warns', UCLA International Institute, 27 January 2003, www.international.ucla.

edu/article.asp?parentid=3010 (date accessed 10 December 2011); Tony Blair's speech to the Labour Party Annual Conference, 2 October 2001, www.guardian.co.uk/politics/2001/oct/02/labourconference.labour6 (date accessed 10 December 2011).

References

Alden, J. (2009) 'Popular Support for Suicide Terrorism in the Muslim World', paper presented at the annual meeting of the Midwest Political Science Association 67th Annual National Conference, the Palmer House Hilton, Chicago, www.allacademic.com/meta/p361672_index.html (date accessed 10 March 2011).

Anderson, E.G. (2011) 'A Dynamic Model of Counterinsurgency Policy Including the Effects of Intelligence, Public Security, Popular Support, and Insurgent Experience', *System Dynamics Review* 27: 111–41.

Baker, A.H. (2010) 'Countering Extremism Locally: A Convert Muslim Perspective', PhD thesis, University of Exeter.

Barnes, M., Newman, J. and Sullivan, H. (2007) *Power, Participation and Political Renewal: Case Studies in Public Participation*. Bristol: Policy Press.

Beck, U. (1992) *Risk Society: Towards a New Modernity*. London: Sage.

Bloom, M. (2004) 'Palestinian Suicide Bombing: Public Support, Market Share, and Outbidding', *Political Science Quarterly* 119(1), 61–88.

Brennan, T., John, P. and Stoker, G. (2007) 'Re-Energising Citizenship: What, Why and How?', in T. Brennan, P. John amd G. Stoker (eds), *Re-Energising Citizenship: Strategies for Civil Renewal*. Basingstoke: Palgrave Macmillan, pp. 8–25.

Briggs, R., Fieschi, C. and Lownsbrough, H. (2006) *Bringing it Home: Community-Based Approaches to Counter-Terrorism*. London: Demos.

Brighton, S. (2007) 'British Muslims, Multiculturalism and Foreign Policy: Integration and Cohesion in and Beyond the State', *International Affairs* 83: 1–17.

Castells, M. (2004) *The Power of Identity*, 2nd edn. Oxford: Blackwell.

Choudhury, T. (2007) *The Role of Muslim Identity Politics in Radicalisation (A Study in Progress)*. London: Department of Communities & Local Government.

Colic-Peisker, V. (2004) 'Migrant Communities and Class: Croatians in Western Australia', in P. Kennedy and V. Roudometof (eds), *Communities across Borders: New Immigrants and Transnational Cultures*. London: Routledge, pp. 29–40.

Crenshaw, M. (1981) 'The Causes of Terrorism', *Comparative Politics* 13(4): 379–99.

Duffy, D. (2009) 'Alienated Radicals and Detached Deviants: What Do the Lessons of the 1970 Falls Curfew and the Alienation-Radicalisation Hypothesis Mean for Current British Approaches to Counter-Terrorism?', *Policy Studies* 30(2): 127–42.

Findlay, M. (2007) 'Terrorism and Relative Justice', *Crime Law & Social Change* 47: 57–68.

Fricker, M. (2000) 'Feminism in Epistemology: Pluralism without Postmodernism', in M. Fricker and J. Hornsby (eds), *The Cambridge Companion to Feminism in Philosophy*. Cambridge University Press, pp. 146–65.

Galam, S. (2002) 'The September 11 Attack: A Percolation of Individual Passive Support', *EJPB – Condensed Matter & Complex Systems* 26(3): 269–72.

Gilroy, P. (2002) 'Diaspora and the Detours of Identity', in K. Woodward (ed.), *Identity and Difference*. London: Sage, pp. 299–346.

Goldsmith, A. (2005) 'Police Reform and the Problem of Trust', *Theoretical Criminology* 9(4): 443–70.

Gregory, F. (2010) 'Policing the "New Extremism" in 21st Century Britain', in Matthew J. Goodwin and Roger Eatwell (eds), *The 'New' Extremism in 21st Century Britain*. London: Taylor & Francis, pp. 85–102.

Hewitt, S. (2010) *Snitch! A History of the Modern Intelligence Informer*. London: Continuum.

Kennedy, P. and Roudometof, V. (2004) 'Transnationalism in a Global Age', in P. Kennedy and V. Roudometof (eds), *Communities across Borders: New immigrants and Transnational Cultures*. London: Routledge, pp. 1–26.

Kohn, B.S. (2002) 'Attacking Islamic Terrorism's Strategic Center of Gravity', Naval War Coll Newport RI Joint Military Operations Dept Handle, http:// Handle.Dtic.Mil/100.2/ADA401841 (date accessed 6 January 2012).

Kudnani, A. (2009) *Spooked! How Not to Prevent Violent Extremism*. London: Institute of Race Relations.

Lambert, R. (2008) 'Empowering Salafis and Islamists Against Al-Qaida: A London Counter-Terrorism Case Study', *PS: Political Science and Politics* 41(1): 31–5.

——. (2010a) *Countering Al-Qaeda in London: Police and Muslims in Partnership*. London: Hurst and Company.

——. (2010b) 'The London Partnerships: An Insider's Analysis of Legitimacy and Effectiveness', unpublished dissertation in partial fulfilment of PhD degree, University of Exeter.

Lambert, R. and Githens-Mazer, J. (2010) *Islamophobia and Anti-Muslim Hate Crime*. London: European Muslim Research Centre.

Lash, S. (1994) 'Reflexivity and its Doubles: Structure, Aesthetics, Community', in U. Beck, A. Giddens and S. Lash (eds), *Reflexive Modernization: Politics, Tradition and Aesthetics in the Modern Social Order*. Cambridge: Polity Press, pp. 110–73.

McGhee, D. (2005) *Intolerant Britain? Hate, Citizenship and Difference*. Maidenhead: Open University Press.

Moisi, D. (2009) *The Geopolitics of Emotion: How Cultures of Fear, Humiliation, and Hope are Reshaping the World*. New York: Anchor Books.

Mythen, G., Walklate, S. and Khan, F. (2009) '"I'm a Muslim, But I'm Not a Terrorist": Victimization, Risky Identities and the Performance of Safety', *British Journal of Criminology* 49(6): 736–54.

Rew, A. and Campbell, J. (1999) 'The Political Economy of Identity and Affect', in J. Campbell and A. Rew (eds), *Identity and Affect: Experiences of Identity in a Global World*. London: Pluto Press, pp. 1–36.

Schmid, A. (2007) 'Terrorism and Democracy', *Terrorism and Political Violence* 10(3): 14–25.

Spalek, B. (2008) *Communities, Identities and Crime*. Bristol: Policy Press.

——. (2010) 'Community Policing, Trust and Muslim Communities in Relation to "New Terrorism"', *Politics & Policy* 38(4): 789–815.

Spalek, B., Davies, L. and McDonald, L.Z. (2010) 'Key Evaluation Findings of the West Midlands 1-2-1 Mentoring Project', University of Birmingham.

Spalek, B., El-Awa, S. and McDonald, L.Z. (2009) 'Police-Muslim Engagement and Partnerships for the Purposes of Counter-Terrorism: An Examination', University of Birmingham.

Spalek, B. and Lambert, R. (2010) 'Policing within a Counter-Terrorism Context Post-7/7: The Importance of Partnership, Dialogue and Support when Engaging with Muslim Communities', in M. Goodwin and R. Eatwell (eds), *The 'New' Extremism in 21st Century Britain*. London: Taylor & Francis, pp. 103–22.

Spalek, B. and McDonald, L.Z. (2010) 'Anti-Social Behaviour Powers and the Policing of Security', *Social Policy and Society* 9(1): 123–33.

Thiel, D. 2009. *Policing Terrorism: A Review of the Evidence*. London: Police Foundation.

Walklate, S. and Mythen, G. (2008) 'How Scared Are We?', *British Journal of Criminology* 48(2): 209–25.

WMPA (2008) 'Preventing Violent Extremism – Communities and Local Government Committee', www.publications.parliament.uk/pa/cm200910/cmselect/cmcomloc/65/65we01.htm (date accessed 16 December 2011).

Youngs, G. (2009) 'Reflections on Research: Media and Mediation in the War on Terror: Issues and Challenges', *Critical Terrorism Studies* 2(1): 1–8.

3
Policing within Counter-Terrorism

Basia Spalek

Introduction

The previous chapter examined the relevance of the notion of community in relation to counter-terrorism. This chapter extends this analysis further by focusing upon community policing in the context of countering terrorism. Within the Prevent strand of the government's counter-terrorism strategy, the police and local authorities have been viewed as taking the lead in any strategies aimed at preventing terrorism, working with wide-ranging bodies including representatives from the education sector, children's and youth services, and the probation and prison services. Muslim communities are also being viewed as key partners (HM Government, 2006). The mainstreaming of the prevention of terrorism within policing is helping to blur distinctions between the role of the police and the security services (Lowe and Innes, 2008), with community policing being viewed as an important resource for counter-terrorism policing (Gregory, 2010). These developments raise many questions for both policing and the prevention of terrorism, some of which have been raised by Gregory (2010).

This chapter focuses on examining community-based policing as a strategy in the 'War on Terror' by drawing upon a significant research study that looked at community-based strategies that have been used in this context. It also focuses on examining the possible tensions relating to the values commonly associated with community policing within a counter-terrorism context, as this is an issue that attracts increasing policy interest but which has so far received little empirical investigation. According to *The SAGE Dictionary of Criminology*, community policing is 'primarily a philosophy of policing that promotes community-based problem-solving strategies to address the underlying causes of crime and disorder and fear of crime and provides reassurance. It is a process by which crime control is shared, or co-produced, with the public, and a means of developing communication with the public, thus enhancing the quality of life of local communities and building police legitimacy' (Virta, 2006: 52–4).

This chapter draws upon empirical data that was gathered as part of an Arts and Humanities Research Council and Economic and Social Research Council-funded project under the auspices of the Religion and Society programme, examining police engagement and partnership work with Muslim communities in London for the purposes of preventing terrorism.[1] During 2007 and 2008, researchers gained access to police officers working within the Muslim Contact Unit (MCU), a counter-terrorism unit within the Metropolitan Police Service (MPS).[2] The MCU has, within a context characterized by suspicion and distrust, engaged with members of Muslim communities and has also entered into partnership with particular Muslim minorities (notably those referred to as 'Salafis' and 'Islamists') for the purposes of preventing terrorism (see Lambert, 2009). This work has included helping to reclaim a London mosque from hardcore extremist supporters and partnering Salafi groups in London in projects that are targeted at young people deemed to be 'at risk' of engaging in terrorism (see Baker, 2009 for an insider's practitioner-based account). The work of the MCU sheds important light upon the role of community-based policing within a counter-terrorism context. As such, the case of the MCU highlights some key issues for counter-terrorism policing, as will be discussed below.

Community-based policing within a counter-terrorism context

According to Virta (2008), although it has previously been argued that community-based policing is no longer 'in vogue', having been replaced by reassurance policing or intelligence-led policing, it is in fact still very prominent in policing agendas. Rather than there having been a paradigm shift from community-based policing to intelligence-led policing, therefore, both styles of policing coexist, albeit that there are different emphases on the different styles in different contexts. Importantly, in the UK since 9/11, and as a result of events such as the urban disturbances in northern English towns in 2001 and the more recent spate of terror attacks in 2005, community-based and intelligence-led policing models have come to be viewed as being complementary. Police services engage with communities as part of a wider strategy of securing community-based intelligence so as to respond to local, regional, national and international security risks (Hughes and Rowe, 2007). Within the post-7/7 counter-terrorism context within England and Wales, links between community-based policing and intelligence-based models of policing can most clearly be seen in the way in which the recently established 'neighbourhood policing' model is explicitly being connected to intelligence gathering. It has been argued that under the neighbourhood policing model, which contains elements of community-based policing, in responding to individuals' routine security concerns on issues such as anti-social behaviour or crime, police officers will be more likely to persuade community members of the benefits of assisting them. Neighbourhood policing is being explicitly linked to counter-terrorism activities in that it is argued that 'neighbourhood policing is a process that can be harnessed to establish the presence of any suspicions about potential terrorist activities' (Innes, 2006: 14). Moreover, it is argued that the indicators for suspecting terror activities may be subtle and not known to any one individual; therefore, neighbourhood policing should be well placed to handle the diffuse information coming from different individuals, due to the beneficial 'weak community ties' developed between police and community members through such a policing model (Innes, 2006: 14). In this approach, communication of intelligence is conceptualized as a vertical, two-way process: from bottom to top with neighbourhood policing teams connecting community intelligence to regional counter-terrorism units (CTUs) through to the National Communities Tension Team (NCTT), and vice versa, with collated national community intelligence and policy from top to bottom – from the NCTT, through to CTUs and down to neighbourhood policing teams. The NCTT is the driving force in this model under the auspices of the Association of Chief Police Officers (ACPO), gathering, analysing and distributing community intelligence relating to the Prevent agenda and community tensions in a weekly bulletin known as Operation Element, and promoting the policy of community engagement and intelligence to all forces.[3]

The developments set out above in relation to the British context can also be seen internationally. In the USA, for example, counter-terrorism has traditionally relied on the analysis of domestic and friendly foreign government intelligence information rather than on the engagement with communities and the development of partnerships between communities and local law enforcement agencies. Nonetheless, recently there has been a movement towards the utilization of community-based policing within a counter-terrorism context, with partnerships being developed between Muslim, Arab, Sikh and South Asian American communities and police. It is argued that these partnerships contain a number of important strands. They are said to provide police with important cultural and linguistic insights, vital information and cooperation, and informed observations that can become part of a productive strategy for terror crime prevention. At the same time, they are said to help to ensure the mitigation of damage to communities that results from 'hard' policing strategies and they also purportedly make it possible for hate crimes to be effectively investigated and prosecuted (Ramirez, 2008). In Canada the Royal Canadian Mountain Police (RCMP) has established a National Security Community Outreach Program (NSCOP). This has drawn heavily upon the model of the MCU in London, adopting community-based policing within its remit of national security policing. Within this context, it has been argued that community-based policing enables trust to be built between the police and communities, particularly those minority communities most affected by national security measures (see Hanniman, 2008 for more details). In Australia new community-based policing initiatives within a counter-terrorism context have also emerged. For example, within the New South Wales Counter-Terrorism and Special Tactics team, there is a newly created Community Contact Unit, and within the Australian Federal Police, there is a new Islamic Liaison Team.

The developments mentioned above raise deeper questions for community-based practices within a counter-terrorism context in relation to policing. If community-based techniques draw upon and utilize religious discourses, what implications does this have for police officers who may have very little knowledge of religious issues and theological questions? What does reassurance policing within a counter-terrorism context comprise? Might an added dimension of reassurance involve police officers giving community partners the space that they need to carry out sensitive work with those deemed 'at risk' from involvement with terrorism without expecting immediate information and direct involvement, because those community partners cannot be seen to be informants by members of their communities? At the same time, community-based policing within a counter-terrorism context raises questions relating to the values commonly associated with community policing. If we draw upon Virta's (2006) conceptualization of community policing as promoting community-based problem-solving strategies to address the underlying causes of crime and to build police legitimacy, then within a counter-terrorism context, the question of what this means needs to be raised. For instance, within this context, the promotion of community-based strategies to address the underlying causes of terrorism raises the issue of which communities and which community groups are best placed to work with police. Moreover, if those groups best placed to counter terrorism are deemed to be 'suspect' by policy makers and influential commentators, then how does this impact upon any attempts at engagement and partnership made by police officers? As demonstrated in the previous chapter, might this lead to community-targeted rather than community-focused approaches? What does building police legitimacy look like within a counter-terrorism context? If community empowerment is an important aspect in building police legitimacy, then what does empowerment mean within a counter-terrorism context? These are just some of the questions that have been raised.

Somewhat worryingly, in England and Wales there now exists a burgeoning policing infrastructure that links community-based policing with intelligence-led policing in relation to the prevention of terrorism, with Prevent indicators and police performance measures being used to assess the effectiveness of any initiatives and engagement work that is being undertaken (Gregory, 2010). However, to date there has been little empirical investigation of community-based policing within a counter-terrorism context, even though this raises many questions. As a result, there is little empirical investigation into, or understanding of, what community-based policing within a counter-terrorism context involves, of the kinds of issues that police officers and communities confront in this context, and whether community policing and intelligence-led policing models may clash and serve to undermine each other. As Ratcliffe has argued, 'where community policing aims primarily for police legitimacy and is organisationally bottom-up and community centered, intelligence-led policing aims for crime reduction, is top-down and hierarchical' (2008: 87, in Virta, 2008). Moreover, within the context of counter-terrorism, Hanniman (2008) argues that the intelligence-led policing model can be linked to national security policing strategies which derive their authority from the state or government, and so do not require public consent or support. In this context, community members are encouraged to watch and share information on suspicious neighbours or friends with police – they are viewed as informants rather than partners. Local police may also be encouraged to use their community–policing programmes and relationships to penetrate local communities and provide intelligence. These strategies, Hanniman (2008) argues, can rapidly alienate a community, particularly since they do not seek to gain community consent and so are community-targeted approaches. At the same time, community policing itself has been criticized for being nothing more than a public relations exercise or for being a form of 'soft power' in trying to get communities to follow wider political agendas (Innes, 2006).

A focus upon the work of the MCU offers a rare insight into the role of community-based policing within a counter-terrorism context. The MCU was established after 9/11 by two Special Branch police officers within the Metropolitan Police Service with long-standing experience in community engagement within a counter-terrorism context, being underpinned by principles of community policing. For the purposes of this chapter, community engagement might be considered to consist of:

> The process of enabling the participation of citizens and communities in policing at their chosen level, ranging from providing information and reassurance to empowering them to identify and implement solutions to local problems and influence strategic priorities and decisions. (Myhill, 2004: 4)

The above definition of engagement suggests that engagement can be an effective tool in developing a community-focused approach, for engagement includes empowering citizens to identify and implement solutions to local problems. Partnership can also be an effective tool here. It might be defined as involving equality, transparency and legitimate cooperation between partners, which may involve different interests forming a partnership to carry out work that they decide to do collectively (Cook, 2006). Partnership work has a number of inherent difficulties. For example, there may be differences in the resources that are available to different groups, and different organizations are also likely to have different sets of priorities, so that there can be considerable difficulties arising from, and tensions within, partnership approaches. At the same time, partnership work can be difficult as it involves power differentials and so community groups may not feel that they are actual partners in the policy process (Thacher, 2001).

Since January 2002, and against the grain of the 'War on Terror', the MCU has built partnerships with minority, often marginalized Muslim community groups – particularly Salafi and Islamist groups – in London with a view to empowering their efforts to counter Al-Qaeda propaganda and recruitment strategies on their own terms, in one case reclaiming Finsbury Park Mosque from Abu Hamza's hardcore extremist supporters (Lambert, 2008). The MCU has also been engaging with wider sections of Muslim minorities in London within a counter-terrorism context, for example, through its interaction with members of the Muslim Safety Forum. An indepth exploration of the work of the MCU, as reported in this chapter, helps to shed important light on what is meant by 'community-based policing' within a counter-terrorism context and what factors serve to enhance and/or inhibit community-based policing in relation to counter-terrorism.

'The new terrorism': Muslim communities as 'suspect'

Since 9/11, government officials and security experts worldwide have used the terminology of the 'new terrorism' to convey the sense of a heightened risk from terrorist activity faced by Western liberal democratic states (Mythen and Walklate, 2006), resulting in the introduction of major pieces of counter-terrorism legislation in the UK (Pantazis and Pemberton, 2009). Importantly, within the notion of the 'new terrorism' is the construction of Muslim minorities as 'suspect', requiring state surveillance and control. Young Muslim men in particular have been viewed as constituting a 'problem group' and a 'fifth column enemy within' by the media, politicians, the security services and criminal justice agencies. They have become the predominant targets of anti-terrorist legislation and counter-terrorism surveillance policing in Britain (Blick *et al.*, 2006; Poynting and Mason, 2006) and other countries such as Australia (Poynting *et al.*, 2004), Canada (Poynting and Perry, 2007), France (Body-Gendrot, 2008), Germany (Bakir and Harburg, 2005) and the USA (Harris, 2006). Muslim minorities have therefore been approached by the security services in order to act as informants. The following extract is a quotation taken from a Muslim participant of the study being drawn upon in this chapter by Spalek *et al.* (2009) examining community policing within a counter-terrorism context:

the other areas of complaint that I'm getting with MI5 are the recruitments that they're trying to do on university campuses and through various other organisations. And sometimes people feel that they're being sort of blackmailed and put into a corner, like if you don't do this, this will happen. And that's not very good. Other times it's an open cheque book, you know, you can have as much money as you want but you know come and spy for us and they clearly don't want to. (Muslim interviewee)

This would suggest that the implementation of community-targeted approaches can make the development and implementation of community-focused approaches more problematic. In this study the research participants also spoke about the effects of being detained without charge and of the effects of people having their homes raided, these 'hard' policing strategies having significant consequences upon the lives of individuals, leading to ostracization from their wider communities, family breakdown and job losses. The following is an extract from an interview on this subject:

A lot of the people who they arrested later on were found to be innocent. So all the damage that was caused, you know, and the whole stigma as well in the community is not something that's easy for people just to say, okay, you know, last night the police came and raided my house and today I'm just normal. It affects the children when they go to school, it affects the elderly when they go to the mosque. It affects the woman when she goes shopping, so all of those things, you know, it's like all the emotional effect of the aftermath of it is not taken into consideration and police, they've done their duty and that's it, but they have a huge responsibility to make sure that if they do some kind of public raids and things, then they make a public announcement to take away that accusation being false, that they need to make sure that they reinforce that this person wasn't guilty and so the police don't do anything after the raids to ensure that they put the public image back the way they had before the raids.

In addition, individuals have been stopped and searched or have been stopped at airports and questioned by customs officials and security service personnel (Spalek *et al.*, 2009).

In keeping with the damaging effects that community-targeted approaches can have, the issue of how 'hard' approaches to counter-terrorism, based on surveillance and the use of other kinds of state powers (Innes, 2005), can significantly undermine any attempts at engagement with Muslim communities was raised by a number of the research study's interviewees. They argued that their experiences of anti-terror laws have reduced their motivations to engage with state authorities:

I was just talking to a friend of mine, I know someone who was picked up and he was kept, detained, for something like seven days. Nothing, nothing. Seven days now in comparison with the 42 days the government wants, absolutely nothing. Seven days. He came back, his wife now wants a divorce. His in-laws don't want him coming into their house anymore. His children, no one will play with them anymore. He was kicked out of his job. His car was taken away. He was refused credit for his mortgage. He's gone back to a broken house. And now that guy who was admired and was a professional working in IT, was a tax-paying citizen, doesn't give a damn about what happens to this country or its people.

Moreover, controversial counter-terror operations that have resulted in physically and psychologically harming those deemed 'suspect', such as the police raid in Forest Gate in 2006, have severely eroded trust between Muslim communities and the police. Indeed, Virta (2008: 30) highlights that 'trust and confidence towards the police is a precondition to community intelligence … It would be very difficult for the police to get community intelligence if people do not trust the police'. This builds on previous research that has established that trust and confidence in the police can be seriously undermined in situations where communities feel that they are being over-policed (Sivanandan, 1981; Bridges and Gilroy, 1982; Smith and Gray, 1985; Jefferson *et al.*, 1992; Macpherson, 1999; Jones and Newburn, 2001; Waddington *et al.*, 2004; Sharp and Atherton, 2007; and Bowling and Phillips, 2007). A breakdown of police–community relations can have serious consequences for policing and in the context of counter-terrorism can halt the flow of vital information from communities, considered to be a key issue within the CONTEST strategy (Hillyard, 1993; 2005).

Within this social context marked by suspicion and distrust, the MCU has been engaging with members of Muslim communities since January 2002 and has built long-term partnerships with particular sections of Muslim minorities through community-based policing. It is therefore important to highlight the key strands to community-based policing as practised by the MCU, as this small policing unit has been working with Muslim communities within a highly charged and difficult social context. Indeed, Pantazis and Pemberton argue that 'it is difficult to see how such skilful, yet ultimately fragile "soft approaches" can thrive, when the full weight of state suspicion and the brutality of "hard" methods have fallen on these communities' (2009: 21).

Community-based policing within counter-terrorism: the MCU

Developing an indepth understanding of complex communities

As illustrated in Chapter 2, much previous research has demonstrated the complexities associated with the notion of 'community', whereby 'community' may be seen as a homogeneous entity, thereby silencing intra-community conflicts by marginalizing those groups and individuals who voice dissent (Crawford, 1997; Hughes and

Edwards, 2002; Spalek, 2008). Moreover, according to Hughes and Edwards (2002), in relation to crime control, the ambiguity over what constitutes 'community' means that in practice the strategies of, and responsibilities for, crime control are a product of struggles between different actors who follow different models about what constitutes community governance.

The work of the MCU illustrates that in relation to community-based policing within a counter-terrorism context, police officers need to spend a considerable amount of time and effort unpicking the multi-layered strands to, and complexities within, the communities that they are engaging with. This approach might be characterized as a community-focused approach, as illustrated in Chapter 2, for it embraces communities for their complexities. As one MCU officer explained:

> Therefore you need to firstly find out who your communities are and how they can actually be part of the process in defeating terrorism. That opens up a whole raft of different areas of work in terms of firstly trying to if you like map out communities, but certainly trying to explain what's going on within communities, who are the Muslims. Because often people talk about the Muslims in a very generalised assumption-based manner of the Muslims, and I see this time and time again throughout officialdom where people talk and refer to in very sort of generalised terms about the Muslims as if they're some homogeneous group of people. To me that indicates a pretty poor understanding of who are Muslim communities and a pretty poorly developed method of communication. There isn't very much access, credible access to the communities so they were people who talked about them from a distance because it's much safer.

Empirical evidence gathered by this study illustrates that developing a nuanced understanding of Muslim communities has taken many years of sustained and focused engagement by MCU officers. The Muslim population of London is extremely heterogeneous in terms of 'race', ethnicity, gender, age, class, culture, politics, country of origin, religious strands within Islam and schools of Islamic thought. Of course, with this level of 'super-diversity', as with other communities, there are intra-community dynamics and at times complex divisions that may have historical, political, doctrinal, familial, tribal and other roots. The issue of representation is key here, particularly as often community leaders can be older and male, so that accessing young people and women has to be a strategy for police officers. At the same time, within the arena of counter-terrorism, social context is essential to interpreting and evaluating pieces of community intelligence that are often far from being clear-cut and further still from constituting criminality. It is therefore vital for police officers involved in community-based policing within a counter-terrorism context to develop an indepth understanding of Muslim communities. This work has to be carried out with sensitivity, and for the approach not to be a community-targeted one, it is not about cross-examining individuals for information about the communities to which they belong. Rather, this work involves interacting with individuals socially and being genuinely interested in their perspectives and experiences, and police officers engaging in trust-building activities, as the following section will highlight.

Grassroots connection and trust building

Police officers within the MCU have developed a methodology of engagement underpinned by an active desire to understand and explore the root causes of terrorism, and ways of countering it, from the perspectives of Muslim minorities. This methodology, implicit within the working practices of the MCU, may be conceptualized as a more grassroots-oriented, horizontal 'bottom-up' approach to engagement. This approach is rare within a counter-terrorism arena that has been dominated by state-centric 'top-down' approaches that fail to understand terrorism and counter-terrorism through the perspectives and experiences of those who comprise 'suspect communities'. The MCU's engagement has enabled police to gain an understanding of community perspectives about a wide range of terrorism-related issues such as the impact of counter-terror operations on Muslim communities. Moreover, in attempting to understand terrorism from the perspectives of those communities who have been particularly affected by extremism, the approach helps the MCU to facilitate working partnerships with community groups for the purposes of preventing terrorism:

> We didn't know a huge amount about Muslim London, you know, it was only through going out to talk to groups and representatives

that we found out, so I think our question was simply you know look, we are very transparent you know, we are counter-terrorism police officers, our interest is Al-Qaeda, do you have any kind of, any broad knowledge of this phenomenon, can we initially have a discussion? (MCU officer)

Empirical evidence gathered by this study shows that MCU officers have openly told community members that they are counter-terror police officers working within a specialist unit. They have argued that in order to be trusted by community members, they have had to build up sincere relationships which are based upon being frank about the unit's remit. Nevertheless, this level of honesty is difficult, as people can continue to be suspicious within a climate of fear generated by counter-terror laws and operations. As one MCU officer observed:

I think you know, this was helpful because although Special Branch had and still has a negative impact in communities, you know it's associated with a secret policing, with spying, nonetheless the fact that we were transparent about that, the fact that we were, you know, as open as possible, I think that helped, not that reticence would be overcome in one meeting ... but we were absolutely adamant that we wanted to put our cards on the table; one of the advantages, again coming back to our own experience, was that community leaders actually do want to talk to fellow experts. Community leaders that are coping with a manifestation of the Al-Qaeda threat in their communities, they want to talk to experts about it, they want to share it.

And another MCU officer, a Muslim, stated:

And I think the unit has often operated in sort of grey man's land in the middle where on the one hand the communities aren't completely sure what you're up to, you're still police officers, are you spying on them or are you not, because you're Muslim, you're part of the police service, very Special Branch, your unit is intelligence, so what do you really want? And trying to reassure them and win over the intellectual battle with the communities in terms of being as blunt as possible with them to say this is what we're doing.

The empirical data also shows that MCU officers have been attending seminars on terrorism organized by Muslim communities, visiting people in their homes for social gatherings, participating in weddings or death ceremonies, being interested in wider community activities that individuals are organizing, etc. This involvement with Muslim communities might be considered as being linked to reassurance policing, whereby in a climate of fear it is particularly important for members of 'suspect' and 'victimized' communities to develop an ongoing and trusting relationship with a counter-terror policing unit. In the context of counter-terrorism, it might be argued that the MCU has played a key role in providing reassurance to Muslim community members, being one identifiable counter-terror unit within London that community members can approach. It has provided a more visible, familiar and accessible policing unit within the context of counter-terrorism, which is generally characterized by secrecy. The MCU also provides reassurance policing in the context of racist and Islamophobic attacks. One individual who was interviewed recounted how he had directly contacted the MCU when witnessing a racist incident because he was concerned by the general (lack of a) police response. At the same time, MCU officers have provided Muslim community members with emotional and practical support in the aftermath of racist and/or Islamophobic attacks, by, for example, visiting victims in hospital. This type of engagement is considered as being a way of building genuine relationships with community members, as the following extract from an interview with an MCU officer highlights:

> There are other examples, people do have various problems, whether it be personal problems to do with their family and X and I have helped people out, someone with personal family problems ... we see that as part and parcel of this ... We're talking about building genuine relationships with people, that's another thing partnership is for, genuine relationship.

Of course, reassurance policing, and community-based policing more generally, has been criticized for being merely a superficial veneer, the sugar coating over a bitter pill (Fitzgerald *et al.*, 2002). Nonetheless, part of the MCU's role, and indeed an important part of building trust with communities, is in helping communities to access the resources they need in order to implement projects. As such, the role of the MCU goes beyond mere appearances or symbolism, but rather also involves empowering members of Muslim communities, as will be described in more detail below.

Bridge-building activities

Empirical data gathered for this study shows that as well as engaging with and partnering Muslim community groups, the MCU has networked with a wide range of other key stakeholders. These have included local authorities, government departments, youth organizations, academics and think-tanks. This has enabled MCU officers to facilitate community projects by building partnerships with other organizations that may be able to provide the kinds of resources necessary for such projects to take place. This approach reflects contemporary developments in governance, whereby responsibility and accountability for preventing terrorism has been progressively shared across statutory, voluntary agencies and community groups in the form of partnership work (HM Government, 2008). The following is a quotation from an interview with an MCU officer:

> We have contacts, a lot of contacts ... Academics. We have an awful lot of academic contacts. We have contacts in the Home Office and so on. Now, if I don't know somebody who these people can go and speak to about funding or even just have a meeting to discuss whether they'd be eligible from the meeting and so on, it's that kind of thing, that's one example.

Rather than working in isolation, the police therefore need to build links with wider society to help facilitate work around the Prevent agenda. According to Oppler (1997), this form of policing can be linked to a multi-agency approach, whereby the police, communities, elected officials and statutory and other agencies work in partnership to address crime and community safety, underpinned by a principle of finding local solutions to address local issues.

Community participation: MCU officers as facilitators

Another important aspect to the work of the MCU which has also helped to generate trust from within Muslim communities is the high level of community participation that MCU officers have facilitated. This provides a good example of how community-based policing can involve a high degree of community participation or even community empowerment. Empowerment might be defined as involving individuals, organizations and communities in the achievement of power not for domination but to act with others to implement change (Wallerstein and Bernstein, 1988).

The interview data suggests that the MCU has facilitated community participation at the highest level by supporting independent community interests. This work is multi-faceted. For example, it involves MCU officers helping community groups access the resources that they require in order to implement the kinds of projects that they want to run, by providing advice on sources of funding, helping to write funding applications and supporting project proposals. MCU officers have also supported Muslim communities in writing a 'Case for Support' as to why a well-known Muslim cleric, who was held in high regard by substantial sections of the Muslim population but who has been deemed 'suspect' by influential political commentators, should be allowed to enter the UK to give talks. The MCU has also worked to help communities obtain permission to organize political demonstrations in London. This strand to the work of the MCU is significant, given that the theory of community participation often falls short, with the supporting of independent community interests rarely being put into practice (Cook, 2006).

It is important to highlight that supporting independent community interests, especially within the highly politicized environment of counter-terrorism, is particularly problematic for police officers. Police officers may find that helping communities to achieve their goals means going against the grain of particular strands of government policy and the top-down approaches which dominate the counter-terror context. Indeed, within the context of counter-terror policing, the adoption of community policing principles may clash with national security policing values. Therefore, police officers working from a community policing perspective within a counter-terrorism context have to be skilled at negotiating their way through conflicting values, an issue raised by Thacher (2001) in relation to community policing in other contexts. This can most clearly be seen in the case of the MCU working in partnership with Salafi and Islamist groups for the prevention of terrorism, these groups having been viewed as 'suspect' by state authorities and other influential commentators (see Gove, 2006; Phillips, 2006). In partnering these groups – groups deemed as 'radical' and viewed as comprising a threat to national security – MCU officers have stood at odds with government agendas that have so far appeared to focus on involving 'moderate Muslims' in partnership work. These agendas appear to be negatively judging as a threat to social cohesion those Muslim community members who are viewed – in a now normative binary – as valuing the Ummah over feelings of 'Britishness' or who appear to isolate themselves from wider society. Empirical evidence gathered by this study shows that the MCU has made an assessment about which groups can best help combat extremism, relegating questions of social cohesion and national identity to other fields of policy and practice (see Spalek and Lambert, 2008 for an analysis of the development of a critically reflective approach to engagement). Another example of how community policing values may clash with national security values is that, contrary to national security requirements which place a high value on gathering intelligence, a partnership-based approach to the prevention of terrorism might involve community members withholding intelligence in order to gain results in the long term. This is because individuals in partnership with the police cannot be viewed as informants by their own community members as they will lose credibility in these communities. It may also involve community partners directly tackling other forms of criminality within their communities, over and above terror-related offences, without involving the police. Of course, this is risk-laden, both for the communities and the police. However, those community members involved in partnership with the police are only effective in preventing crime, including terrorism, if they have legitimacy and credibility amongst members of their own communities. Informing on individuals to the police can only be an option that is used as a last resort, when all other options have been explored (Spalek, 2010).

Muslim police officers within the MCU

Another key feature of the MCU is that Muslim police officers have been employed on the unit, this being a rare feature of CTUs. MCU Muslim police officers have brought with them not only operational policing and community-based policing experience but also social and cultural capital that has enabled the MCU to build trust with particular minorities of the Muslim population. As one police officer interviewed said:

It's about cultural understanding and it's also about recognizing where the police service is in relation to the minority communities, you know, if you can look at every major poll the number, the level of trust and confidence within the BME communities is lower than the trust and confidence in the white community. So it's about actually having Muslim officers who understand the community, [that] the community are going to trust and have confidence in.

MCU Muslim police officers have played an instrumental role in building bridges with members of mosques, developing trusting relationships with mosque communities and then extending these relationships to the non-Muslim police officers working on the MCU. This study has found that in order for Muslim police officers to gain access to certain communities, they must have credibility with those communities and respect for the religious identifications of community members, particularly when some members of Muslim communities have viewed the 'War on Terror' as being a war against Islam. Muslim MCU officers participating in this research suggested that in order to partner people for whom religion is important, it is often necessary for police officers who are making initial contacts with community members to show religious sincerity and credibility. The following is a quotation from a Muslim MCU officer:

I'm a Muslim, a very serious practising Muslim if you like, you know, I don't take my religion lightly, and people in the community who know me know full well where I stand on these issues. So therefore ... it takes something like that to build ... to overcome these deeply, deeply difficult issues of trust or mutual mistrust. And it's very nice using our own personal credibility, you're putting that on the line to say, hold on, if there's something going on against Muslims and I'm a Muslim and I take my religion really seriously, then I want to know what. And whatever your issues are let's talk about them. And it's really trying to break down this problem and trying to get people to discuss it with us first and then trying to bring that back into officialdom.

It has to be stressed, however, that the Muslim police officers working on the MCU have had to negotiate their dual identities as police officers and Muslims on an ongoing basis. They have had to draw upon significant personal resources in order to operate in a wider counter-terrorism context whereby police and community alike tend to operate around the binaries of 'insider' and 'outsider' and/or 'innocent' or 'suspect'. Muslim police officers working on the MCU are in a particularly difficult position as their identities as Muslims and police officers mean that they challenge these simplistic binaries and as a result may experience suspicion from both communities and police officers.

Conclusion

Since 9/11, there has been unprecedented interest in the issue of terrorism across policy-making, media and academic arenas. Whilst critiques in relation to the 'War on Terror' have dominated discourse and analysis, the issue of countering terrorism has received less attention. This chapter highlights the important role that community-based policing can play in a counter-terrorism context. Within a context of fear and distrust generated by 'hard' policing strategies, it seems that community-based policing has an important role to play in building trust between Muslim communities and the police. However, the utilization of community-based policing within a counter-terrorism context is not without its difficulties. In order for community-based policing not to be viewed as little more than a public relations exercise or as a form of 'soft power' whereby communities are viewed primarily as informants, it is important for police officers to engage with communities so as to empower communities and support independent community interests. However, this work is itself difficult, given that the values associated with community policing may clash with the values more commonly associated with intelligence-led models of policing, and so effective police practitioners within this field need to be able to negotiate conflicting values. Furthermore, whilst the work of the MCU has included a focus upon police–community partnerships for the purposes of counter-terrorism involving mosques, this issue merits further examination. It may be the case that young people are not generally actively involved in mosques and do not see existing religious leaders as exercising authority. A study by Lowe and Innes

(2008) has found that some Muslim youth have reported feeling angry and resentful towards elders and community leaders. Moreover, in the case of working to prevent terrorism, the limits of any work is often set by wider factors, for example, international foreign policy or the spread of religious misinterpretation in theological circles. The role of Muslim police officers within counter-terrorism also merits further exploration. Chapter 4 focuses on engagement and partnership in community-based approaches to counter-terrorism more substantively, building on the literature in Chapters 2 and 3. It considers the challenges involved in developing and implementing a community-focused approach to counter-terrorism against a backdrop of traditional, community-targeted approaches.

Case study

Spalek and McDonald (2011) use the following model to conceptualize police–community engagement in relation to counter-terrorism.

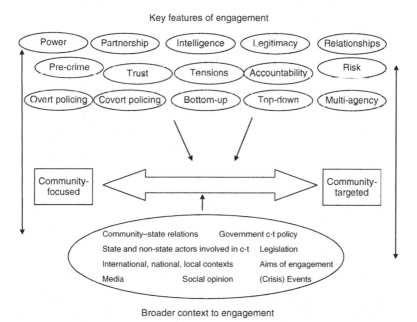

Figure 3.1 A model of police and community engagement

At the core of the model is a central descriptor which helps us to understand the nature of police–community relations regarding counter-terrorism and ultimately how effective community-based strategies are. The descriptor consists of a continuum. On one side of the contiuum is a counter-terrorism approach that can be conceptualized as being community-focused, while on the other side of the continuum is a counter-terrorism approach that might usefully be conceptualized as being community-targeted. Spalek and McDonald (2011) argue that this model can be used to help assess where a programme of activities, or a particular initiative or a set of initiatives, lies on this continuum in order for policing, community and other bodies to be able to implement future policies and practices. Spalek and McDonald (2011) also argue that they have purposefully moved away from using the often-utilized notion of community-based counter-terrorism because this is an over-used notion that fails to distinguish between community-based strategies that are targeted at communities and those community-based strategies that are focused upon communities, and they argue that this distinction is fundamental to understanding counter-terrorism policy and practice.

Notes

1. The study was undertaken by Basia Spalek, Salwa El-Awa and Laura Zahra McDonald, based at the University of Birmingham, with Robert Lambert, MBE, Lecturer, Centre for the Study of Terrorism and Political Violence (CSTPV), University of St Andrews and Research Fellow, Department of Politics, University of Exeter, acting as a consultant. I would like to thank the Arts and Humanities Research Council and Economic and Social Research Council's Religion and Society programme for funding the research study presented here, reference AH/F008112/1.
2. This is a small policing unit within the Metropolitan Police Service, comprising of approximately eight counter-terrorism police officers.
3. See www.communities.idea.gov.uk/comm/landing-home.do?id=158743 (date accessed 10 January 2012).

References

Arksey, H. and Knight, P. (1999) Interviewing for Social Scientists. London: Sage.
Baker, A.H. (2009) 'Countering Extremism Locally: A Convert Muslim Perspective', PhD thesis, University of Exeter.

Bakir, S. and Harburg, B. (2005) 'German Anti-Terror Law and Religious Extremism', www.humanityinaction.org/knowledgebase/224-die-geister-die-ich-rief-the-ghosts-that-i-awoke-german-anti-terror-law-and-religious-extremism (date accessed 6 January 2012).

Blick, A., Choudhury, T. and Weir, S. (2006) *The Rules of the Game: Terrorism, Community and Human Rights*. York: Joseph Rowntree Foundation.

Body-Gendrot, S. (2008) 'Muslims: Citizenship, Security and Social Justice in France', *International Journal of Law, Crime and Justice* 36(4): 247–56.

Bowling, B. and Phillips, C. (2007) 'Disproportionate and Discriminatory: Reviewing the Evidence on Police Stop and Search', *Modern Law Review* 70(6): 936–61.

Breen Smyth. M, (2007) 'A Critical Research Agenda for the Study of Political Terror', *European Political Science* 6: 260–7.

Bridges, L. and Gilroy, P. (1982) 'Striking Back', *Marxism Today*: 34–5.

Burnett, J. and Whyte, D. (2005) 'Embedded Expertise and the New Terrorism Thesis', *Journal of Crime, Conflict and Media Culture* 1(4): 1–18.

Cook, D. (2006) *Criminal and Social Justice*. London: Sage.

Crawford, A. (1997) *The Local Governance of Crime: Appeals to Community and Partnerships*. Oxford: Clarendon Press.

Fitzgerald, M., Hough, M., Joseph, I. and Qureshi, T. (2002) *Policing for London*. Cullompton: Willan.

Gove, M. (2006) *Celsius 7/7*. London: Weidenfield & Nicolson.

Gregory, F. (2010) 'Policing the "New Extremism" in 21st Century Britain', in M. Goodwin and R. Eatwell (eds), *The 'New' Extremism in 21st Century Britain*. London: Taylor & Francis.

Hanniman, W. (2008) 'Canadian Muslims, Islamophobia and National Security Royal Canadian Mounted Police', *International Journal of Law, Crime and Justice* 36(4): 271–85.

Harris, D. (2006) 'US Experiences with Racial and Ethnic Profiling: History, Current Issues and the Future', *Critical Criminology* 14: 213–39.

HM Government (2006) *Countering International Terrorism: The United Kingdom's Strategy*, July (presented to Parliament by the Prime Minister and the Secretary of State for the Home Department by Command of Her Majesty).

Hillyard, P. (1993) *Suspect Community: People's Experience of the Prevention of Terrorism Acts in Britain*. London: Pluto Press.

——. (2005) 'The "War on Terror": Lessons from Ireland', essays for civil liberties and democracy in Europe, European Civil Liberties Network, www.ecln.org/essays/essay-1.pdf (date accessed 14 December 2011).

Home Office (2008) Home Secretary's speech on the threat of international terrorism, Institute for Public Policy Research Commission on National Security by Home Secretary Jacqui Smith, 15 October.

Hopkins, P. (2004) 'Young Muslim Men in Scotland: Inclusions and Exclusions', *Children's Geographies* 2(2): 257–77.

Hughes, G. and Edwards, A. (eds) (2002) *Crime Control and Community*. Cullompton: Willan.

Hughes, G. and Rowe, M. (2007) 'Neighbourhood Policing and Community Safety: Researching the Instabilities of the Local Governance of Crime, Disorder and Security in Contemporary UK', *Criminology & Criminal Justice* 7(4): 317–46.

Innes, M. (2005) 'Why "Soft" Policing is Hard: On the Curious Development of Reassurance Policing, How it Became Neighbourhood Policing and What this Signifies about the Politics of Police Reform', *Journal of Community & Applied Social Psychology* 15: 156–69.

——. (2006) 'Policing Uncertainty: Countering Terror through Community Intelligence and Democratic Policing', *Annals of APSS* 605: 1–20.

Jackson, R. (2007) 'The Core Commitments of Critical Terrorism Studies', *European Political Science* 6: 244–51.

Jefferson, T., Walker, M. and Seneviratne, M. (1992) 'Ethnic Minorities, Crime and Criminal Justice: A Study in a Provincial City', in D. Downes (ed.), *Unravelling Criminal Justice*. London: Macmillan, pp. 138–64.

Jones, T. and Newburn, T. (2001) *Widening Access: Improving Police Relations with Hard to Reach Groups*, Police Research Series Paper 138. London: Home Office.

Lambert, R. (2008) 'Empowering Salafis and Islamists Against Al-Qaida: A London Counter-terrorism Case Study', *PS: Political Science and Politics* 41(1): 31–5.

——. (2009) 'London Police and Muslim Londoners: Countering Al-Qaida in Partnership', unpublished PhD thesis, University of Exeter.

Lowe, H. and Innes, M. (2008) 'Countering Terror: Violent Radicalisation and Situational Intelligence', *Prison Service Journal* 179: 3–10.

Macpherson Inquiry (1999) *The Stephen Lawrence Inquiry, Report of an Inquiry by Sir William Macpherson of Cluny*. London: Stationery Office, Parliamentary papers, Cm 4262-I.

Myhill, A. (2004) *Community Engagement in Policing: Lessons from the Literature*. London: Home Office.

Mythen, G. and Walklate, S. (2006) 'Criminology and Terrorism', *British Journal of Criminology* 46(3): 379–98.

Oppler, S. (1997) 'PARTNERS AGAINST CRIME: From Community to Partnership Policing', Crime and Policing Project, Institute for Security Studies, Occasional Paper No. 16 (March): http://dspace.cigilibrary.org/jspui/bitstream/123456789/31596/1/paper_16.pdf?1 (date accessed 6 January 2012).

Pantazis, C. and Pemberton, S. (2009) 'From the "Old" to the "New Suspect" Community: Examining the Impacts of Recent UK Counter-Terrorist Legislation', *British Journal of Criminology* 49(5): 646–66.

Phillips, M. (2006). *Londonistan: How Britain Is Creating a Terror State Within*. London: Gibson Square.

Poynting, S. and Mason, V. (2006), '"Tolerance, Freedom, Justice and Peace"?: Britain, Australia and Anti-Muslim Racism since 11th September 2001', *Journal of Intercultural Studies* 27(4): 365–92.

Poynting, S., Noble, G., Tabar, P. and Collins, J. (2004) *Bin Laden in the Suburbs: Criminalising the Arab Other*. Sydney Institute of Criminology.

Poynting, S. and Perry, B. (2007) 'Climates of Hate: Media and State Inspired Victimisation of Muslims in Canada and Australia since 9/11', *Current Issues in Criminal Justice* 19(2): 151–71.

Ramirez, D. (2008) 'Partnering for Prevention', www.northeastern.edu/law/academics/institutes/pfp/index.html (date accessed 6 January 2012).

Ratcliffe, J. (2008) *Intelligence-Led Policing*. Cullompton: Willan.

Sharp, D. and Atherton, S. (2007) 'To Serve and Protect?: The Experiences of Policing in the Community of Young People from Black and Other Ethnic Minority Groups', *British Journal of Criminology* 47: 746–63.

Silke, A. (2008) 'Holy Warriors: Exploring the Psychological Processes of Jihadi Radicalization', *European Journal of Criminology* 5(1): 99–123.

Sivanandan, A. (1981) 'From Resistance to Rebellion', *Race and Class*: 111–52.

Smith, D. and Gray, J. (1985) *Police and People in London: The PSI Report*. Aldershot: Gower.

Smith, J. (2008) Home Secretary's Speech, Manchester, www.britishpolitical speech.org/speech-archive.htm?speech=289 (date accessed 6 January 2012).

Spalek, B. (2008) *Communities, Identities and Crime*. Bristol: Policy Press.

——. (2010) 'Community Policing, Trust and Muslim Communities in Relation to "New Terrorism"', *Politics & Policy* 38(4): 789–815.

Spalek, B. and Lambert, R. (2008) 'Muslim Communities, Counter-terrorism and De-radicalisation: A Reflective Approach to Engagement', *International Journal of Law, Crime and Justice* 36(4): 257–70.

Spalek, B. and McDonald, L.Z. (2011) 'A Study Exploring Questions in Relation to Partnership between Police and Muslim Communities in the Prevention of Violent Religio-Political Extremism amongst Muslim Youth', University of Birmingham.

Thacher, D. (2001) 'Conflicting Values in Community Policing', *Law & Society Review* 35(4): 765–98.

Virta, S. (2006) 'Community Policing', in E. McLaughlin and J. Muncie (eds), *The SAGE Dictionary of Criminology*, 2nd edn. London: Sage.

——. (2008) 'Community Policing Meets New Challenges', in S. Virta (ed.), *Policing Meets New Challenges: Preventing Radicalization and Recruitment*. Tampere, Finland: University of Tampere, Department of Management Studies, CEPOL, pp. 15–41.

Waddington, P. Stenson, K. and Don, D. (2004) 'In Proportion: Race, and Police Stop and Search', *British Journal of Criminology* 44: 889–919.

Wallerstein, N. and Bernstein, E. (1988) 'Empowerment Education: Freire's Idea Adapted to Health Education', *Health Education Quarterly* 15(4): 379–94.

Wilkinson, P. (2006) 'Terrorism', in M. Gill (ed.), *The Security Handbook*. Basingstoke: Palgrave Macmillan.

4

Engagement and Partnership in Community-Based Approaches to Counter-Terrorism

Abdul Haqq Baker

Introduction

Following the terrorist attacks in London on 7 July 2005, questions were raised regarding the levels of disengagement among Muslims communities in Britain, particularly relating to the second/third generations and converts. The realization that such attacks were perpetrated by British citizens highlighted the need for the government to examine and address the causes behind home-grown extremism. Engagement with grassroots local communities was emphasized as a priority, with think-tanks like Demos (Briggs *et al.*, 2006) being among the first to highlight the sense of urgency required. Statutory agencies like the Metropolitan Police's Muslim Contact Unit (MCU) had been involved in engagement with various communities at a grassroots level since early 2002 and, following reports like that mentioned above, began to get recognition for the collaborative approach it had adopted due to the success it yielded.

Against the backdrop of the MCU's pioneering strategy to both engage and empower Muslim communities in their fight against violent radicalism, this chapter will examine and discuss the effectiveness of partnership approaches between statutory agencies and Muslims, particularly insofar as they precede the more recent and arguably flawed former government's Prevent strategy, which was aimed at empowering and facilitating the very same communities (Kundnani, 2009). It will also outline key arguments in support of this approach as well as those against it, whilst illustrating particular examples of grassroots partnership engagement in the counter-radicalization field. The final section of the chapter provides insight to newer programmes and collaborative projects that have evolved from the earlier partnership initiatives.

The previous Labour government's immediate response after the attacks of 7 July 2005 was as predictable as it was reactionary. Its engagement with organizations and personalities with whom it had already existing and established relationships only exacerbated perceptions of its inability to identify credible and more representative voices from Muslim communities. Furthermore, many of the personalities and groups chosen to engage at this critical period came from traditionally and culturally orientated Muslim communities and were therefore largely non-representative of the second- and third-generation British Muslims or converts, which is the group from which the four suicide bombers emerged. The problem facing Muslim communities who were now prepared to engage with statutory agencies and the government in order to address the issue of homegrown terrorism was how to define the nature and parameters of such engagement. Pre-existing arrangements were considered both unsatisfactory and unacceptable from a grassroots community perspective in view of their coercive and hierarchical top-down approaches designed to elicit intelligence to serve the agendas of statutory agencies. As demonstrated in Chapter 2, counter-terrorism policies and practices have been dominated by state-led approaches that have placed nation-state security above that of the security and other needs of some communities. In fact, as this chapter will highlight, community concerns over new statutory intervention programmes such as the Channel Project may be considered a rebranded form of the informant process (Kundnani, 2009). Some police authorities are themselves rephrasing informant relationships with newer, more subtle terminologies like 'Covert Human Intelligence Source(s)' (CHIS), Human Source(s) (HS) or Human Intelligence Sources, which all contain connotations not too dissimilar from traditional informant roles (Crous, 2009). This chapter will also examine community engagement within the more recently defined 'new terrorism' context under Prevent, especially insofar as it relates to new or re-defined relationships between communities, government and statutory bodies.

Engagement and partnership: intelligence gathering in disguise?

Prior to the inception of the MCU, a common grassroots perception of police interaction with various communities – irrespective of religious affiliation – was that it was based primarily on informant relationships, using and/or coercing communities to provide intelligence on its members who were suspected of criminal activity. Thus, there existed a perception that approaches to communities were largely community-targeted. This unsavoury perception of the police also exists among many Muslim communities in view of the experiences of a significant number of individuals who have been approached by sections of the intelligence services (Verkaik, 2010). Some communities felt almost compelled to enter and negotiate new, more palatable terms of reference relating to communication and liaison with various authorities due to high-profile events post-9/11, which inadvertently linked them to violent extremist propaganda or terrorist acts. For example, engagement was considered paramount in the cases of the Brixton and Finsbury Park Mosques in order to mitigate the ensuing climate that surrounded these communities following the terrorist attempts of Zacarius Moussaoui (the twentieth 9/11 bomber), Richard Reid (the shoe bomber) and Abu Hamza al-Misree (the extremist preacher who had forcibly taken possession of Finsbury Park Mosque in the mid- to late 1990s). Brixton Mosque's initial stance against extremism drew a mixed response among Muslim communities due to its public condemnation and naming of key propagandists that it believed to be responsible for propagating violent extremist propaganda in the UK following the 9/11 attacks. Despite the stratagem to distance Brixton Mosque and its community from Moussauoui, Reid and, by extension, violent extremism, criticism was levelled against it following media interviews, due to impressions given to the effect that they had provided intelligence on innocent Muslims to the authorities. These accusations were countered by the Mosque with a clarification about such warnings being restricted to outlining the adverse effects of extremist propaganda and its effect among susceptible Muslim youth in south London; however, in spite of this, accusations continued to proliferate regarding the Mosque being an informant entity. As a result of these emerging conflicts, the Mosque felt compelled to address challenges relating to both its members' identity as predominantly British Muslim converts and the level of engagement now required with the wider non-Muslim community and statutory bodies in particular. In view of its members' negative encounters and experience with institutions like the police pre-conversion, consideration surrounding any level of engagement or interaction was, unsurprisingly, treated with extreme caution. The legacy of police community-targeted strategies against 'suspect' communities was all too familiar to Mosque members; however, as a community emerging from an inherently local and insular context, it was necessary for the Mosque leadership to re-define and explore the parameters of interaction with such bodies due to its arrival on the international stage as a possible conduit/haven for violent extremism. Instead of adopting an entirely defensive strategy to counter the unprecedented media attention that had been thrust upon it, the Mosque's leaders became proactive by defining its terms upon which it was prepared to engage with any entity that wanted to cooperate with it in tackling violent extremism in the UK. It had, in effect, outlined its objectives for community-focused engagement where the acknowledgement of its experience and expertise would enable it to continue operating independently and effectively at a grassroots level without overt or covert interference from statutory agencies, whose roles would be solely facilitory.

A significant proportion of the young Muslim population in Britain continues to view the police and other statutory authorities with mistrust. Negative pre-conversion experiences of African-Caribbean converts add to this sense of mistrust due to indelible impressions and scars to the racial psyche of such individuals. The murder of Stephen Lawrence in 1993 and the ensuing ineptitude that followed in the wake of a public inquiry are among some of the significant reasons for such sentiments, as the incident revealed the extent of institutionalized racism within the police force (Hall, 2009). Unfortunately, post-conversion experiences and similar Islamophobic attitudes towards second- and third-generation South Asian Muslims have only served to reinforce pre-existing mistrust and suspicions. The increase in anti-Muslim sentiment in recent years has led to some academics embarking on new research to determine the extent of Islamophobia in Britain (Githens-Mazer and Lambert, 2011). Since the Runnymede Trust Report of 2000 (Githens-Mazer and Lambert, 2011), very little research has explored British sentiment or perceptions regarding

Muslims, especially post-9/11 and 7/7. In the event, the European Muslim Research Centre (EMRC) report observed difficulties in obtaining accurate data relating to hate crime in general, let alone that related specifically to Islamophobic hate crime, thus making it all the more difficult to gauge the latter's adverse effect on the psyche of the Muslim population (Githens-Mazer and Lambert, 2011). This handicap, together with the former government's response and strategy post-9/11 and 7/7 further exacerbated feelings of alienation among many British Muslims:

> In 2001, the UK joined the US in invading Afghanistan … Two years later, they joined the US again to invade Iraq and overthrow the regime of Saddam Hussein. Both invasions were successful in achieving their immediate objectives, but the political fallout from these conflicts would be felt on the streets of UK cities in the following years. Since 2003, there has been a dramatic increase in terrorist activity in the UK by individuals and groups based within the Muslim population. (Cole and Cole: 2009: 111)

In this climate, the forging of any symbiotic partnerships or relationships between grassroots Muslim communities and statutory agencies or the government would always be viewed with suspicion from many angles. Some Muslims, averse to establishing any type of relationship of this nature, would consider their colleagues to have betrayed the religion. At worst, Muslim individuals or organizations embarking upon such relationships would be considered to have apostatized from Islam (Baker, 2010). More recently, this position has increasingly found resonance among a number of younger second- and third-generation Muslims due to perceptions (with some apparently supporting evidence) of the former government's Prevent strategy being inherently anti-Muslim (Kundnani, 2009). Communities like that at Brixton Mosque have emerged in this climate of uncertainty and mistrust to test the validity and extent of engagement and partnership arrangements with particular statutory bodies, including the police. Contrary perceptions of a pre-existing top-down and coercive relationship, typified by an informant/police arrangement between the Mosque and the police, are easily dismissed by Brixton Mosque's leadership due to the well-established fact that they had seldom liaised or communicated with the police and local council on anything other than superficial levels. This was due to previous unproductive encounters, which often resulted in either confrontations or conflicts that are well documented in the history of local police and community relations (Baker, 2010). Rare exceptions to these apprehensive stand-offs witnessed very occasional and periodic meetings where community issues relating to Lambeth's increasing Muslim communities were discussed (Baker, 2010). Despite this, the prevailing climate and suspicions between the parties failed to provide a springboard for a collaborative arrangement to be forged. A greater combined effort was required to bridge the increasing vacuum between Muslim and other communities in Lambeth if the effects of violent extremist propaganda were to be thwarted. Moussaoui and Reid disappeared from the local Muslim community radar and were certainly not detected by statutory agencies, thus providing a fertile opening through which they became violently radicalized. They provided immediate examples of what could transpire if this inter-community/statutory agency vacuum was not effectively bridged. Figures 4.1 and 4.2 below provide illustrative examples of the effects of this vacuum.

The key factor in any potentially successful working partnership between community and police lies in the nature and terms of engagement. This would subsequently determine the parameters of an ensuing agreement. The controversial issue of Muslims providing intelligence on their own communities, i.e. informing or spying on

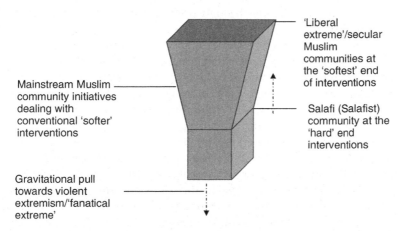

Figure 4.1 The Funnel Model (Baker, 2010)

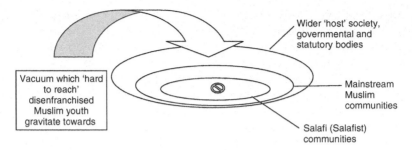

Figure 4.2   Cross-section of the Funnel Model (Baker, 2010)

members, must, in view of its position in Islam[1] and among Muslims generally, therefore be considered unviable from the outset. This position should not, however, conflict with a firm commitment towards civic responsibility and, within a counter-terrorist context, reporting identified or potential terrorists or terrorist actions provided sufficient and robust mechanisms that can identify such threats are in place. In the absence of comprehensive systems of identification of such trends, it would be almost impossible to avoid the existing local/cultural prejudices and/or inter-religious factionalism that currently permeates some community decisions on who and what actually constitutes violent radicalism or extremism. Examples of biased accounts occasionally surface under the guise of academic reports but are easily discernable through their lack of academically based research (Dyke, 2009). Parameters similar to those discussed above were suggested by Brixton Mosque and were actually accepted by the MCU – a first for the Metropolitan Police in this context. This is perhaps due to the latter's understanding that communities like Brixton's Muslims were more suitably placed to address and tackle extremist propaganda among their own community. This acceptance removed some of the initial mistrust held by the Brixton Mosque leadership regarding the MCU's intentions. It was the first time in the community's history that consideration had been given to engagement with police authorities at this level. Subsequently, the Mosque leadership was able to provide assurances to the MCU regarding its civic and social responsibility to the extent that, in the event of it facing insurmountable challenges or threats from extremists, it would request the MCU's assistance to intervene and support the community's attempts to repel such threats. This marked the first phase of the symbiotic relationship between Brixton Mosque and the MCU, with both parties conceding previously immutable ground regarding what concessions each was prepared to make. In order to illustrate the success of the MCU's grassroots partnership approach, one need only refer to its intervention at Finsbury Park Mosque, which had been taken over by Abu Hamza al-Misree in the late 1990s. Together with local Muslim community leaders, it developed a collaborative approach to oust Abu Hamza and reclaim the premises (Lambert, 2010). Its success arguably underscored the call for a comprehensive 'bottom-up' approach to tackle and address the threat of radicalization among British Muslims. Spalek *et al.* observed the pioneering nature of this work:

> The Muslim Contact Unit ... developed a close working partnership with black convert community groups ... and many others of a similar nature. The essence of this work is to empower and facilitate local Muslim Community groups and their efforts to educate and support convert Muslims and, where they have been released from prison, to re-integrate them into a devoutly practicing faith community. (Spalek *et al.*, 2009: 176)

Empowerment and facilitation were key components that distinguished the initial partnership between the Mosque management and the MCU. Subsequent partnerships began to emerge with other statutory bodies like the probation services and the local council, which enabled a more comprehensive and consolidated way of working with socially conservative communities like Brixton for the first time. The success of these relationships meant that such communities were able, to some extent, to deflect:

> opposition from powerful commentators who regularly conflate[d] Salafism (and Islamism) with extremism and terrorism. (Spalek *et al.*, 2009: 176–7)

Spalek *et al.* further suggested that, in the absence of this facilitation:

> These groups would have otherwise been excluded from engagement processes as a result of their perceived links with terrorism,

or because of their real or perceived opposition to established secular values. (Spalek *et al.* 2009: 177)

The partnership arrangement described above predates the former government's Prevent strategy by almost four years and is indicative of the foresight often required by many communities and a few statutory bodies that have been tackling violent radicalization and extremist propaganda at a grassroots level for over 20 years (Lambert, 2010). The partnership arrangement reflects a community-focused approach, as highlighted in Chapter 2, since there is community consent and participation in the actual governance of the partnership and there is trust between the police officers and community members involved in the partnership.

The government's recognition of collaborative efforts to effectively tackle extremism at a grassroots level was reflected in the launch of the Preventing Violent Extremism Fund (PVEF) and agenda by the Department for Communities and Local Government (DCLG), which cited initiatives like Strategy To Reach Empower & Educate Teenagers (STREET UK) among its case studies as models of good practice (DCLG, 2007). STREET UK encapsulated many of the PVE objectives, including the government's commitment to:

support priority local authorities, or groups of local authorities, to take forward a programme of activities to tackle violent extremism at a local level. (DCLG: 2007: 3)

By expressing this commitment, the government acknowledged the necessity of engagement with grassroots communities. The MCU's innovative approach enabled Lambeth – the local authority under which Brixton Mosque and STREET UK were located – to support and develop effective intervention models once it had also successfully bid for money from the PVEF. However, the local authority's collaborative approach was not without criticism and think-tanks questioned the wisdom of its alignment with allegedly non-violent extremists, who were considered to be part of the problem so far as violent radicalization and extremism were concerned (Maher and Frampton, 2009).

Negative perceptions of existing and successful partnerships continue to be stoked by entities warning that support is being afforded to extremists who are considered to be at either the embryonic stage of violent extremism or precursors to it:

> The central theoretical flaw in PVE is that it accepts the premise that non-violent extremists can be made to act as bulwarks against violent extremists. Some within government and the police service believe that only non-violent radicals – otherwise known as 'political Islamists' – possess the necessary 'street cred' to control angry young Muslims. Genuine Muslim moderates are regularly dismissed by key authority figures as 'spoken for', and thus marginalised. Non-violent extremists have consequently become well dug in as partners of national and local government and the police. Some of the government's chosen collaborators in 'addressing grievances' of angry young Muslims are themselves at the forefront of stoking those grievances against British foreign policy; western social values; and alleged state-sanctioned 'Islamophobia'. PVE is thus underwriting the very Islamist ideology which spawns an illiberal, intolerant and anti-western world view. (Maher and Frampton: 2009: 5)

Other Muslim-led think-tanks, particularly the Quilliam Foundation, supported the assertions of the former government funding non-violent extremists, attempting to promote itself as the viable counter-radicalization alternative.[2] The Quilliam Foundation's leaked report (July 2010) to the Office for Security and Counter-Terrorism (OSCT) highlighted the extent of its concerns regarding a variety of Muslim organizations and while it was ambitious in its attempt to convey findings and recommendations within an academic framework, its content was undeniably subjective and based upon the observations of its co-authors.[3]

Questions that could be posed to any government averse to Prevent's more successful counter-radicalization programmes are as follows: 1) what alternatives do they propose to replace these programmes in the event of scrapping them?; and 2) if there are alternatives, what evidence exists to support their effectiveness at a grassroots level? In view of the continued threat of terrorist attacks against UK interests and the present sentiment among many young Muslims regarding British foreign policy, successful intervention initiatives must either remain or be replaced with viable alternatives that can continue to address the above-mentioned challenges. To date, no *credible* or *proven* alternative has been recommended to replace the more effective programmes which have, thus far, received support from various statutory agencies that have partnership agreements with them. Until proven and viable alternatives exist, any new government would do well to carefully evaluate existing programmes and identify other established and credible initiatives before simply abandoning the former. Leaving a vacuum in this very sensitive and volatile area of the counter-terrorist arena is likely to result in a fomenting of further extremist propaganda among susceptible youth.

Grassroots partnerships: a successful strategic approach or an additional method of alienating Muslim communities?

If the above considerations are to be made regarding the nature of community–statutory agency relationships or agreements, it is even more imperative to deliberate over the damage caused by aspects of Prevent which have caused the further stigmatization and, as a result, marginalization of Muslim communities. The indiscernible criteria by which a significant number of organizations managed to successfully apply for and receive money from the PVEF suggested that they were all tackling problematic areas within their respective communities insofar as it related to the threat of violent extremism (Bartlett and Birdwell, 2010). One only had to look at some of the entities that received funds from the DCLG alongside the 'interventions' and activities they delivered to ascertain that violent extremism was certainly not a priority issue in their communities.[4] Arguments that suggested, on the one hand, that public funds were being wasted and, on the other, that Muslim communities were being stigmatized could be considered credible in light of these observations. As discussed in the previous section, grassroots, bottom-up initiatives need to provide clear terms of reference regarding the parameters within which they would be prepared to work with statutory partners and the government. The suggestion that communities need not work with any one of these at all is one that, in today's climate, can be considered ineffectual due to the microscopic lens under which Muslims have been placed as a result of the pressure to tackle the issue of violent radicalization and extremism in their respective communities. Another counter-argument that can be proferred against suggestions of disengagement and insularity is that there are an increasing number of entities erroneously claiming the mantle of representation for Muslim communities or purporting to have expertise on the identity of radical or extremist individuals or groups.[5] In the absence of credible grassroots counter-radicalization organizations, new, unrepresentative claimants will continue to emerge and communities will continue to be misrepresented or suspected of not doing enough to tackle the problem of extremism. The disbandment of organizations with established track records in this field would, no doubt, be welcomed by influential voices such as the former Assistant Commissioner of the Metropolitan Police Andy Hayman, who believes the funding of present counter-radicalization initiatives in preference to conventional intelligence-led policing is 'a lost cause' (Hayman, 2010). His position is likely to have resonated with the present government, particularly as it considers austerity cuts to its various departments and initiatives across the UK (Lyall, 2010). This position reflects, perhaps, a community-targeted approach, as it favours top-down, traditional nation-state security approaches to countering terrorism, as discussed in Chapter 2.

Partnership problems and impenetrable obstacles: the Channel Project

Hayman's preference for conventional intelligence-led policing may be considered by some to be the way forward. Others will deem it regressive. The author would suggest that Hayman's position is already being reinforced by the Channel Project, which continues to cause consternation among Muslim communities but satisfaction among present government circles. The Channel Project was launched as a pilot scheme across two areas in the UK during 2008 – Lambeth in south-west London and Preston in the north of England. The success of at least one of the pilots enabled the roll-out of the Channel Project across London. It was during this expansive phase that the Project began to encounter problems with other PVEF organizations due to the perceptions by the latter that it was designed to enlist intelligence from community partners about suspects on a police watch list. Instead of adopting the successful model of the earlier pilot schemes and referring to the terms of those Service Level Agreements (SLAs) which were mutually representative of each party's requirements and parameters of operation, the Channel Project was re-defined with new terms of agreement reflecting perhaps a more one-dimensional but inherently top-down approach. The new agreement could therefore be perceived as protecting, first and foremost, the interests of the Metropolitan Police Service (MPS) more than its community partners.[6]

The Channel Project may arguably become the single defining feature of what Prevent will come to represent. It should come as no surprise that the new government favours this project above other existing counter-radicalization initiatives involving communities under Prevent. The immediate difficulty that the government will invariably face, in the event of abandoning the community-led approach, is the Channel Project being rendered redundant in the absence of established and credible partners at a grassroots level. The Project will no longer be suitably placed to evaluate its own intelligence, leaving itself exposed to potential flaws in its strategy to recognize uncharacteristic trends or behavioural traits of Muslims which in themselves may not denote extremist tendencies. It is widely accepted that only Muslim communities are in a position to identify and address these sensitivities, which then begs a rather obvious question: in the absence of credible grassroots organizations and/or community voices to advise statutory agencies and the government, would Muslims again become subject to new interrogative legislation similar to s. 44 of the Terrorism Act 2000, recently scrapped in July 2010 by the Home Secretary, Theresa May, following a ruling by the European Court of Human Rights that the powers used by the police, i.e. stop and search, were unlawful (Travis, 2010)? Legislation akin to the 'Suss' laws of the 1980s, when many from African-Caribbean communities were subjected to sporadic stop and search arrests on account of their ethnicity, accentuated a negative era of the previous Conservative government and its relations with the Black community. The ensuing public disorder[7] that spread across parts of the UK during the early 1980s should serve as a timely reminder of the consequences of top-down strategies directed at communities considered to be 'suspect'. Concerns regarding the revisiting of strategies or approaches from that period could understandably be considered by some to be regressive in today's multicultural and multi-religious society, particularly in light of the findings highlighted in the Scarman Report at that time (Scarman, 1983).

New partnership arrangements under counter-terrorism frameworks

Despite the difficulties surrounding the nature of the Channel Project requirements, new productive partnerships can be developed between less contentious statutory agencies. This section will examine some of the relationships established between Prevent intervention programmes and a few agencies.

Youth Justice Service Referrals

Agencies from the Youth Justice Service (YJS) can form part of a trilateral arrangement with community partners and other agencies like the police when dealing with ex-offenders. However, the nature of this arrangement should be such that it is not dominated by one party's terms. For example, referrals established between the YJS and the community group whereby ex-offenders are directed by the former to the latter should not require an Information Sharing Agreement (ISA) with the third party – the police in this instance – due to the likelihood that the individual being referred is not considered vulnerable to violent radicalization or extremist propaganda; his or her referral is merely on the basis of rehabilitation and engagement with Muslim mentors, etc. If, however, the YJS has information regarding the vulnerability of this individual to extremism, it is within its jurisdiction to first refer him or her to the police on the premise that the community partner is included to discuss an effective intervention strategy of engagement to reduce this susceptibility.[8]

This trilateral approach formed the initial basis of the Channel Programme, although in some cases it has departed from the original format. A bilateral arrangement is also an effective approach to dealing with Muslim ex-offenders and provides more fluidity in view of the fact there are fewer parties with fewer stipulations. The YJS has the autonomy to refer its cases directly to another third party without including the community-based partner if there are issues beyond the remit of the latter. For example, if the community group's resources are restricted to education and employment training and the referral has social and psychological issues or vulnerabilities regarding extremism, etc., another, more suitable organization could be approached. Thereafter, once those issues have been addressed, the individual could be referred at a later and more progressive stage of his or her development to the organization at the 'softer' end of the intervention programmes spectrum.

Probation service referrals

The key objectives of the remit of some probation services accord with the Prevent strategy, but should also sit comfortably with community partners and groups involved in the counter-radicalization field at a grassroots level.[9] Like the YJS, but unlike the Channel Project, ex-offenders are conversant with the reasons for their referral between probation services and community partners. However, unlike the YJS, where, in some instances, young Muslims request referral to a Muslim organization, the probation service first assesses the needs of its client in more detail and then matches these with the relevant intervention partner. The nature of the probation service's approach is such that it has forged strong and successful relationships with many of its community partners. Its symbiotic and collaborative approach towards grassroots organizations and communities has yielded largely positive results.

Cross-cultural bridges: working with the families of victims of terrorist attacks

Perhaps the most innovative work done among some grassroots community groups is their collaborative work with family members of victims of terrorist attacks. The most poignant example to be cited is that of Carie Lemack[10] and John Falding's[11] work with the Brixton Mosque community via STREET UK. In February 2008, Ms Lemack and Mr Falding held a workshop with pupils of Iqra Independent VA Primary School in Brixton. The workshop explored common themes related to common hopes and aspirations shared by the pupils and their guests. Ms Lemack and Mr Falding also met parents of the pupils at the conclusion of the workshop. It is important to highlight how such collaboration evolved. The initial introduction of the parties was made through the MCU – again highlighting the success of a community-based partnership approach. The main impetus behind this introduction was Ms Lemack's commitment to meeting Muslims and sharing both her and their experiences of terrorism and its adverse effects on communities regardless of faith. This initial event provided the momentum for Lambeth Council, who, as mentioned earlier in this chapter, had already established partnerships with

Muslim communities in Brixton, to petition for additional funds from central government to host a subsequent event on a larger scale in schools across the borough.[12] The relationships between the parties continue to some extent today and they support each other in various areas of community, cross-cultural and counter-radicalization work.

Emotional intelligence: understanding the stages of individual development and deconstructing extremist narratives

Emotional intelligence is an intrinsic aspect of the psychological mosaic of young Muslims and to date there do not appear to be many organizations with a comprehensive programme to address this area. Emotional intelligence as it relates to youth at a grassroots level can be summarized in the following manner:

> Th[e] sustainable element of the programme would provide young Muslims with the skills to benefit their own community. However, this project would not focus solely on fundraising and delivering activities within the target community, but rather [would] be a diversionary process with an ethos based on conditioning the mindset away from radicalisation. This will be achieved by developing the emotional intelligence of young Muslims through authentic Islamic teachings. This will help young Muslims interpret and visualise current affairs in way that is more reflective of an authentic approach, as oppose[d] to a more radical interpretation being obtained by young Muslims today. Th[e] project would employ a more targeted approach towards those young Muslims that do not usually access [conventional mainstream] services. As is increasingly evident, a large majority do not access mainstream services as the feelings of isolation and discrimination felt by young Muslims are more prominent in the UK. Suffice it to cite the examples of Richard Reid (aka the Shoe Bomber) and Zacarius Moussaoui who both divorced themselves from all mainstream avenues, including their local mosques (Brixton Mosque being one of them). Their backgrounds provide sufficient proof of their susceptibility to extremism if social, ideological and political concerns – all surrounding their Muslim identity within the context of their immediate society and environment – are not

adequately addressed. Their backgrounds are not dissimilar to a significant number of British Muslims, particularly second/third generation Muslims, and converts. (STREET UK, 2007: 5)

The attraction of violent extremist propaganda is found in its ability to highlight and relate various strands of injustices across the Muslim world with the young, susceptible individual whose own circumstances, in many instances, is not too dissimilar so far as disengagement and/or disillusionment from society is concerned. While there exist various approaches to addressing these socio- economic, socio-religious or socio-political dynamics, increasing evidence suggests that a theological degree of engagement is required to remove the 'hard-wiring' effect of extremist propaganda on the emotional psyche of the individual. Deconstructing the extremist narrative is perhaps an effective way of engagement as it provides an opportunity to examine theological interpretations within discernable and societal contexts in which the individual is living. This in turn enables a paradigmatic shift from previous (mis)understandings:

> The deconstruction attempts to isolate the various media components that have been utilised to construct the media text in question ... This report will identify the various messages being encoded within the text and the subtleties at play that are deliberately put together for effect and impact upon the viewer.[13]

Additionally, the theological thread provides:

> a counter-narrative from an Islamic perspective, using authentic sources to repel justifications offered by the producers of the named video. [The counter-narrative is] aimed at devaluing the arguments put forth by highlighting the weaknesses ... in light of the Qur'an and Sunnah. (Hussain, 2009: 44)

Also, and in conclusion, Hussain suggests that:

> This discussion [regarding a Deconstruct programme] has demonstrated that in the existing discipline of media studies there is a framework that can be developed to expose the manipulative encodings employed by al-Qaeda. Such an approach would

better equip the most vulnerable in society with the necessary tools to at least decode a different reading to the one preferred by al-Qaeda as well as potentially reject it ... The Media Deconstruction approach presented ... becomes the foundation of further extensive deconstructions of material like the text analysed above. The fact that the approach is widely used in schools and colleges teaching Media Studies supports the notion that it can be made easily accessible for the susceptible young Muslims that al-Qaeda's propaganda clearly targets. (Hussain, 2009: 45)

Recognizing the effects of extremist propaganda on the emotional psyche of a young, vulnerable Muslim is perhaps a precursory stage to understanding what angle of approach should be taken in relation to his or her emotional intelligence. Arguably, one of the reasons for the inability of more culturally orientated Muslims to address the issue of violent radicalization among their own communities is because of their failure to comprehend both the emotional capacity and therefore the intelligence of young second- and third-generation Muslims whose religious understanding in twenty-first-century Britain has become alien to their own traditional and cultural roots.

The process of engagement, counselling and mentoring

One particular organization – STREET UK – has developed various workstreams across which it engages and eventually counsels or mentors members of its target audience who have either been identified as possessing particular vulnerabilities or have themselves approached staff seeking advice/assistance. Each workstream provides a range of services that cater for individual needs, as can be seen in the illustration provided in Figure 4.3 below.

Counselling, advice and mentoring may occur following interaction between target audience members and staff in workstreams 1 and/or 2. These workstreams cover the more general areas of activities where audiences feel more comfortable to engage and socialize with peers and staff alike. 'Safe spaces', which foster a degree of trust and reassurance, are created within these two structured remits and it is among these environments that issues are identified and initially assessed before attempts are made to address individual needs head-on. Once counselling and advice are offered

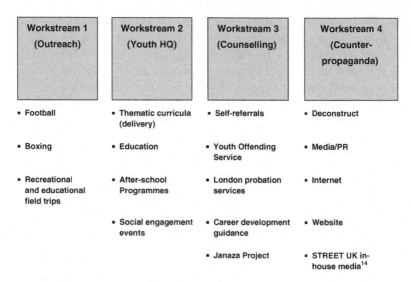

Workstream 1 (Outreach)	Workstream 2 (Youth HQ)	Workstream 3 (Counselling)	Workstream 4 (Counter-propaganda)
• Football	• Thematic curricula (delivery)	• Self-referrals	• Deconstruct
• Boxing	• Education	• Youth Offending Service	• Media/PR
• Recreational and educational field trips	• After-school Programmes	• London probation services	• Internet
	• Social engagement events	• Career development guidance	• Website
		• Janaza Project	• STREET UK in-house media[14]

Figure 4.3 STREET operational workstreams

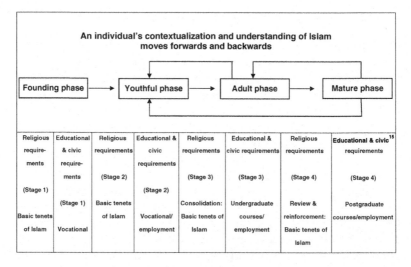

Figure 4.4 Adapted model for the life cycle of a convert's post-conversion process (Baker, 2009)

and accepted, workstream 3 provides the necessary level of expertise to the individuals requiring such engagement and a mutually agreement between the mentor and mentee is devised to facilitate a rehabilitative path towards positive societal re-engagement. The identification and understanding of the stage of the mentee's religious and social/educational development are essential if he or she is to be successfully engaged with at this sensitive stage. The following theoretical framework has been implemented in order to assess the various stages of an individual's development.

The above illustration can be explained using the following summary of each developmental stage.

1) Founding (conversion) phase (STREET UK, 2010)

This stage of conversion addresses the formative stages of conversion and the influences/drivers that caused individuals to convert to Islam (STREET UK, 2010). The foundational tenets of Islam and introductory programmes relating to identity and civic society will be introduced to target audience members who enter STREET UK at this stage of their lives. Research has indicated that this stage is one at which new converts and second- and third-generation 'returnees' to Islam are most susceptible to violent radicalization and/or extremist propaganda (Roald, 2004).

2) Youthful (formative/overzealous and idealistic) phase

This is another phase where converts/second- and third-generation returnees are considered to be susceptible to extremist propaganda and teachings. Overzealousness is a common feature of many conversions as, in many instances, new converts/second- and third-generation returnees possess heightened senses of self-righteousness with a desire to directly address/tackle the perceived ills of society (Roald, 2004). Social affiliations, if not effected at the founding phase of conversion, can possibly still occur at this stage.

3) Adult (foundational) phase

This phase looks at more established Muslim converts/second- and third-generation returnees who have practised the religion long enough to have perhaps progressed from the earlier understandings and practices of the first two phases. Their respective *actualization* of the religion, as opposed to practising it in the *abstract*, means that individuals at this phase have better understood and experienced the religion as a way of life, i.e. they have lived or travelled abroad to Muslim countries and engaged/participated in those societies, thereby enhancing their understanding and practice of Islam. This is contrary to their previous understanding and practice which, as mentioned above, was previously applied in an abstract form, i.e. learned from books, cassettes and videos in a predominantly non-Muslim environment. Research results are intended to show whether converts have come to terms with their new-found and often dual identities or whether conflicts still ensue during this phase.

4) Mature (reflective) phase

An individual's perceptions may further develop or, indeed, change if they have not at earlier stages of post-conversion due to a multiplicity of socio-economic and/or religious factors. For example, marriage, the birth of a new child or even the death of relatives or friends (irrespective of their religion) may be contributory factors towards an individual reflecting on his or her religious understanding, practice and development. These potential drivers are similar to Roald's theory describing a three-stage conversion process which, to some extent, lends support to the four-stage model proposed above (Roald, 2004). When suggesting the 'culturalization' of new Muslims into the cultural contexts of their spouses or friends, she identifies a preliminary stage of: '"falling in love with Islam", where one wants to practise every Islamic precept' (Roald, 2004: 288). The second stage is described as a period of discovery where the convert realizes the difficulty or, indeed, impracticality of implementing Islamic practices in their entirety. He or she therefore realizes the 'discrepancy' between Islamic ideals and Muslims' actual practice. In other words, the new convert recognizes the difference between 'the Ideal Islam' as it is illustrated in Islamic books and that of Muslim understanding/practice in various parts of the world (Roald, 2004). Roald's observations accord to 'abstract' and 'actualized' understandings of the religion. Finally, she mentions the third stage of conversion being the convert's ultimate realization that Muslims are not too dissimilar to their non-Muslim counterparts and that 'it is possible to understand Islam in a Scandinavian framework' (Roald, 2004: 288).

The British context is obviously the setting for the descriptive process outlined above with an additional but important pretext that staff who engage with youth at the various stages of this developmental chart must themselves be at a more advanced stage than their audience in order to effectively mentor and advise them.

Conclusion

The previous section endeavoured to highlight a few strategies being implemented by the 2009 award-winning STREET UK programme in relation to its methodology of engagement with its target audiences. The work described perhaps supports arguments in favour of the grassroots bottom-up approach to countering not only violent radicalization but also social issues which continue to affect the 'Big Society' at its core insofar as it relates to the disconnection and disaffection of some second- and third-generation Muslims and converts. Arguably it is only these communities and organizations that are equipped to address such challenges. The acknowledgement, support and facilitation of some statutory agencies to enable these groups to get on with the work they have, to a greater extent, always been doing further strengthens this assertion.

This chapter has endeavoured to outline differing perspectives as to whether a requirement continues to exist for statutory agency partnerships with grassroots organizations in the field of counter-radicalization. The need to define clear parameters of engagement between the two entities was also briefly examined, with the discussion focusing on the effectiveness of the grassroots, bottom-up approach and the value of community-focused approaches. However, it is apparent that, although a general consensus remains concerning the inclusion and necessity of grassroots, community-led organizations in successful counter-radicalization initiatives, there is disagreement regarding the *type* or *ideological profile* of communities and organizations that should be involved or should receive public funding. Given the applicability and indeed success of intervention strategies deployed at a grassroots level by community-led initiatives, it may come as a surprise to some communities if such projects cease to exist without suitable and equally robust alternatives being put in place. Additionally, when considering the role of statutory-driven projects like the Channel Project, consideration must be given to their ultimate direction and whether they are in fact indicative of a return to a previous hierarchical, essentially top-down, coercive and community-targeted approach towards tackling violent extremism among British Muslim communities.

While the above synopsis may provide a somewhat grim scenario insofar as it relates to police–community-led partnerships, the success of other statutory community-led alliances perhaps provides a more optimistic picture for the immediate future. However, until the existing government evaluates and chooses to remain with some of the existing and more successful intervention programmes or develops a newer, more comprehensive counter-terrorist strategy, indecision over what actually constitutes effective or ineffective counter-radicalization models will prevail, enabling proponents of violent extremism to continue to develop their strategies relatively unchallenged, as well as exploit the current climate of uncertainty surrounding the UK's present ability to devise a comprehensive and effective strategy of counter-terrorism which can stand the test of time and not be discarded if a subsequent government happens to replace it in the near future.

Case study: Peer Audio Visual Engagement (PAVE)

PAVE is intended to act as a precursor to the more intense Deconstruct project. It is in essence a project where the identified groups of youth participate in sessions of watching documentaries and YouTube links of subjects of topical and specific interest to them. An interactive discussion then ensues, with them providing feedback on their observations and understandings of what they have watched. Viewings are arranged according to the developmental stages of the youths – the earlier the stage of development, the more basic the footage in content and duration. The general outline of the project can be defined as follows:

- It is a key development of STREET UK's objectives to initiate and maintain open and useful dialogue with attendees.
- Video viewings will be based mainly on DVD documentaries and TV recordings where the overall content is seen to be of relevance to attendees. Content themes may vary across strands such as personal development, morality, community, parenting, diversity, environment and globalization.
- Attendee audiences will be grouped according to their perceived Islamic maturity using the STREET UK progression model.
- Each viewing session is to be properly facilitated by a youth worker who will also guide attendees to complete a double-sided

prompt/feedback sheet. The prompts will give the viewing group pointers to discuss their pre-existing ideas on the video topic with the youth worker and fellow attendees. The feedback section will give attendees the opportunity to say how relevant or beneficial they found the video.

* The pre-viewing discussion and post-viewing feedback should guide attendees to consider how the video themes relate to their circumstances and their Islamic understanding. The PAVE session should therefore be constructive and interactive rather than a passive experience.
* Youth workers delivering this initiative will need to view video programmes in advance of PAVE sessions to ensure they are prepared to field the anticipated themes for discussion.
* Youth workers should be responsible for monitoring the attendance at each viewing session (particularly where a series of videos is being shown) to ensure that attendees are involved in an appropriate progression of PAVE sessions.[16]

Notes

1. The Qur'an, Chapter 49 (al-Hujurat), verse 12: 'O you who have believed, avoid much negative assumption [suspicion]. Indeed, some suspicion is sin. *And do not spy* or backbite each other...': Abul Qasim Publishing House, 1997.
2. Secret Quilliam memo to the government: www.scribd.com/doc/34834977/Secret-Quilliam-Memo-to-government (date accessed 14 December 2011).
3. *Ibid.*
4. See Hazel Blear's video highlighting entities receiving PVEF in 2008: www.lga.gov.uk/lga/core/page.do?pageId=664688 (date accessed 6 January 2012).
5. See Bora, 2008.
6. Information Sharing Agreement for the purposes of the Channel Project: prepared by the MPS, 2009.
7. The Toxteth, Brixton and Tottenham riots.
8. Channel Project Service Level Agreement between the YJS, the Youth Support Services (YSS), the MPS and a community-based intervention project, 2007.
9. The following is an example of the joint objectives of one probation service and community partnership: all identified partners will work together within the vision of the Prevent strategy:

   * to reduce the risk and vulnerability to violent extremism of Muslim offenders that the probation service refers to the community-based partner in question;

- to reduce associated risk factors while identifying and promoting positive attributes within Muslim offenders;
- to provide offenders with positive alternative diversionary activities together with Islamic counselling and Deconstruct management for selected offenders.

An SLA between the probation service and a community-based partner, 2009.
10. Ms Lemack lost her mother, Judy Lacroix, in the Twin Towers terrorist attacks on 9/11 in New York, 2001.
11. Mr Falding lost his partner, Anat Rosenberg, on the bus targeted in the terrorists attacks on London, 7 July 2005.
12. 'Building Bridges 2': workshops for four Lambeth primary and secondary schools – 6, 9 and 10 February 2009, STREET Report and 'Families of Terror Victims Warn Pupils of Extremism', *Evening Standard*, 10 February 2009, p. 25.
13. Media deconstruction and counter-narrative of 'as-Shahab Video 1', STREET UK Ltd Deconstruction Team, August 2008, p. 2.
14. STREET UK organizational and operational structure, 2009.
15. STREET UK framework for identifying the target audience's developmental stages and implementation of schedule, 2010.
16. V. Chung, STREET PAVE Outline, 26 August 2010.

References

Baker, A.H. (2010) 'Countering Extremism in the UK: A Convert Community Perspective', PhD thesis, University of Exeter, Chapter 8, Case Study 3: Abdullah el-Faisal.
——. (2011) *Extremists in Our Midst: Confronting Terror*. Basingstoke: Palgrave Macmillan.
Bartlett, J. and Birdwell, J. (2010) 'From Suspects to Citizens: Preventing Violent Extremism in a Big Society', Demos, www.demos.co.uk/files/From_Suspects_to_Citizens_-_web.pdf?1279732377 (date accessed 14 December 2011).
Bora, M. "2008) 'Sssh! It's the Silent Majority', *The Guardian*, 16 May, www.guardian.co.uk/commentisfree/2008/may/16/ssshitsthesilentmajority (date accessed 14 December 2011).
Briggs, R., Fieschi, C. and Lownsbrough, H. (2006) 'Bringing it Home. Community-based Approaches to Counter-Terrorism', DEMOS, www.demos.co.uk/files/Bringing%20it%20Home%20-%20web.pdf (date accessed 14 December 2011).
Cole, J. and Cole, B. (2009) *Martyrdom: Radicalisation and Terrorist Violence Among British Muslims*. London: Pennant Books.
Crous, C. (2009) 'Human Intelligence Sources: Challenges in Policy Development', *Security Challenges* 5(3): 117–27.
DCLG (Department for Communities and Local Government) (2007) 'Preventing Violent Extremism Pathfinder Fund 2007/08 Case Studies',

April, www.communities.gov.uk/documents/communities/pdf/324967.pdf (date accessed 14 December 2011), p. 4.

Dyke, A.H. (2009) *Mosques Made in Britain*. London: Quilliam Foundation.

Githens-Mazer, J. and Lambert, R. (2011) 'Islamophobia and Anti-Muslim Hate Crime: UK Case Studies', Exeter: EMRC, University of Exeter: http://centres.exeter.ac.uk/emrc/publications/Islamophobia_and_Anti-Muslim_Hate_Crime.pdf (date accessed 18 January 2012).

Hall, N. (2009) 'Policing Racist Hate Crime: Policy, Practice, and Experience', in H.S. Bhui (ed.), *Race & Criminal Justice*. London: Sage.

Hayman, A. (2010) 'We Experts were Totally Wrong-Footed by 7/7', *The Times*, 7 July, www.thetimes.co.uk/tto/opinion/columnists/article2590043.ece (date accessed 14 December 2011).

Hussain, T. (2009) 'As-Sahab: A Semiotic Analysis of *The Wills of the Knights of the London Raid*', MA Islamic Studies, Final Dissertation, Birkbeck College, University of London.

Kundnani, A. (2009) *Spooked! How Not to Prevent Violent Extremism*. London: Institute of Race Relations, available at www.irr.org.uk/pdf2/spooked.pdf (date accessed 16 December 2011).

Lambert, R. (2010) The London Partnerships: An Insider's Analysis of Legitimacy and Effectiveness', PhD thesis, University of Exeter.

Lyall, S. (2010) 'Britain Reels as Austerity Cuts Begin', *New York Times*, 9 August, www.nytimes.com/2010/08/10/world/europe/10britain.html (date accessed 14 December 2011).

Maher, S. and Frampton, M. (2009) 'Choosing Our Friends Wisely: Criteria for Engagement with Muslim Groups', London: Policy Exchange, www.policyexchange.org.uk/images/publications/pdfs/Choosing_Our_Friends_Wisely.pdf (date accessed 14 December 2011).

Roald, A.S. (2004) *New Muslims in the European Context: The Experience of Scandinavian Converts*. Leiden: Brill.

Salafi Manhaj.com (2007) 'The Devil's Deception of Abdullah el-Faisal: A Critical Study of His Statements, Errors and Extremism in Takfeer', www.Salafimanhaj.com (date accessed 14 December 2011).

Scarman, L.G. (1983) *The Scarman Report: The Brixton Disorders, 10–12 April 1981*. Harmonsworth: Penguin.

Spalek, B., Lambert, R. and Baker, A.H. (2009) 'Minority Muslim Communities and Criminal Justice: Stigmatized UK Faith Identities Post 9/11 and 7/7', in H.S. Bhui (ed.), *Race & Criminal Justice*. London: Sage.

STREET UK (2007) 'Proposal' (final draft), 25 July, p. 5.

——. (2010) 'Framework for Identifying Target Audience's Developmental Stages and Implementation of Schedule'.

Travis, A. (2010) 'Anti-Terror Stop and Search Powers to be Scrapped', *The Guardian*, 8 July, www.guardian.co.uk/law/2010/jul/08/anti-terror-stop-and-search-scrapped (date accessed 14 December 2011).

Verkaik, R. (2010) 'MI5 "Still Using Threats to Recruit Muslim Spies"', *Independent on Sunday*, 5 January, www.independent.co.uk/news/uk/home-news/mi5-still-using-threats-to-recruit-muslim-spies-1857750.html (date accessed 14 December 2011).

5
Gender within a Counter-Terrorism Context

Laura Zahra McDonald

Introduction

In researching the evolution of community-based approaches to countering terrorism, an important finding has been the development of innovative practices by community organizations in relation to women's roles – potential and actual – in violent extremism and in its prevention. While both the definition of 'community' and the approaches explored throughout this book necessarily include women, the gender-specific nature of some of the work deserves separate analysis. Additionally, the inclusion, indeed active participation and leadership, of women in this arena challenges a number of academic theories and social discourses in relation to Muslim women, their perceived social roles and their relevance to understanding security. This chapter will therefore unpick the multiple strands surrounding these issues, beginning with the broader historical discourses which act as the backdrop for the way in which Muslim women are viewed within the security arena and ending with an exploration of grassroots work by and for Muslim women that contributes towards countering terrorism.

The impact of Orientalist and community misogyny

In order to understand the context of security discourse in relation to Muslim women, the history of Orientalism – Said's (1979) conceptual tool for the Eurocentric and racist body of images and social processes by which the 'West' has normatively viewed the

'East' – must be discussed in relation to gender. While Said himself has been criticized for a lack of gender consciousness, the scholarly input since has illustrated the highly gendered nature of Orientalist discourse, in which Muslim women are constructed through a number of exoticized, sexualized and misogynist motifs (McClintock, 1995; Zine 2002). From the artistic Victorian fantasies of the *harem* and *hammam*, in which Muslim and Arab women are portrayed as sybaritic chattels of barbarian men, to the twenty-first-century concern with the Afghan burqa and the suicidal Palestinan, Muslim women and their spaces have been reduced to one-dimensional opposites of the Western perception of self. Within this process, Western women are also constructed and their image appropriated to act as a contrast to their Muslim sisters. Thus, the self-image of Western civilization and moral conservatism, which baulked at the perceived sensual lifestyles of Muslims in the nineteenth century, has given way to a binary of Western liberation of women with the supposed submission and fanaticism of their Muslim counterparts under Islam (Freedman, 2007: 39). What has remained constant, however, is the way in which these varying, adapting forms of Orientalism have acted as a prejudicial lens through which Muslim societies and communities have been viewed and judged in the European West and as a benchmark for understanding the lives of Muslim women.

In opposition to this Orientalism is its parallel, a 'reverse-Orientalism' (Abu Lughod, 1993: 10) in which Orientalist perceptions are recast as positive, alongside a crude Occidentalism and appropriation of women's images found within certain popular discourse in various Muslim societies. Like Orientalism, these narratives are espoused for ideological and social purposes. In these internal Muslim constructions, cultural mores and Islamic ideals are employed and in many cases misinterpreted to create a further set of images to which women are expected to conform or avoid, and by which their behaviours are assessed. While Western women are often portrayed as wanton or subjugated by a perceived Western pornocracy, Muslim women are also offered various dualities in which to fit according to context, from the pious Muslim sister to the disruptive source of sexual power and *fitna*.

What is interesting and important to our analysis are the ways in which these disingenuous and sexist images pervade the corresponding security paradigms, illustrated at their most explicit and extreme within the discourses of New Terror and Al-Qaeda, and through which Muslim women are understood in relation to the state and human security.

Muslim women, gender and security

While gender and security has become an area of increasing academic interest, the normative position has been one of disinterest. More specifically, the male-dominated arenas of terrorism and counter-terrorism may be viewed as having an embedded and invisible assumption that security is the business of men: where women are included in discourse or practice, it is usually as an interesting aside or an aberration to the security context. Analyses that include women are often overtly sexist, the depiction of female Eta operatives as 'menstruating through their guns' (Hamilton, 2007: 141, 145) illustrating the level of misogyny found in security texts (Brunner, 2007). Moreover, the relegation of women to the sidelines (Talbot, 2001: 8) and the gendered nature of understandings of terrorism and its prevention are so prevalent as to have been rendered invisible – natural facts which are neither noted nor questioned. Yet, in recent years these assumptions have been carefully deconstructed by feminists, who argue that it is neither just an interesting but academic social phenomenon nor an exercise in gender consciousness, but a necessary examination in order to reveal the ways in which political violence and its prevention operate within societies both at micro- and macro-levels. Such scholarship calls for an acknowledgement of the 'complexities of the gender-politics of conflict, including the roles of women as perpetrators' (Feinman, 2000; Moser and Clark, 2001; Hasso, 2005; Krylova, 2005) and a move away from the binaries of victim/perpetrator and man/woman (Hamilton, 2007: 133).

This need for gender-sensitive investigation is particularly pertinent to the context of the New Terror era, in which gendered discourses and practices are embedded within broader narratives relating to Muslims, Islam and security. Summarized, the imagery dominating post-9/11 debates around terrorism and security draws from the aforementioned long tradition of Orientalist and Occidentalist imagery of the Self and Other. The security narratives thus reveal stereotypes of violent Muslim men committing acts of terror and oppression, in diametric opposition to 'Western' men (non-Muslim/ Christian/White) acting to save and protect, or, alternatively, heroic mujahideen brothers resisting and protecting the Ummah in the wake of devilish 'Western' hegemony. The discourses vary in sophistication and theme, but, as discussed throughout this book, create an overwhelmingly divisive flow of narrative about the relations and nature of the apparently monolithic communities of Muslims and non-Muslims. It is not surprising, therefore, that a gender-conscious reading of New Terror as put forward by both self-proclaimed 'sides' also reveals imagery of Muslim women that even further exaggerates the deletion and exceptionalization of women in relation to security. Within these narratives 'terrorism' is the violence of the Other, and countering terror is the method of prevention, disruption and resistance.

From the Orientalist tradition, Muslim women appear relevant to terrorism only in states of victimhood, remaining worthy of interest only as rather exotic subjects. This victim trope has two dominant forms. First, Muslim women are cast as passive onlookers or victims maimed by their menfolk in the terrorist attacks and insurgencies of the Middle East and Asia (Silber and Bhatt, 2007: 23). Alternatively, and illustrating the inherent sexism of normative security discourse, they are cast as active, deviant victims. The 'Black Widows of Chechnya', for example, are reduced and pathologized, constructed as women whose 'gentle nature', damaged by social, psychological or personal trauma and oppression, turn to terrorism. Their acts of violence are thus depoliticized and explained away as desperation, vengeance or social defiance (Brunner, 2007). In relation to counter-terrorism, as will be discussed further, constructions are equally problematic yet more active: as potential informers on their terrorist menfolk, as social barometers, whose progress to emancipation indicates the cleansing of extremist ideologies from Muslim society, or as community pillars whose womanly gentle nature can be used to pacify violent tendencies.

Echoing the Orientalist use of Muslim women in the binaries of Self and Other – Western freedom versus Islamic oppression – narratives employed by self-proclaimed 'jihadi' groups use women in their appropriation of Quranic ethical imperatives, including justice, righteousness and the command of God. Using very similar tropes to those of the Orientalists, Muslim women are constructed and their images co-opted as passive victims or useful participants. The former is simple, casting Muslim women as passive victims of Western war-mongering and corrupt regimes; the latter, however, is dependent on the interpretations of jihad in relation to women – whether or not they can or should be involved – as a distraction or a support. These are the tropes of the idealized 'supportive sister', who supports or even joins acts of violence despite her propensity towards womanly passivity or distracted sensuality, or the 'disruptive wife', who draws her man away from jihad through her worldly nature and seductive but ultimately destructive, limited sexuality (Cook, 2005). Compare, for example, the following quotes, in which varying interpretations of extremist theology and gender intersect and appropriate the Islamic concept of jihad and image of Muslim women for political and ideological purposes:

> It is a woman who teaches you today a lesson in heroism, who teaches you the meaning of Jihad, and the way to die a martyr's death ... It is a woman who has shocked the enemy, with her thin, meagre, and weak body ... It is a woman who blew herself up, and with her exploded all the myths about women's weakness, submissiveness, and enslavement. ('It's a Woman!', Editorial, *Al-Sha'ab*, 1 February 2002, OSCE Technical Expert Workshop on Suicide Terrorism, Warsaw, May 2005: 2)

> If you say [wanting to avoid jihad]: My heart is not comfortable parting from my wife and her beauty, the companionship I have close to her and my happiness in touching her – even if your wife is the most beautiful of women and the loveliest of the people of the time, her beginning is a small drop [of sperm] and her end is a filthy corpse. Between those two times, she carries excrement, her menstruation denies her to you for part of her life, and her disobedience to you is usually more than her obedience ... (Cook, 2005: 378, quoting Ibn al-Nahhas al-Dumyati (d. 1414), *Mashari' al-ashwaq ila masari' al'ushshaq* (Beirut: Dar al-Basha'ir al-Islamiyya, 2002), I, p. 129 (no. 60); see also I, pp. 215–17)

> It should be noted that physical fighting has been a role assigned primarily to men, both by the Prophet (peace be upon him) and those after him. However, when the need arose, our brave sisters never held back from fighting, and neither should they now! (*Qoqaz/NEFA*: 3)

Each set of imagery thus reduces the Muslim woman to one-dimensional, stereotypical constructs at the sidelines of political violence and security, whose involvement is generally understood to be personal, social and irrational – categories traditionally considered within patriarchal frameworks as feminine rather than considered and political. The process acts to erase the possibility of female agency and prevent the recognition of women as important actors – either actual and potential – in the creation and prevention of political violence. It is in this context that the developments in both recent British policy towards countering terrorism and the community responses and alternative frameworks are situated. As will be discussed further, these narratives flavour the attitude of the state towards Muslim women, and community attitudes, and are at the centre of a series of implicit and explicit forms of negotiation that Muslim women perform in their engagement with both the state and human security.

The British context, Muslim women and 'Prevent'

As stated above, the body of transnational misogynist and patriarchal discourse provides a context to the central subject of this chapter – the involvement of Muslim women in community approaches to countering terror crime. The phrase 'community approaches' is one that indicates inclusivity not only in relation to the involvement of Muslims with diverse ethnicities, social backgrounds and religious interpretations, but also to the inclusion of women in this grassroots alternative to state-driven security. However, grassroots initiatives and responses are not detached from wider contexts, and before proceeding with a discussion of Muslim women's involvement, it is important to reiterate the British situation in which community approaches are being developed that, in addition to the New Terror discourse discussed above, shape the landscape in which community work must operate.

As this book has explored, the post-9/11, post-7/7 era may be characterized in the UK by its highly politicized social context and a number of these social and political developments are of particular relevance in understanding Muslim women's interactions with security. The increase in Islamophobia, the generalized suspect status of Muslim communities, the ascription of the categories of 'moderate' and 'radical' to delineate differing interpretations and practices of Islam, and the securitization of the cohesion/integration agenda all impact negatively on Muslim women. The impact is particularly strong for women whose modes of dress publically signify Islam, such as head scarves or face coverings, which allow for their public identification as Muslim.

Muslim women have found themselves simultaneously marginalized and at the centre of intense – even hysterical – public, political debate, subject to judgments ranging from their status in Islam to their relations with Muslim men and their ability to integrate with British society. Treated as social, cultural and religious barometers of their communities, such scrutiny not only challenges individuals at a personal level but also forces individuals to negotiate their agency, interacting socially and politically within a hypercritical, objectifying framework. As such, the woman who chooses to cover her body as an act of spirituality is subjected to hostile ascriptions and outsider interpretations that proclaim her as oppressed and extremist. For example, an individual may suffer the violence of anti-Muslim hate crime, of which women are most often the victim (Githens-Mazer and Lambert, 2011: 12), with the accompanying physical and psychological impacts. Yet, on another level she must also interact with political discourse: the hijab in particular has become a metonym for Muslim difference (McDonald, 2006: 160–97), with women's acts of religiosity linked for political ends to issues of cohesion, immigration and national identity throughout Europe, with countries such as Belgium and France going as far as to outlaw items of dress. In Britain, the infamous statement of Jack Straw, an MP and public servant who suggested his constituents remove their niqabs to alleviate his discomfort at what he viewed as a 'visible statement of separation and of difference',[1] illustrates the Orientalism, prejudice and imbalance of power relations inherent in the relationship between the state and Muslim women. As such, an individual, in order to resist the reduction or relativization of her agency, must through her attitude, behaviours and actions negotiate the place she seeks within British society rather than the one which she is given.

Against such a background, in which Muslim communities are under great strain, and merely being Muslim and female appears a political, social and existential struggle, interacting with the security agenda is a challenging and sensitive undertaking. For many, the circumstances mean that such interaction is neither desirable nor possible. However, there are individuals and groups who are doing so, who negotiate with and resist dominant discourse, and choose to engage with the security paradigm, in some cases contributing to alternative community frameworks.

Before detailing women's involvement in community-based approaches, it is important to outline the complexities of Muslim women's involvement in state-led approaches, which may be characterized as predominantly top-down and developed in response to the events of 9/11 and 7/7. Within the CONTEST strategies (1 and 2) and inherent to the notion that 'communities defeat terrorism', women were identified as important community members, particularly in relation to Prevent (Home Office, 2009: 90; 2010: 14). Under the New Labour governments of Tony Blair and Gordon Brown, Prevent policy explicitly identified Muslim women as a group to engage and co-opt for the purposes of countering terrorism, their gender and faith drawing government interest alongside a range of assumptions, expectations and offers. This role was outlined more specifically in related Prevent-specific documents, as the following quote illustrates:

Strengthen the role that women can play within their communities

Women can play a vital role in building strong communities and tackling violent extremism. It is important to enable their voices to be heard and empower them to engage with disillusioned youths. There is already important work underway across Government to help Muslim women get on in the workplace and to play a bigger role in civil society. But further specific action is required. We have funded a range of local initiatives aimed at enabling women to play a part in tackling violent extremism. For example, leadership training enables women to develop the skills and build the confidence necessary to be able to influence members of the community more widely. (DCLG, 2007: 9)

Muslim women were thus explicitly linked to the Prevent agenda, in particular as key to 'building resilience in communities' (Home Office, 2009: 90) and 'supporting and promoting moderate voices' (HM Government, 2008: 19). These phrases reveal two understandings about Muslim women from a policy perspective: that they are viewed as the building blocks of community and are inclined to moderation and non-violence – images drawn from normative sexist discourse in which women are meek, mild and nurturing, crucial to creating and sustaining human relations. This is also reflected in wider opinions regarding the role of women and conflict: the UN, for example, highlights the important role of women in the prevention and resolution of conflicts and in peace-building (UN Security Council, 2000). Additionally, a reading of the New Labour Prevent policy suggests that they have, by virtue of their gender and experience as Muslim women, a tendency towards the British state's interpretation of 'moderate Islam'. This 'call of duty' is also tacitly aimed at activist Muslim women, those who are in a position of knowledge and influence to work with and within communities. Muslim women were thus officially and explicitly included in the British state's counter-terrorism policy, creating a number of opportunities but also challenges.

For a group so problematized within British society, inclusion and recognition in the state's security programme presented a great opportunity for Muslim women to participate in, contribute to and even shape the ways in which acts of terror crime are prevented. Thus, the Prevent strand between 2005 and 2010 included a very broad understanding of 'preventative work', from hard-ended interventions with individuals considered vulnerable to violent extremism to cohesion-related community projects, including the funding of Muslim women's groups and networks. This blurring of state security with community development thus opened up a space for individuals and groups willing to be categorized under their gender and religious identities as 'Muslim women' to raise issues and lead community projects within the security framework.

The state-led approach has therefore arguably increased the opportunity for Muslim women to voice their concerns, represent themselves and the needs of their communities, and increase community activism. Additionally, issues considered important to the promotion of women's welfare and participation were often championed through official channels created between government departments and the groups they formed to act as representatives of Muslim women. While arguably a top-down initiative, the National Muslim Women's Advisory Group, a group appointed by the Department for Communities and Local Government (DCLG) in order to represent and speak for British Muslim women, functioned to inform the government regarding issues such as Muslim women's participation in religious institutions and wider British society. The scrutiny of the post-7/7 environment and increased political consciousness that this has raised amongst Muslim community groups has also meant that women are increasingly involved in active leadership roles within broader issues rather than gender-specific organizations, including the Muslim Safety Forum and the British Muslim Forum.

However, state-led developments also represent a series of challenges. On a general level, the divisive nature of funding in which community groups compete for legitimacy and financial support, and the tendency to recreate colonial-style relations between minorities and the state through the creation of in-group representatives have heightened tensions at a time of great sensitivity. Collective memories within many Muslim communities may recall the colonial co-opting of 'native' groups and their mimicry (Bhabha, 1984), with the complex and mutually destructive relations sustained through the imperialist framework. The highly politicized and often difficult relationships between British Muslims, the state, the media and the wider public impact on engagement and create a difficult context in which the security agenda is rooted, further contributing to feelings of stigma and vulnerability within communities.

The breadth of the Prevent programme and its ascendency over cohesion, particularly in relation to Muslim community groups, also resulted in many community activists, including under-funded women's groups, faced with little choice but to engage with the top-down securitized framework in order to secure funding. Community activism, viewed through a lens of security that muddled community development and women's empowerment with counter-terrorism, has been subjected to the appropriation of its issues and the co-optation of individuals and activist groups. For example, issues such as Muslim women's mosque access and empowerment initiatives have not only been funded through Prevent but also brought up within policy documents as ways in which to bolster state security (HM Government, 2008: 25).

Additionally, the idea that Muslim women's groups can and will help state security by building resilience and promoting moderation rests on a highly gendered, feminized assumption about women's natural 'soft power' (Adnan, 2006) – the ability to charm and persuade rather than force (Nye, 2004)[2] – and, as illustrated previously, an ability to 'bridge' or provide access to Muslim men and young people considered more hard to reach, a problematic and rather insulting supposition. And while it may be argued in the wider sense that women are vital in arbitration:

> [This is] not an expression of a biologically determined predisposition to peace, but is rather a function of greatly restricted access to the means of violence within the gender dichotomy ... and also a consequence of their greater degree of social integration and responsibility for children and other family members. (Feminist Institute of the Heinrich Böll Foundation, 2005: 16–17)

The assumptions inherent in the current contexts and policies appear to be underpinned by unhelpful stereotypes. Once more, the focus on 'soft', social aspects to countering terrorism adds to the ongoing failure to recognize the role of women in preventing and supporting political violence.

To illustrate such challenges, it may be useful to present two examples from primary research (Spalek *et al.*, 2008–9). The first involves a young woman actively engaged with the security agenda through her participation as member and organizer of a coalition of Muslim community groups who engage formally with the police, politicians and the security services. Enjoying the engagement, which she finds empowering and interesting, she finds that her position as one of the few women involved and as a visibly identifiable, conservatively dressed Muslim means that she is perceived as a representative of Muslim women. This pressure is compounded by the apparently well-meaning but misinformed attitudes of colleagues who treat her differently from her male counterparts. From over-anxious interaction to patronising comments, her dealings are coloured by the intersection of several processes: attitudes towards women in general and Muslim women in particular, ignorance regarding Muslims and Islam, and a heightened sense of anxiety within the current securitized, politicized context:

> ... the first few times I went ... they were too careful, they wanted to know if I'm allowed to drink tea or not. I don't know what they feel a Muslim woman can or can't do. I know they were trying to be nice but I thought that was really, really ignorant. To say are we allowed to drink tea? We don't have a special Muslim drink, you know! ... Obviously they've been told you have to be very nice

to these people ... you need to go beyond the call of duty which is excellent, which is really nice, but at the same time, you think do you not know how to approach someone who is a Muslim, a normal person ... I do feel as a woman you get undermined a lot. (Spalek *et al.*, 2008–9)

The second example relates to the experience of a community organization that deals with issues relating to domestic violence. While concerns regarding women's rights and empowerment were adopted by the Prevent strategy, the direct engagement of such an organization seems unlikely and the link between domestic violence and state security unclear. Yet the research conducted (Spalek *et al.*, 2008–9) revealed covert approaches by security services working on the assumption that Muslim women using the organization's services could be co-opted into informing on their partners – the assumption allegedly being that a violent husband could be a violent extremist. Members of the organization, concerned about the confidentiality of their work and the ethics of such a proposal, along with the fear elicited by persistent and aggressive attempts at recruitment, felt completely disenfranchised, stigmatized by the way in which their work was perceived by a state institution and within the security framework in general.

The experience of this community organization highlights an important tension created by top-down state approaches: the concern with state security over human security. Activists and community workers interviewed over the course of the research repeatedly questioned the apparent lack of concern for their well-being, arguing that if communities are to be expected to help defeat terrorism, the security and safety of those communities must also be considered important:

Security for the people, security for the country, the government or for the community? I mean for the government and the country security has become a priority so it is already [a] priority from the point of view [of] protecting interests of the nation. But of course what is not really in the public discussion very much is the consequences of what's happening and its impact on ordinary people on the ground ... I quite often feel not safe ... I don't go out of my way to make myself vulnerable, if I'm by myself, walking around, in particular, you know, and I'm always with my kids, very conscientious about that. (Spalek *et al.*, 2008–9)

This is not only an ethical point, a call for a recognition of the equality of suffering (Lambert, 2010) but is also a point of pragmatism: if community members – especially women – are marginalized and threatened by the apparatus of state security, their vital participation will remain tentative and their relationship with the state ambivalent.

State-led approaches have thus created a dilemma for Muslim women and their engagement with security. To engage may benefit individuals and groups on a number of levels – fulfilling the desire to practise Islamic and civil duties to protect other citizens, to act against crime and violence, to promote social justice and to actively shape the policy and practices of the state. On the other hand, disengagement or non-engagement may appear necessary in the face of stigmatizing discourse, divisive policies and oppressive practices which women may feel are strengthened by their involvement, especially for women who are themselves – by virtue of their political or religious positionality – considered 'immoderate' by state definitions. From a personal perspective, overt and implicit Islamophobia and sexism experienced by women, coupled with the stigma of 'collusion' with the state, whether financial or ideological, as well as criticism for the perceived public airing of community 'dirty linen', can be extremely disconcerting. These challenges have created a complex context within which Muslim women's activism may at any one time be promoted, rejected or appropriated for the perceived benefit of state security. The inclusion of Muslim women in Prevent presented numerous challenges, yet the shift in the latest government review has resulted in a total exclusion of Muslim women's activism from mention within the revised Prevent policy (HM Government, 2011). Muslim communities remain stigmatized within security discourse, and Muslim women's contributions, despite the previous policy's problematic assumptions, are now linked to social cohesion instead of, rather than in addition to, security policy. Furthermore, activists with affiliations to groups deemed or self-identifying as Salafi or Islamist are increasingly excluded from engagement between the state and Muslim communities, potentially limiting the important contributions of community approaches to countering terrorism.

However, this problematic state-led framework shaping and limiting women's engagement with counter-terrorism is not the only route: community approaches to the prevention of terror crime have been in part driven by women wishing to engage on their own terms with security issues, providing an alternative space in which community members – including women – can lead but also tackle issues which state-led approaches have so far failed to acknowledge or address.

Grassroots initiatives: women and community security

As discussed in previous chapters, it is important to understand the development of community approaches to countering terror crime and the contribution of women to this, their experiences offering an invaluable insight into the provision of state and human security.

While the state-led inclusion of communities came from a reaction to a tragic, violent event – the London terrorist attacks of July 2005 – and was centred around the creation of policies to be applied generally to the British Muslim public, it may be argued that community-led work developed as a evolution of internal dialogue and nuanced response to specific ideas, ideologies and practices over a period of many years before 9/11 (Lambert, 2011). The resulting body of expertise has therefore been tailored from within and for specific groups, communities and situations according to necessity and means. As such, the participation of Muslim women has differed significantly from their inclusion in state-led efforts.

State-led approaches have divided communities into categories with which to partner or isolate – moderates and radicals, mosque leaders and youth workers, young people and women. From this perspective Muslim women are a distinct, demarcated group, engaged in policy-driven and defined ways. The approach ensures the inclusion of women, however tokenistically, but, as discussed above, places limits on their participation via implicit assumptions rooted in simplistic discourse. In contrast, the pragmatic, informal development of community approaches has resulted in the inclusion of women as part of the process rather than as an end in itself: while state policy has reactively focused on the specific inclusion of women, community initiatives have tended to involve women as part of their natural development. For example, women have been involved in the establishment and running of various organizations engaging with security with and without gender as an overtly identified issue, from women's networks to street-based youth clubs. Nevertheless, as a result of normative security and social contexts, the most hard-ended community work – with violent extremist groups, gangs and prisoners, for example – has been male-dominated. On a practical level, the small pool of community expertise such as youth workers and mosque leaders, in addition to the common Muslim practice of gender separation, has resulted in men dealing with men.

In spite of this male orientation, a number of grassroots organizations, particularly those actively engaged in intervention work, have begun to focus with more interest, and in some cases urgency, on women's participation. There are several reasons for this: first, the continued high profile of the security agenda has led to the greater participation of community members generally, a number of whom happen to be women; secondly, the resources and expertise of community groups specializing in countering terror crime and related issues have grown, from a realization that women are involved in supporting and committing acts of political violence to a capacity to involve women able to engage with such issues from a preventative perspective. Community members have for some time understood the need for women to engage with the entire spectrum of security-related issues, and now a burgeoning, integrated knowledge and related practice is growing. Crucially, this form of Muslim women's participation is grassroots-led, legitimate and effective.

A further pair of case studies drawn from current and continuing research illustrate the developments of these community approaches. The first is a woman-focused project established by an organization specializing in hard-ended youth work. Tackling a spectrum of challenges facing young people, including gang violence, drug dealing and use, sexual abuse and prostitution, the organization has an established and respected record by both state institutions and Muslim community members for intervention work with regard to violent extremism, which it views as a further strand in the problems which it addresses. Over the course of time, its leaders have noted an increasing number of young Muslim women caught up in these issues and have felt that a specialist strand was necessary to provide a safe space for vulnerable Muslim women to address their situations, with sensitivity towards faith, culture and gender. This has been particularly important in relation to community denial: as a result of internal gender discourses, the involvement of Muslim women as victims and perpetrators of such forms of criminality is commonly unacknowledged within many Muslim communities.

As well as addressing the needs of victims of gang rape, homelessness and substance abuse, the organization is developing expertise in intervention work with women vulnerable to and in some cases holding violent extremist ideologies. In particular, this work is unique in its ability to access the most isolated individuals and closed networks of women whose 'hard-to-reach' status not only stems from their desire to remain true to conservative interpretations of physical gender separation – requiring only women to make contact – but also from the ideological positions they hold, including violent extremist interpretations of Islam, through which they occupy the fringes of communities. In this way, the organization is at the forefront of community-led preventative approaches to countering terrorism, including the development of expertise in intervention work by Muslim women with Muslim women.

The second example relates to a woman's initiative within a community organization which has developed expertise in relation to theologically-based interventions with Muslim prisoners identified by prisons and/or community members as vulnerable to or already holding violent extremist views, including individuals convicted under counter-terrorism laws. The organization has also developed a specific strand with and for Muslim women, recognizing the need to engage women within the prison system, and with whom they carry out intervention work and mentoring, and also to develop family outreach programmes. In this case, female members of the organization have developed a unique skillset, not only dealing directly with female prisoners but also locating, approaching and working with family members of both male and female prisoners. This not only tackles individuals whose records indicate a threat to the state, the community and their own security, but also functions to deal with the wider impact that the beliefs and actions of violent extremist individuals and their subsequent arrests and convictions have on wider society: the communities and families traumatized, marginalized, ostracized and in some cases themselves radicalized by the functioning of security apparatuses.

Muslim women involved in community-led approaches to countering terror crime are thus contributing significantly – engaging individuals with violent extremist ideas, supporting community members affected in various ways by terror crime and counter-terrorism practices, and consequently building trusting relationships between different community groups and state actors. As members of Muslim communities, as women and as British citizens, they are contributing to the building of a more holistic approach to security, one which highlights the need for human and community security as well as state security, and in which women are acknowledged as actors who must be recognized and engaged with.

Muslim women and the future of security

As this chapter has explored, the intersection of racist discourse, gender constructions and security frameworks creates a complex and difficult backdrop for Muslim women to engage in the prevention of terror crime and its related issues. Top-down, state-led approaches created a double-edged sword: an opportunity to engage and influence, yet limited by their location within a security framework developed with little input from Muslim communities, their experiences and their expertise. However, Muslim women continue not only to successfully participate on these grounds but also to contribute to and in many cases lead within the alternative human-focused security frameworks developed at a grassroots level. While the woman-focused aspects in the British context are in their nascent stages at the time of writing, their contribution not only appears fundamental to the development of community-led approaches to countering terror crime but sets a new benchmark for Muslim women's participation in the demand for the recognition and inclusion of the public – individuals, organizations and communities – in achieving safety and security for all.

Case study

A community group whose work focuses on tackling vulnerabilities in relation to violent extremism amongst Muslim prisoners convicted under terrorism laws or identified as vulnerable to violent extremist ideas within prisons has recently developed a holistic community outreach programme, led by and aimed at supporting women. Through it:

- The needs and experiences of Muslim women within the British prison system are acknowledged, the organization actively seeking to further understandings in relation to gender-specific issues.
- The project aims to work not just with prisoners themselves but also with the communities and families of prisoners. This may include family members whose understanding of violent extremism is negligible, especially for those from non-Muslim backgrounds.
- The project has developed an innovative approach to security which takes into account the intersection of gender and the wider impact of terrorism and counter-terrorism on communities, families and women in particular.

Notes

1. www.guardian.co.uk/commentisfree/2006/oct/06/politics.uk (date accessed 15 December 2011).
2. See also www.rhodeshouse.ox.ac.uk/page/engaged-intellectual-joseph-nye-speaks-on-leadership-in-the-21st-century (date accessed 15 December 2011).

References

Abu Lughod, L. (1993) *Writing Women's Worlds: Bedouin Stories*. Berkeley, CA: University of California Press.

Adnan, I. (2006) 'Men, Step Aside: Tackling Terrorism is Women's Work', *The Guardian*, 27 July.

Bhabha, H. (1984) 'Of Mimicry and Man: The Ambivalence of Colonial Discourse', *Discipleship: A Special Issue on Psychoanalysis* 28: 125–33.

Brunner, C. (2007) 'Discourse – Occidentalism – Intersectionality Approaching Knowledge on "Suicide Bombing"', *Political Perspectives* 1(2): 1–25.

Cook, D. (2005) 'Women Fighting in Jihad?', *Studies in Conflict & Terrorism* 28(5): 375–84.

DCLG (Department for Communities and Local Government) (2007) 'Preventing Violent Extremism – Winning Hearts and Minds, www.communities.gov.uk/documents/communities/pdf/320752.pdf (date accessed 15 December 2011).

——. (2008) 'Empowering Muslim Women: Case Studies', www.communities.gov.uk/documents/communities/pdf/669801.pdf (date accessed 15 December 2011).

Feinman, I.R. (2000) *Citizenship Rites: Feminist Soldiers and Feminist Antimilitarists*. New York University Press.

Feminist Institute of the Heinrich Böll Foundation (2005) 'Security for All – A Feminist Critique of the New Security Agenda', Discussion Paper by the Feminist Institute of the Heinrich Böll Foundation, based on the expert input of the Working Group 'Gender in Security Policy and Civil Conflict Prevention', September.

Freedman, J. (2007) 'Women, Islam and Rights in Europe: Beyond a Universalist/ Culturalist Dichotomy', *Review of International Studies* 33: 29–44.

Githens-Mazer, J. and Lambert, R. (2011) 'Islamophobia and Anti-Muslim Hate Crime: A London Case Study', European Muslim Research Centre (EMRC), University of Exeter, http://centres.exeter.ac.uk/emrc/publications/Islamophobia_and_Anti-Muslim_Hate_Crime.pdf (date accessed 15 December 2011).

Hamilton, C. (2007) 'The Gender Politics of Political Violence: Women Armed Activists in ETA', *Feminist Review* 86: 132–48.

Hasso, F.S. (2005) 'Discursive and Political Deployments by/of the 2002 Palestinian Women Suicide Bombers/Martyrs', *Feminist Review* 81: 23–51.

HM Government (2008) *The Prevent Strategy: A Guide for Local Partners in England Stopping People Becoming or Supporting Terrorists and Violent Extremists.* London: HMSO.

Home Office (2009) *The United Kingdom's Strategy for Countering International Terrorism,* http://merln.ndu.edu/whitepapers/UnitedKingdom2009.pdf (date accessed 18 January 2012).

——. (2010) *The United Kingdom's Strategy for Countering International Terrorism,* Annual Report, www.official-documents.gov.uk/document/cm78/7833/7833.pdf (date accessed 18 January 2012).

Krylova, A. (2005) 'Stalinist Identity from the Viewpoint of Gender: Rearing a Generation of Professionally Violent Women-Fighters in 1930s Stalinist Russia', in S. D'Cruze and A. Rao (eds), *Violence, Vulnerability and Embodiment.* Oxford: Blackwell, pp. 132–60.

Lambert, R. (2010) 'Practical Solutions', paper presented at the Perspectives on Terrorism, Resistance, and Radicalization Al Jazeera & EMRC Conference, Doha, 27 September.

McClintock, A. (1995) *Imperial Leather: Race, Gender and Sexuality in the Colonial Contest.* London: Routledge.

——. (2011) *Countering al-Qaeda in London: Police and Muslims in Partnership.* London: Hurst.

McDonald, L.Z. (2006) 'Islamic Feminisms: Ideas and Experiences of Convert Women in Britain' unpublished thesis, University of York.

Moser, C.O.N. and Clark, F.C. (eds) (2001) *Victims, Perpetrators or Actors? Gender, Armed Conflict and Political Violence.* London: Zed Books.

Said, E. (1979) *Orientalism.* New York: Vintage.

Silber, M.D. and Bhatt, A. (2007). *Radicalization in the West: The Homegrown Threat.* New York Police Department Intelligence Division.

Spalek, B., El-Awa, S., McDonald, L.Z. and Lambert, R. (2008–9) 'Police-Muslim Engagement and Partnerships for the Purposes of Counter-Terrorism: An Examination', Report and Summary Report, University of Birmingham with AHRC.

UN Security Council (2000) Resolution 1325. Adopted by the Security Council at its 4213rd meeting, 31 October, www.un.org/events/res_1325e.pdf (date accessed 18 January 2012).

Zine, J. (2002) 'Muslim Women and the Politics of Representation', *American Journal of Islamic Social Sciences* 19(4): 118–21.

6
Engaging Young People within a Counter-Terrorism Context

Laura Zahra McDonald

The development of state and Muslim community engagement in the wake of 7/7, as explored in the previous chapters, has impacted on the experiences of individuals, communities and grassroots organizations in multiple and complex ways. But for one group, the impact has been felt more acutely: at the interface of engagement, identified as most vulnerable to violent extremism and in many ways otherized by both the state and their own communities, young Muslims – in general but especially those considered vulnerable to violent extremism – have become a focal point for the security agenda. Yet, despite this difficult context, grassroots initiatives are succeeding in engaging young people, not to neutralize or suppress but to empower and support. This chapter draws upon ongoing, qualitative research relating to forms of engagement between Muslim communities, the British state and counter-terrorism policing for the purposes of preventing extremist violence amongst young people (Spalek *et al.*, 2011). In particular, data from indepth interviews and focus groups with young people and Muslim youth workers is used to explore the challenges that people face, the ways in which they are engaged through specialist youth work, and the contribution that tackling these issues has made not only in relation to countering terrorism but also in developing ways for individuals to contribute as socially and politically engaged Muslims.

It is also important to note at this point that in writing about the binary constructed between the British state and Muslim youth, it is all too easy to perpetuate the idea that 'Muslim youth' is an easily defined, neatly bounded community, for whom research data with a sample group may act as a representation of community experience. The truth is obviously to the contrary. As such, the analysis articulated throughout this chapter makes a distinction between young Muslims as a group constructed and constricted through the discourses and practices of the security era, and the diversity of individuals and their realities, which, as the later sections will explore, provides alternative frameworks and modes of engagement. Furthermore, the research on which these analyses are based (Spalek *et al.*, 2008–9; Spalek *et al.*, 2011) did not focus on a general cross-section of Muslim youth. The ethnic and cultural heritage of participants was diverse, but their experiences as young people between the ages of 16 and 22 who consider themselves marginalized socially, politically[1] and in relation to their own communities and wider British society were remarkably similar. All were being engaged to some extent either by communities or the state as vulnerable to or involved in a number of issues, including gang membership, crime, drug abuse, sexual exploitation and violent extremism. This grouping is therefore part of a significant section of the demographic considered of interest to state security, but does not reflect or represent Muslim communities and Muslim youth in general.

Context: young people and the security agenda

Since the level of threat from international terrorism – identified as predominantly 'Islamist' and Al-Qaeda-related – was first made public by the British security services in 2006, it has been considered 'severe' or 'critical' for the majority of this time period.[2] The state assessment in relation to the level and type of threat to security has therefore resulted in a focus on preventing and disrupting possible violence emanating from Muslim communities at home and abroad. More specifically, despite the discrediting – conceptually and in practice – of profiling within the counter-terrorism arena (Horgan, 2008: 84), it appears that a form of pragmatism in the face of actual and potential multiple, independent cells or lone individuals across whole populations has resulted in a focus on young, male Muslims as a probable demographic (House of Commons, 2006: 31; Lowe and Innes, 2008: 5). High-profile cases provide the evidence, including: five of the 'Seven in Yemen' (1999), shoe bomber Richard Reid (2001), Omar Khan Sharif and Asif Mohammed Hanif, the Tel Aviv 'Mike's Place' bombers (2003), shoe bomber Saajid Badat (2005), the four 7/7 London bombers (2005), the 'Aircraft Plot' (2006), Dhiren Barot (2006), the 'Fertilizer Plot' (2007), Nicky Reilly (2008), the 'Beheading Plot' (2008), the Christmas Day bomber Umar Farouk Abdulmuttallab (2009), Roshonara Choudhry (2010) and the Birmingham suicide bombing plot (2011) (Abbas, 2007; Lowe and Innes, 2008).[3] The legitimacy of the concern is thus supported by the chronological regularity of actual and attempted attacks committed by young British-born or British-based Muslims.

Within this counter-terrorism context and linking to wider discourses built around the highly problematic notion of a 'War on Terror' has been the predominance of New Terror theory. This academic narrative has permeated counter-terrorism policy (Spalek and McDonald, 2009; McDonald, 2011) and promoted the identification of young Muslim people in the West as 'potentials', vulnerable by the nature of their youth and religion to succumbing to the ideology of violent Al-Qaeda-related extremism (Abbas, 2007: 435; NCTB, 2007: 36; Schmid, 2007: Conway and McInerney, 2008: 1; 12; Lowe and Innes, 2008: 5; Roy, 2008: 11; Silber and Bhatt, 2007: 22; Briggs and Birdwell, 2009: 6). As explored throughout this book, there are three assumptions that often underpin this viewpoint: that the process of radicalization can not only be identified through a range of contributing factors and drivers, but that each factor contributes to an increased level of potential threat; that youth and an identification with Islam are factors in themselves; and that communities must be viewed as layers of subgroups graded in relation to their level of potential vulnerability to violent extremism. This understanding supports a wide net approach and appears to have influenced the policies and practices of counter-terrorism. Coupled with the notion that 'communities defeat terror', a phrase which implicitly distances the state from citizens while defining community responsibility, counter-terrorism tactics have thus become a commonplace feature in the lives of many young British Muslims. From soft security approaches, such as youth-focused community projects under the Prevent strategy,[4] and broad-brush intelligence gathering and spying, such as the use of covert cameras in Birmingham (Project Champion), to more direct, hard-ended security practices, including stop and search and raids on premises, the practices of state security are located within communities and are focused upon young people.

Yet in this effort to maintain state and public security and to avoid the victimization created by terrorist attacks, counter-terrorism methods have created primary and secondary forms of victimization amongst young Muslim people. Even if an individual has not experienced stop and search themselves, the knowledge that it has happened to a friend, or a friend of a friend, or indeed *could* happen is enough to create a climate in which young Muslims may experience a sense of fear, of being unfairly suspected and of being targeted by the state (Spalek *et al.*, 2008; Spalek, Lambert and Baker, 2009; Spalek and McDonald, 2009). It is this self-perpetuating cycle of victimization and insecurity which not only creates a barrier to effective engagement within the counter-terrorism context, polarizing the state and young Muslims, but, crucially, appears to actually escalate the issues, exacerbating and intensifying both the process of violent radicalization and state counter-measures. This is a cycle of violence and it permeates and defines the forms of engagement that young Muslims may experience with the state.

Understanding the cycle of violence

In order to more deeply understand the ways in which this destructive cycle is maintained, it is useful to look at the wider social and political context and corresponding layers of discourse which operate as a backdrop and as a drip-feed of contributing and sustaining factors operating at macro- and micro-levels. For the purposes of analysis, it is helpful to explore each concentric layer according to scale, from the transnational to the local, which – crucially – link directly to the personal. As these layers are multiple, complex and situational, the analysis will focus on the impact of violence – actual, and perceived, physical and epistemic – which pervades each layer.

Violence is the main business of the security agenda, which uses forms of violence in order to prevent it, and it is the main business, or at least the means and sometimes the end, of terrorist action. In relation to our discussion of engaging young people in the counter-terrorism context, violence is a central theme from the perspective of the state and of young people, acting concurrently as the main contributing factor, and the most devastating result in the cycle of victimization and insecurity. The aim of this section, then, is to identify each layer and its sub-cycles and relate it to the central sequence of victimization.

Discourses of inevitable violence

In the first instance, the role of discourse must be highlighted. It is through discourse, the powerful reductionist narratives that shape our social and political relations, that the world is often understood and, in the case of state and community security, influences perceptions of what is going on and how to end it. A number of competing narratives may be identified in relation to the security agenda and the understanding of state and non-state violence. Here, the dominant discourse will be explored, illustrating the way in which violence between young Muslims and the nation state is constructed as inevitable. The notion of inevitability directly perpetuates the cycle of victimization, trapping individuals into polarized and relational positions and shaping their subsequent actions.

As discussed above, directly associated with the current British security agenda is the dominant discourse of the 'War on Terror', within which a binary is recognized and generated between those mis/represented as the 'West' and 'Al-Qaeda' (Jackson, 2005), each grouping attempting to co-opt ever-larger groupings of people to its side in order to resist the terror of the other. The category 'West' has come to signify a coalition of willing states and allies, their peoples and their 'civilization', while 'Al-Qaeda' has correspondingly been labelled and has claimed for itself Islam, Muslims and the power of a 'borderless loyalty' (McDonald, 2011; ISCR Insight, 2011) to resist hegemony, corruption and the violence of states, and to build an alternative order. The construction and ensuing action of these competing, symbiotic narratives are built on violence – violence being the basis on which each side justifies its existence and its means (Joseph and Sharma, 2003: ix). The narrative is dramatic and polemic: slogans of justice, righteousness and superiority abound, and through physical aggression and as well as epistemic brutality, each 'side' attempts to dehumanize the other and legitimize bloodshed.

This vision of the security agenda remains normative in popular discourse, played out on news screens and political rhetoric, to the extent that our understanding of state violence, Al-Qaeda-related terrorism and the violent radicalization of young Muslims must be understood in relation to it. Through it we understand the young Muslim person as an actual or potential victim of Al-Qaeda-related ideology and violence, as well as the corresponding state response through counter-terrorism policies and practices that target young

Muslims as vulnerable or dangerous. The discourse (from either of the two perspectives – and in this discourse there can only be two) forces itself onto a diverse and complex set of contexts, asserting a version of history and simplistic account of cause, effect and violent remedy. This promotes a culture of violence and terror that distorts social relations and interactions, as witnessed repeatedly in the context of the colonial experience and explored by scholars such as Fanon (2001 [1961]) and Taussig (1987). The power imbalance, brutality and paranoia between state and colonized other that were sustained by the binaries of popular and political discourse from Algeria to Colombia echo in the contemporary relationship between the state and Muslim minorities in the 'War on Terror'.

Equally damaging is the ability of the narrative, in its construction and assertion of a dominant world view, to obscure the multiple realties and possibilities at the ground level. The result is a blinkered narrative of the world, in which the threat, if not the actual act and indeed need of violence, whether physical or symbolic, looms expectantly. Thus, discourse normalizes and promotes the sense that violence is inevitable and necessary, and as such colours the way in which we interpret and interact with the world. For many young people, the impact is particularly devastating: for the post-9/11 generation, the 'War on Terror' permeates the ways in which the world is understood and subsequently interacted with, acting as a lens through which the global, national and local are viewed.

Global insecurity

At the global level, a number of events and issues in which violence is central and on which young people have articulated concern through the research dominate: wars, insurgencies and terror attacks act as the physical proof that the 'War on Terror' not only exists but also overshadows the world stage. At a time when communication technology makes it possible to witness the full horror of war and oppression in real time and in pornographic detail, from the mutilated bodies of children to beheadings, young people whose voices are rarely heard or given space can nevertheless see and hear the violence on their own mobile phones and computers. Violence committed at a geographical distance is thus brought into the personal space of individuals, creating vicarious victimization amongst the young people who view it. Furthermore, transnational links extend beyond the geographical to the realm of the social and theological. Young Muslims in the UK, often holding diverse and multiple heritages, draw upon familial and community links to many other parts of the world, so that violence and oppression far away is not happening to 'other people' but, echoing the sentiments of the 7/7 suicide bomber Mohammad Sidique Khan, is happening to 'my people'. This sense of identification with global victimization and, potentially, related acts of vengeance, strategic violence or violent empathy is given further strength by the social and theological concept of the Muslim Ummah. It is the sense of community and commonality arising from shared faith and identity, and the emotion, sense of duty and unity that is experienced by many Muslims which, in the context of oppression, may be appropriated by the violent extremist narrative. As Roshonara Choudhry illustrated with her explanation for stabbing Stephen Timms MP, 'as Muslims we're all brothers and sisters and we should all look out for each other and we shouldn't sit back and do nothing while others suffer. We shouldn't allow the people who oppress us to get away with it and to think that they can do whatever they want to us and we're just gonna lie down and take it'.[5]

Research participants not only highlighted these processes but underscored the emotional responses from anger to helplessness; in the words of one participant:

> They feel no one cares. You can relate to the victims, to the suffering. There's a lot of grievance. They relate to the people who suffer.

Global violence and its impact on individual young people – social and political consciousness, a sense of outrage and of grievance – thus reflects the feminist assertion that the personal is political and the political personal.

The national context: British Muslim communities

The national context in Britain also plays a role in the cycle of victimization encircling many young Muslims. As well as the security agenda and its direct and indirect impacts on individuals and communities, political and social discourse since 9/11 has had a pernicious effect. In particular, dominant interpretations of violent events and state policy reactions – the Northern Disturbances of 2001, the London bombings of 2005 and the widespread media coverage of insignificant but vociferous 'protestors' at the funerals and remembrance services of British soldiers – are used to construct Muslim communities as other. Muslims (and young Muslims especially) are not only viewed as lacking in a desire and ability to achieve social cohesion and rejecting British values, but also as characterizing an innate violence. The resulting Islamophobia, stigma and marginalization of young Muslims as a group creates further violence – a powerful epistemic hostility providing a backdrop to physical and verbal attacks on individuals and on community institutions, such as mosques and Muslim-owned shops (Githens-Mazer and Lambert, 2011). The national context therefore impacts directly on individual young people and through high levels of awareness – of the news, of politics – more widely as waves of indirect victimization of an entire social/religious grouping.

The local context

As microcosms of the national picture, local contexts also colour the experiences of young Muslims in relation to their families, friends and local communities. For many young research participants, their local environment is also informed by violence: for some, brutality within the home and for more, outside as victims and perpetrators of gang violence and street crime, and poor, often hostile relations with the police. The forms of disconnect and otherization many feel at the hands of older generations are also damaging, who often appear unable and unwilling to recognize and deal with the complex challenges that young people's lives present. Research participants talk of the intense need for trusting relations and, in the face of widespread hostility and marginalization, a source of support in the form of retreat. This retreat is also multi-layered – a shrinking of geographical location to a few streets or a single postcode, of social relations into highly localized, exclusive groups of friends (gangs) and sometimes into ideas that through their simplicity and action-orientated call to resist all these forms of marginalization – lower the horizons of young people through a narrow, violent and extreme world view. This is where vulnerability to religious misinterpretation and associated violence becomes a major issue, an area that community approaches working from within an Islamic framework are able to tackle most effectively, as will be explored later in this chapter.

From this perspective, social and political events and discourse, from the transnational to the local, always impact upon the personal, contributing repeatedly and in multiple ways to the cycle of victimization and culture of terror in which, as a research participant noted, *violence is normal*. The young Muslims who live this as direct and vicarious victims, and sometimes contributors, can remain trapped in the cycle.

As explored in previous chapters and highlighted here, the role of the state, through traditional, top-down and reactive policies, particularly within the arena of counter-terrorism, may be held directly responsible for this contagion of violence. This is in part because of the nature of violence itself since, as Crenshaw Hutchinson argues, violence:

> suffered or performed, contains a part, more or less large, of traumatization. This traumatization ... can then only result in a repetition of the violent act. (Ivernel, 1962: 392–3, quoted in Crenshaw Hutchinson, 1972: 393)

Yet even when the state's own forms of violence are replaced by forms of fire-fighting, of top-down attempts at Prevent, the result appears to be a jamming of the cogs: while the violence may be prevented, its threat remains. The following sections of this chapter therefore aim to explore the development of community approaches to engaging, supporting and empowering young people within and indeed despite the counter-terrorism context as an alternative, grass-roots framework.

Engaging young people: development and recognition of formal and informal Muslim youth work in the UK

As illustrated in Chapter 4, in which Baker explores the practicalities of Muslim youth work in the counter-terrorism context, the development of community approaches has not been easy. While the importance of Muslim inclusive, centred and/or Islamic frameworks has been increasingly recognized within youth work and more generally (McDonald, 2011), it has not been without its controversies. Particularly for youth workers operating from explicitly Islamic frameworks, a nervousness and in many cases hostility from the state and the wider public have created barriers, from health and safety concerns and funding problems to ideological attack (Spalek *et al.*, 2011).

Despite or perhaps because of these challenges, a very carefully thought out, practice-orientated and specialist form of Muslim youth work has been created (McDonald, 2011). Nationally, the number of organizations and individuals working in this arena remains, at the time of writing, very small, perhaps less than 50, working both in specific localities with groups of young people and on a case-by-case basis with individuals who have been identified by the state, for example, through the Home Office-based Channel Project, or by communities concerned about a person who have asked for help. The work is both formal and informal, in partnership with state and public institutions or independent. Yet the core methodologies of this youth work are strikingly similar and may be identified as the major difference between community approaches and top-down tactics. First, community approaches necessarily involved youth workers who are respected and wholly trusted by young people – who have experienced many of the challenges themselves, who remain independent and can therefore assert a level of legitimacy that state actors cannot. As one youth worker explained (quoted in Spalek *et al.*, 2008):

> Intervention has got to be grass roots, it's got to be on the ground. It's got to be face to face. And you can't do that if they don't relate to you, you don't relate to them.

This face-to-face, 'dirty' style of working consequently operates by creating safe spaces not only in localized, physical locations, but also psychologically, facilitating young people to address their issues at a holistic and personal level. Such an approach means that the factors and sustainers explored above in relation to cycles of violence and victimization can be tackled directly: this is hard-ended youth work that embraces the challenges posed by a gamut of serious social, political, religious and personal issues. The issue of violent radicalization, then, is often just one element of multiple issues and according to the individual's specific needs is addressed either from a preventative or a remedial perspective. This is not the 'deradicalization' of state programmes and cults, but a personalized, context-specific form of support, which works with an individual over the necessary period of time to find ways forward.

The power of this approach is in its ability to address the multiple forms of violence experienced and perpetrated by young people, using diverse methods including mentoring, public debate, theological education, mediation and conflict mediation. The results are successful interventions – as acknowledged by, for example, the police. The following section provides examples of these interventions, including a case study.

Addressing violence with honesty

In the rush to address issues relating to violent extremism and to develop concepts and practices, the most fundamental, apparently obvious questions are often ignored: what exactly is violent extremism and why should it be prevented? The frameworks used in this context are rarely pacifist, objecting to violence per se; rather, they seek to legitimize some forms of violence over others. From a state perspective, it appears straightforward – attacks on state security and citizens must be stopped. But this answer fails to look beyond its inherent creation of an 'us' and 'them', in which state violence through warfare, injustice to its own citizens or the sustaining of epistemic violence through discourse is not acknowledged. Violent extremism is the crime of the other, of terrorists and those vulnerable to terrorist viewpoints.

For those working with young people from a grassroots perspective, this understanding of violence can be highly problematic. First, the broader context results in the stigmatizing of community voices which challenge state viewpoints. For Muslims, questioning the relationship between state and non-state violence can lead to accusations of extremism and radical politics. The result is fear, a high level of sensitivity around the issue of violence and a shutting down of debate and discussion. This is particularly problematic in relation to notions of deradicalization: for community members engaging in the counter-terrorism agenda, the accusation from young people or indeed anyone coming from a critical perspective is that they are actually engaged in the pacification of non-state actors who hold legitimate grievances. Why, as research participants asked, 'should one remain passive in the face of attack? Why shouldn't violence be used to resist oppression? If conditions are extreme, then the extreme measure of violence is surely legitimate'. Furthermore, the legitimacy of jihad within Islamic frameworks cannot be wished or legislated away by the state, and once more, for Muslim community members this may represent a conceptual challenge. If Islam permits the defence of innocent civilians, albeit within a tightly regulated framework, to what extent can we condemn the actions of fighters in occupied territories from Palestine to Kashmir? And how might this relate to the definitions of violent extremism in state policies? From an academic perspective, particularly a critical perspective, these questions not only relate to questions of defining forms of political violence but also to the concept of revolution and the legitimacy of violence as a means of disrupting and subverting entrenched forms of political and social oppression. The possibility of popular political violence as legitimate is also tentatively embraced by Western states in the name of democracy – contemporary examples, including the 'Arab Spring' and the NATO-backed rebellion in Libya, have been supported, at least for the sake of political expediency at home and abroad.

This complex and competing set of frameworks, especially when applied to contentious situations such as the Palestinian struggle against Israeli occupation in which support for violence on both sides has become radically polarized and politicized, allows for a sense of possibility and ambiguity in relation to violence as desirable, necessary or effective. To promote a framework in which violence is discouraged therefore poses a number of conceptual problems, particularly for those whose political and personal leanings might include empathy for oppressed populations. Crucially, however, it is these challenges – to refrain from doublethink or hypocrisy – that the research has identified as creating a strength and a legitimacy for community approaches which state tactics cannot replicate. For individuals involved in the development of community approaches to countering violence, addressing these issues directly has resulted in the construction of new frameworks from which to operate. The concept of violence itself is challenged in relation to its legitimacy, effectiveness and long-term impact, with the violence of both state and non-state actors being challenged. From ethical and theological perspectives relating to the protection of human and all forms of life to the rigorous rulings of jihad that resist Al-Qaeda's anarchic and individualistic conceptions of violence, community approaches create a sense of interconnected human security, motivated by a sense of social justice, community protection and to some extent that Muslims and Islam should be defended from the image of violence emanating from outside and within Muslim communities. This approach therefore demands recognition of all perspectives and a commitment to creating a sense of safety for people beyond state-defined borders or religious, ethnic, political or cultural identities.

Addressing cycles of victimization

> I don't want to see what I've witnessed happening in my own country, my own land. Ever again. 7/7. That's one of the motivational factors. (Muslim practitioner)

With a clear sense of a community-based framework and what a bor-derless, human-centred – rather than state-centred – security might be (Alkire, 2003), youth and community workers are able to find legitimate ways in which to work with young people and attempt to stop the cycles of victimization. This starts with connecting with and supporting vulnerable individuals:

> i am in a situation where i do not have a friend, i have no one to speak too, no one to consult,
>
> no one to support me and i feel depressed and lonely. I do not know what to do. (Umar Farouk Abdulmuttallab's Internet 'chat')
>
> Until we feel security, you will be our targets. (Mohammad Sidique Khan, from his suicide video)

As explored above, the violence found at global, national and local levels relates directly to the personal experiences of individual young Muslims. This not only creates vulnerability to violent extremism and other issues but also builds barriers to the creation of solutions. Community approaches not only seek to tackle the cycles directly but also challenge the actual factors and sustainers themselves in order to break the cycle and create new frameworks. Layers of politically related issues, for example, the grievances created by Western foreign policy, can be channelled. From the sense of disen-franchisement, helplessness and vicarious victimhood that global politics builds, youth workers attempt to harness anger as a way of inspiring activism, providing education around subjects of concern and creating opportunities to do something about it:

> Because actually anger is good; we like anger. It's an emotion. And that's not a bad thing. Erm and with all young people, for them to express emotions is, is good. (Youth worker)

Case study 1

> What exactly are you doing to help? When your sisters are being abused on your doorstep? (Youth worker)

One youth worker described challenging an individual whose justification for supporting terror attacks was political oppression and violence, to do something in the face of local oppressions – to help the women in his local community suffering from the violence of pimps, to find ways of feeding children suffering malnutrition on his own doorstep. The message was loud and clear – instead of contributing to the violence, use the emotion, the empathy and the passion to really change people's circumstances. The youth worker was then able to provide the means for this individual to work as a volunteer within the community alongside continued intervention in relation to other issues.

Similarly, where individuals have already developed an adherence to violent extremist interpretations of theology, specialist youth workers have been able to use their indepth knowledge of Islamic jurisprudence to challenge beliefs and assumptions, and provide answers in what often turns out to be a void in an individual's Islamic knowledge. From opening out debate in relation to Al-Qaeda-related propaganda, as described by Baker in Chapter 4, to exploring, through educational sessions – both formal and informal – community approaches can tackle issues that the state cannot and should not. This ranges from specific theological themes, such as jihad as a bounded and complex religious duty which by definition excludes acts of terrorism, to notions of active citizenship and relations with non-Muslims.

Specialist youth work also involves partnering specialist support in relation to mental health. A significant number of youth workers described cases in which a number of issues faced by an individual were exacerbated by psychological problems.

Case study 2

A common theme within the research is that of the 'dirty Muslim'. For individuals whose lives have been so chaotic, marked by violence and unsurprisingly affected by mental health issues, a sense of being a 'bad' Muslim – for example, for committing crimes or for feeling sinful – had become linked in the individual's mind to the idea of martyrdom and its 'cleansing' properties. In these cases a warped sense of martyrdom – i.e. the concept of suicide bombing – had become an attractive solution to a painful life and an opportunity for redemption: by killing themselves and others, the act of death would end the life of the individual and of perceived enemies and would result in the cleansing of sins through the act itself. In such cases youth workers partner mental health specialists and also use theological interventions similar to those described above.

Broader psychological approaches include addressing the process of otherizing by working on increasing integrative complexity (Savage *et al.*, 2011) and exploring the sense of self and linking to discussions of identity in relation to belonging and the social space. These themes also include an acknowledgement of emotion as a factor in creating and suffering violence, but also in healing and developing alternatives. For example, frustration, anger and disaffection in response to the violence of events and discourse are often associated with love, empathy, a sense of community and a desire to affect change, emotions which may be channelled into creating the alternative frameworks and positions that community approaches are able to bring about. Crucially, however, the psychological elements are understood in relation to the social and political contexts, avoiding the danger of individualizing and pathologizing vulnerability to violent extremism or hiding the external drivers for which we are all responsible.

Conclusions

Community approaches which utilize the expertise of community practitioners directly at a grassroots level and which address issues of violence with empathy are able to engage young Muslims in ways that top-down, state-led models are unable to do. This is predicated on a willingness to risk personal reputation as community members and suspicion as citizens challenging state norms. Yet, at the time of writing, many of these practitioners, having taken the steps to engage with the state and with young people, have been labelled 'part of the problem of extremism', with government departments withdrawing not only funding but also willingness to engage, with explicit attempts to re-define the partnerships that have been nurtured over time. A controversial development has been the introduction of funding contracts which require a 'declaration of British values' which not only construct a state-led (and ill-defined) notion of Britishness to which individuals are expected to conform but also assert a clear message of power, dominance and insulting assumptions pertaining to the 'values' of those individuals.

Resisting these challenges, community approaches are continuing to develop and to contribute to the construction of a framework based on an inclusive sense of security, wherein state and community, local and global are understood as interconnected and interdependent. An analysis of those rare individuals and organizations equipped to do this identifies the necessity of multiple factors, including insider legitimacy, an ability to use individualized holistic approaches as opposed to standardized and regulated models, and a level of understanding that can only be achieved from working on a long-term basis and on an equal footing with young people. Trust, as explored throughout this book, is of vital importance, along with levels of dedication that go well beyond the demands of the profession, to make these forms of specialist Muslim youth work a rare expertise. Through these fundamental characteristics, community members developing community approaches are able to identify and unpick the multiple strands which contribute to and maintain the cultures of violence in which young people may be trapped. They provide young people with the support and most importantly the tools with which to understand their situations and to find alternative frameworks and spaces through which they may view and experience the world around them. Community approaches do not attempt to 'deradicalize' or pacify young people; rather, they remove them from the cycles of victimization, allowing them to construct their own ways forward. This also carries implications for a re-definition of security, wherein state and communities are pulled out of the current binaries and a human-centred security is created (Alkire, 2003).

Notes

1. Economic issues also commonly affected research participants. However, it seems that young people articulate their concerns in relation to social and religious rather than economic capital, although poverty magnifies the challenges that many of them face.
2. www.mi5.gov.uk/output/threat-levels.html#history (date accessed 15 December 2011).
3. See also https://www.mi5.gov.uk/output/terrorist-plots-in-the-uk.html (date accessed 15 December 2011).
4. Funded through the Department of Communities and Local Government under New Labour.
5. www.guardian.co.uk/uk/2010/nov/03/roshonara-choudhry-police-interview (date accessed 15 December 2011).

References

Abbas, T. (2007) 'Ethno-Religious Identities and Islamic Political Radicalism in the UK: A Case Study', *Journal of Muslim Minority Affairs* 27(3): 429–42.

Alkire, S. (2003) 'A Conceptual Framework for Human Security', Working Paper 2, Centre for Research on Inequality, Human Security and Ethnicity, CRISE, University of Oxford: www.crise.ox.ac.uk/pubs/workingpaper2.pdf (date accessed 18 January 2012).

Briggs, R. and Birdwell, J. (2009) *Radicalisation among Muslims in the UK*. MICROCON Policy Working Paper 7. Brighton: MICROCON.

Conway, M. and McInerney, L. (2008). 'Jihadi Video & Auto-Radicalisation: Evidence from an Exploratory YouTube Study', EuroISI 2008 – First European Conference on Intelligence and Security Informatics, Esbjerg, Denmark, 3–5 December.

Crenshaw Hutchinson, M. (1972) 'The Concept of Revolutionary Terrorism', *Journal of Conflict Resolution* 16(3): 383–96.

Fanon, F. (2001 [1961]) *The Wretched of the Earth*. Harmondsworth: Penguin.

Githens-Mazer, J. and Lambert, R. (2011) 'Islamophobia and Anti-Muslim Hate Crime: UK Case Studies. Exeter: EMRC, University of Exeter: http://centres.exeter.ac.uk/emrc/publications/Islamophobia_and_Anti-Muslim_Hate_Crime.pdf (date accessed 18 January 2012).

Horgan, J. (2008) 'From Profiles to Pathways and Roots to Routes: Perspectives from Psychology on Radicalization into Terrorism', *ANNALS of the American Academy of Political and Social Science* 618(1): 80–94.

House of Commons (2006) *House of Commons Report of the Official Account of the Bombings in London on 7th July 2005*. London: HMSO.

ISCR Insight (2011) *Inspire Magazine*, January edition: http://icsr.info/publications/newsletters/1305032088ICSRInsight_AlQaedaintheArabian PeninsularreleasesnewcopyofInspireMagazine.pdf (date accessed 18 January 2012).

Ivernel, P. (1962) 'Violence d'hier et d'aujourd'hui', *Esprit* 30: 186–98.

Jackson, R. (2005) *Writing the War on Terrorism: Language, Politics and Counter-Terrorism*. Manchester University Press.

Joseph, A. and Sharma, K. (2003). *Terror, Counter-Terror: Women Speak Out*. London: Zed Books.

Lowe, T. and Innes, M. (2008) 'Countering Terror: Violent Radicalisation and Situational Intelligence', *Prison Service Journal* 179: 3–10.

McDonald, L.Z. (2011) 'Listening to the Experts: Muslim Youth Work in the UK and its Implication for Security', *Religion, State & Society* 39(2–3): 177–89.

NCTB (Netherlands) (2007) 'Radicalisation in Broader Perspective': http://english.nctb.nl/current_topics/reports/index.aspx?q=o&p5=rapport&p7=2000-06-21&select=6 (date accessed 18 January 2012).

Roy, O. (2008) 'Radicalisation and De-radicalisation in ISCR', Perspectives on Radicalisation and Political Violence: Papers from the First International Conference on Radicalisation and Political Violence, London, 17–18 January.

Savage, S., Liht, J. and Williams, R. (2011) 'Being Muslim Being British: Preventing Extremist Violence through Raising Integrative Complexity', in M. Sharpe (ed.), *The Intangibles of Security*. Netherlands: IOS Press.

Schmid, A.P. (2007) 'Why Terrorism? Root Causes, Some Empirical Findings, and the Case of 9/11', Strasbourg, 25–26 April, Conf Prev Terr (2007) 18 rev., pp. 20–1.

Silber, M.D. and Bhatt, A. (2007). *Radicalization in the West: The Homegrown Threat*. New York Police Department Intelligence Division.

Spalek, B., El-Awa, S. and McDonald, L.Z. (2008) 'Police-Muslim Engagement and Partnerships for the Purposes of Counter-Terrorism: An Examination', Arts and Humanities Research Council.

Spalek, B., El-Awa, S., McDonald, L.Z. and Lambert, R. (2008–9) 'Police-Muslim Engagement and Partnerships for the Purposes of Counter-Terrorism: An Examination', Report and Summary Report, University of Birmingham with AHRC.

Spalek, B., Lambert, R. and Baker, A.H. (2009) 'Minority Muslim Communities and Criminal Justice: Stigmatised UK Faith Identities Post 9/11 and 7/7', in H. Bui (ed.), *Race and the Criminal Justice System*. London: Sage, pp. 170–87.

Spalek, B. and McDonald, L.Z. (2010) 'Terror Crime Prevention: Constructing Muslim Practices and Beliefs as "Anti-social" and "Extreme" through CONTEST 2', *Social Policy and Society* 9: 123–32.

Spalek, B., McDonald, L.Z. and El-Awa, S. (2011) 'Preventing Religio-Political Extremism Amongst Muslim Youth: A Study Exploring Policy-Community Partnership', University of Birmingham with AHRC.

Taussig, M. (1987) *Shaminism, Colonialism and the Wild Man: A Study in Terror and Healing*. Chicago University Press.

7
Religion, Theology and Counter-Terrorism

Salwa El-Awa and Basia Spalek

Introduction

As highlighted in Chapters 3 and 4, historically – in a pre-9/11 world – communities were primarily viewed by the police on the basis of their 'race'/ethnicity rather than their religious identities. As such, social tensions giving rise to crime and thus meriting police surveillance were not understood as arising from specifically religious questions, as is perhaps the case with the issue of religiously endorsed violence today. But the events of 9/11 and 7/7 brought religion, and Islam in particular, abruptly and forcefully to the forefront of policing issues. In doing so, the focus turned from policing an ethnically diverse community in general to specifically policing a religiously identified and identifying community – a community of one religion, Islam – that is often described by its adherents as 'a complete way of life' and by many outsiders as 'the most political religion in the world' that is 'determined to take over the world'.[1] However, it was a religion about which the British police knew very little.

After the events of 7/7, terrorism began to be viewed as an internal affair rather than a 'foreign problem'. The view developed from this point has been that 'home-grown terror' was an issue which the police *and* Muslim communities had to deal with, each from a very different positionality. Underpinning this is a fundamental and problematic question: whether the Muslim community is a suspect community or a community that can help to solve the problem of terrorism. On this controversial issue, both the police and the community were – and remain – internally divided. As argued in Chapter 2, whilst some counter-terrorism policy officials, practitioners and communities actively promote a community-targeted approach, others involved in counter-terrorism promote a community-focused approach.

When Sir Ian Blair, the Commissioner of the Metropolitan Police, made his famous statement that 'communities defeat terrorism' in the 2005 Dimbleby Lecture,[2] he also made a conclusive position on the issue, committing the government and Muslim communities to engaging with each other in the fight against violent extremism. It appeared to be an announcement of trust in and expectation of Muslim communities, but at the same time it placed a level of responsibility in the hands of both the community and the government. For the community it meant an expectation to cooperate with the government and support it in fighting violent extremism; however, in order for that to happen, the government also had to put systems and mechanisms in place through which such cooperation could be achieved. Both had to be seen to actively play their part.

Against the above background, this chapter asks questions pertaining to the role of religion and religious knowledge in counter-terrorism work between the police and communities. The main areas of exploration around this topic are as follows:

- Does religion come into counter-terrorism work?
- Do religion and religious belief help or hinder counter-terrorism?
- Have partnerships with individuals and groups who have particular religious affiliations been useful to the police in counter-terrorism work or has religion been a cause of tension in these cases?
- Additionally, what is the nature and role of individuals' religiosity in relation to motivating Muslim community members in the field of counter-terrorism?

The chapter reveals that, contrary to the common assumption that commitment to Islamic values and religious doctrines is a root cause of terrorism, religion can provide a stronger commitment and a feeling of moral responsibility – *a duty* or *a religious obligation* – to help solve the problem of violence committed in the name of Islam, build bridges and form positive relations with other UK communities. At the same time, however, religious and religio-political perceptions can hinder cooperation with the police. This chapter draws heavily upon the research findings of an Economic and Social Research Council/Arts and Humanities Research Council-funded study exploring police–community engagement and partnership in relation to counter-terrorism, which included extensive interviews with members of Muslim communities and police officers working in countering terrorism (Spalek *et al.*, 2009).

Islam and the 'War on Terror'

From its conception, the 'War on Terror' has been perceived by many Muslims as a war on Islam, causing reluctance within Muslim communities to help the police. Research reveals that some members of Muslim communities view it to be a mistake on the part of the British government in following American rhetoric within counter-terrorism discourse when the remit of police work is based on public safety rather than political standpoints. It seems that one of the main reasons for some Muslims not to have taken a proactive role in supporting counter-terrorism was the British role in the highly contested 'War on Terror' – a synonym for a war on Islam in many minds (Spalek *et al.*, 2009). Nonetheless, it may also be argued that this position primarily relates to a political matter and that if sensitively handled, there remains room for understanding the issue as a matter of public safety beyond politics. This highlights the importance of dialogue and partnerships between communities and the police in fighting religiously endorsed violence, an issue previously highlighted and discussed in Chapter 4.

This type of dialogue remains challenging and complex, as the discourses that require such careful deconstruction are both emotive and ingrained. In particular, perceptions of the USA's war campaign launched in the aftermath of 9/11 were very much shaped by President Bush's political discourse against 'those who envy the Western values and the Western freedom'.[3] By taking this stand, not only did Bush offend the feelings of the general Muslim populations around the world, he also recalled the history of some of the worst conflicts between the Christian and the Muslim worlds through reference to the Crusades.[4] This notion was thus seen as a hostile attack on Muslims whose faith is often viewed as defining freedom differently from the Western world, yet who do not necessarily 'envy' the West for its 'values'. Many Muslims across the globe have not yet forgotten the history of centuries of Western colonialism and exploitation, and, as a consequence, think of the Crusades as a series of wars proving the Western/Christian ambition to control Muslim lands. By framing the response to 9/11 as a 'crusade' and a 'War on Terror', alongside the launching of attacks on Afghanistan and Iraq, Bush elicited strong popular and intellectual reactions from across the Muslim world.[5] Specifically, his remarks provoked animosity towards what has been perceived as a new colonialist era, echoing the historical exploitation of resources of developing countries by Western/Christian civilizations.

Despite the subsequent attempts to tone down the rhetoric and explain away Bush's reference to the Crusades, the USA's political discourse, which was to some extent reiterated in Tony Blair's subsequent speeches,[6] alarmed Muslim communities and created a deep feeling in many that their religion and their communities were coming under attack.

Terrorism as crime

The charged and politicized climate set out above has resulted in the overshadowing, to a large extent, of dialogue and discussion as to what terrorism and counter-terrorism truly are. Muslim populations largely adhere to the strict Qur'anic prohibition of killing civilians and killing altogether, outside of a battlefield[7] or within the criminal justice system.[8] As such, terrorist acts are seen as terrible crimes despite the political and religious justifications of their perpetrators. Research has shown that the religious justification of terrorism has caused initial conflict in some parts of Muslim communities between religious doctrines of the sanctity of the human soul and the political argument used by Al-Qaeda to gain support for what Muslims would normally see as a crime. However, from a community security point of view, this confusion can be eliminated if terrorist acts are re-explained to the Muslim population as a pure crime – stripped of their political and religious propaganda. Research has shown that clarifying the distinction between crime and ill-formed religious justification can lead to community members making a decision to take an active role in supporting counter-terrorism (Spalek *et al.*, 2009).

Theology

Debate within Muslim communities over the legitimacy or illegitimacy of using intelligence to uncover political crime or to confirm or remove suspicion[9] reveals important gaps in contemporary Islamic jurisprudence that can only be filled by scholars of Islam whose work addresses the concerns of contemporary Muslims. The study by Spalek *et al.* (2009) has shown that positive examples of work carried out in partnership between the police and the community has been, to a great extent, reliant on credible community leaders who enjoy popularity as well as indepth knowledge of Islamic texts and jurisprudence, being able to argue the ideological case against violent extremism based on Islamic sources. As illustrated in Chapters 3 and 4, the Muslim Contact Unit's efforts in supporting and empowering those leaders to access their communities and debate with those supporting and perpetrating violent extremism, refuting their interpretation of the Qur'an and *Sunnah* and exposing its weaknesses, provide rich examples of deradicalization of both mosques and individuals, from which many lessons can be learned.

Policing and religion

Secularism and modern society

Secularism has been viewed as an integral part of modern Western society, where religious considerations are excluded from civil affairs and issues in relation to equality are viewed largely through the secular framework of multiculturalism (Caraballo-Resto, 2006). Modern societies have also been viewed as undergoing a process of secularization, where secularization is a widespread alienation from organized churches and religious institutions (Berger, 1999). The philosophical and historical underpinnings of secularism lie within the European Enlightenment, where scientific reasoning progressively replaced theological frameworks of understanding. At the same time, the influence of religious institutions on civil society declined with the emergence of modern institutions and professional bodies that came to be separated out from their religious roots (Beckford, 1996; Jürgensmeyer, 2003).

Secularism and the criminal justice system

Historically, religious convictions have been a motivating factor for those individuals who have volunteered their services towards rehabilitating offenders and reducing crime. Thus, historical accounts of the influence of evangelical Protestantism on the penal system can be found (Beckford and Gilliat, 1998) and the historical roots of the probation service lie in the police court missionaries in England in the late eighteenth and early nineteenth centuries, many of whom had religious convictions. The 1907 Probation of Offenders Act put this work onto a statutory footing, which meant that courts could now appoint and pay probation officers, thereby absorbing the original court missionaries into these new services. The 1920s was the period when probation work moved away from religious, missionary ideals to become a professional-based service (Whitfield, 1998).

At the same time, it is important to consider multiculturalism in Britain, as this has adopted a secular-based model in that cultural and other identities in relation to race/ethnicity have been the primary lens through which the state has approached diversity issues, with religion largely being viewed as something that is confined to private space and is therefore outside of state interest and regulation. Equality and diversity issues have thus traditionally been approached through the lens of 'race'/ethnicity rather than religious identity. Within the criminal justice context, agencies of the criminal justice system have approached diversity issues through a secular, race relations framework, whereby 'race'/ethnic identities/groupings have been identified and used to guide service delivery and provision, so that religion/spirituality have traditionally been overlooked within contemporary criminal justice policy and practice. This can be seen most clearly in the monitoring procedures used by agencies of the criminal justice system to record the identities of suspects, offenders, victims and employees, whereby racial and/or ethnic (rather than faith) categories have traditionally been used, with only the prison service systematically recording offenders' religious identities. Thus, for example, statistics in relation to stop and searches conducted by the police under counter-terrorism legislation use ethnic rather than religious categories. This means that although statistics may suggest an increase in the number of Asians stopped and searched, it is not possible to gauge the circumstances of young Muslims from these statistics (Garland *et al.*, 2006). This means that direct evidence of the number of Muslims who have been targeted by the police, either as part of wider anti-terror operations or due to more general policing initiatives, is generally unavailable because of the ways in which data is collected by agencies of the criminal justice system. This is due, in part, to the secular nature of the race relations movement, whereby researchers who have documented racial disadvantage and discrimination have, for many years, argued that public bodies should routinely assemble information about ethnicity (and not religion) in order to help monitor disadvantage and to ensure that their policies and practices are not disadvantaging particular communities. It was decided that all agencies of the criminal justice system should, from 1 April 2003, begin to collect data using the 16-point classification used in the 2001 National Census in order to create a single common system for the collection of ethnic data in all agencies. However, in practice, the ways in which statistics are collected, the ways in which this data is presented and the ways in which research is conducted and statistically analysed is according to a modified five-point system of racial classification, generally relating to White, Black, Asian, Other and Mixed. This means that Muslims' experiences are subsumed within very general categories, which do not reflect, or indeed even consider, the religious affiliation of individuals (Spalek, 2008). As demonstrated in Chapters 3 and 4, a result of the post-9/11 'new terrorism' climate, community-based approaches to countering terrorism have developed whereby state–community engagement has gone beyond engagement with ethnic/racial groupings to engaging with religious groups, notably Muslim communities.

Although Chapters 3 and 4 have tended to focus upon partnership approaches between Muslim communities and police and other statutory agencies in relation to counter-terrorism, it is important to note that partnership is but one type of engagement and is perhaps quite an uncommon form of engagement due to the challenges raised by partnership work. It is important to stress in this chapter that engagement between Muslim communities, the police and other statutory agencies is complex and multi-layered because engagement can take place at individual and organizational levels, at local and national levels, involving 'harder' and 'softer' approaches, in multiple and complex ways. There is also significant variation in the types of engagement that exist. Studies by Spalek *et al.* (2009) and Spalek and McDonald (2011) demonstrate that one type of engagement that exists might be referred to as general, ongoing police–community engagement, whereby a number of organizations and individuals have developed a good relationship with one or two individual police officers from their local area or from units such as the Muslim Contact Unit (MCU) or the National Communities

Tension Team (NCTT), who will make regular face-to-face contact through informal meetings and attendance at community events and police meetings. This type of contact may be best described as informal and dialogic engagement, and the research indicates that this is a fairly standard, commonly found practice, particularly since 7/7 and the shift towards community policing.

Importantly, whereas the notions of engagement and disengagement may, at first sight, be viewed as separate, comprising of binary opposites, the interview data suggests that a more realistic conceptualization views engagement as being comprised of a continuum – from full engagement to full disengagement – and that individuals (both community members and police officers), community groups and policing units will at different points in time in different contexts be located on different points of the continuum vis-à-vis each other, being in constant flux, their positionings influenced by wide-ranging factors. Therefore, it is important to note that what may appear initially as being 'disengagement', whereby community members may leave existing processes and protocols of engagement with the police, may not always in fact comprise 'full disengagement' as these individuals may create new ways of engaging with the police, outside of existing processes and structures, with officers and policing units that they trust. At the same time, for some individuals and groups, disengagement may be temporary and may be used strategically to help negotiate a more empowered position within any future engagement that takes place.

It may be that in some instances individuals choose to fully disengage from the police, particularly those who live and/or work in areas which have had an ongoing history of poor police–community relations, who describe a complete lack of positive engagement with police officers. In these cases, negative experiences of police activity – from sustained, low-level incidents of police harassment to the over-use of stop and search and in some cases being subjected to 'hard' counter-terrorism techniques – have contributed to disengagement. For these participants, contact with the police is felt to be inevitably negative. Of particular concern are the experiences of participants who have engaged previously with the police – either individually or as members of organizations – but whose experiences have been so negative that they have chosen to fully disengage. This is significant as it may be the case that it is more difficult to make links with those individuals and groups who have fully disengaged from the police than those individuals and groups who have only partially or temporarily disengaged. Furthermore, the Muslim population in the UK is extremely diverse, ethnically, culturally, religiously and politically, posing significant challenges for engagement. It may be that some groups place a higher value on organizing demonstrations and vociferously expressing their concerns to the police, whereas other groups prefer an approach that involves implicitly expressing their concerns whilst maintaining good relationships with the police. These different styles and viewpoints of engagement inevitably lead to tensions between groups and individuals and may lead to some groups and individuals partially disengaging from established police–community structures. However, it is important to point out that this kind of disengagement is not necessarily negative because those individuals/groups who disengage from existing structures of engagement may continue to engage with police, albeit in new ways. Other intra-community tensions that may impact upon community–police engagement include the lack of representation and the perception that this has been reduced through intra-community dynamics and political manoeuvrings, including the marginalization of certain ethnic and religious groups from engagement, the competition between groups for voice and influence, internal leadership disputes and in some cases ineffective grassroots communication so that any engagement between community members and the police does not filter down to a wider population (Spalek *et al.*, 2009).

Salafi and Islamist groups in particular have been viewed as a security threat. Islamism is diverse and a category that encompasses many different movements and ideals. Islamist groups can be identified primarily by their core objective of bringing about divine justice, which whilst in theory implies respecting and implementing 'sharia law', in practice urges to a commitment to 'social justice' and 'political reform' (Silvestri, 2009: 1). Salafism is equally diverse. According to Silvestri (2007), Salafism has in particular been used as a synonym for jihadism and terrorism, thereby neglecting the nuances and multiple positionings of Salafis and the evolution of different currents of Islamic thought. The categories 'Salafi' and 'Islamist' are complex and contain vast diversity between individuals thus classified, thereby reflecting generally the endemic problem to social categorizations of identity (Woodward, 2002). According to

Silvestri (2007: 3), 'salafism is often discussed as if it were a clearly defined violent and radical ideology and set of precepts, whereas in fact it is a recurrent *topos* in the history of Islam, a broad approach that emphasises the exemplary life and religiosity of the "ancestors" or "predecessors" (in Arabic, *Salaf*), the companions of the Prophet. So, the importance of the *Salaf* and of the return to the original sources of the faith has inspired different generations of Muslims and has been interpreted in different ways'.

To draw upon and to use Islamic identities and practices that potentially might be construed as 'radical' (which in some cases may be simply because individuals are religiously conservative and have a real or a perceived opposition to established secular values: see Spalek *et al.*, 2009) runs the risk that these are negatively labelled and attract the attention of approaches to security that might be considered as requiring counter-insurgency and/or counter-subversion tactics. According to Kilcullen (2007: 112–13), counter-insurgency involves 'all measures adopted to suppress an insurgency' where insurgency is 'a struggle to control a contested political space between a state (or group of states or occupying powers) and one or more popularly based, non-state challengers'. According to Lambert (2008), a counter-subversion perspective in the UK posits that those described as being Islamist, whether or not they are suspected of terrorism or violent extremism, are to be targeted and stigmatized in the same way as terrorists influenced or directed by Al-Qaeda. Thus, there is a danger that the expression of Islamic identities considered to be 'radical' may attract the attention of certain security sectors and groupings that are striving to influence the kinds of Islamic identities that are made manifest in the UK and in other Western democratic contexts. Islamic identities may be influenced through the penetration of Muslim communities by covert and largely ungoverned and ungovernable security operatives that draw upon multimedia and other strategies that aim to influence the kinds of Muslim identities and Islamic practices that are being expressed and practised. Nonetheless, it is important to highlight that according to Schmid (2007: 13–14), 'a disproportionately large number of European Muslims feel they are underprivileged. Not feeling accepted by host societies, some of the young Muslims have been radicalized by Muslim clerics who warned them against integration and offered them a Salafist or even jihadist version of

Islam'. It is therefore important to consider the structural experiences of alienation and marginalization amongst Muslim minorities when researching terror crime prevention.

The utilization of Salafi and Islamist groups for counter-terrorism is a neglected issue and research area, for the debate around preventing terrorism and community policing has tended to be one dominated by a generalist approach. Although this highlights the importance of local contexts, it nonetheless posits that neighbourhood policing, through responding to Muslim communities' concerns regarding particular signal crimes like burglary, hate crime and drugs, can help build enough of a rapport with community members for them to provide the police with community intelligence (Innes *et al.*, 2007). It is important to stress that more research and policy attention needs to be paid to specific partnerships between police officers and members of Muslim communities where young Muslims deemed at risk of committing acts of terrorism are targeted for intervention. It is not necessarily the case that intelligence regarding young people at risk is widely available amongst members of Muslim communities, but rather that this intelligence is perhaps concentrated amongst particular groupings and networks, and so preventing terrorism is not a question of necessarily engendering trust between all Muslim communities and the police but instead developing trust between specific Muslim groups and the police (see Spalek, 2010).

At this stage it is perhaps useful to distinguish between counter-terrorism responses that problematize identities and those that emphasize liberal freedoms associated with liberal democracy. Approaches that emphasize liberal freedoms seek not to problematize or securitize particular identities, but rather seek to enable individuals to draw upon the liberal freedoms associated with liberal democracy in order that a wider range of actions are considered legitimate, so that individuals no longer see violence as a means to pursue their aims. This work includes wide-ranging activities like encouraging political participation from within Muslim communities, enhancing education about Islam among Muslims themselves and supporting social and political activism. This work also seeks to draw upon individuals formerly and/or currently practising 'securitized identities' as mentors in order to attempt to rehabilitate those deemed at risk of committing acts of violence, so that they are no longer vulnerable to pursuing violent action. However, as highlighted in Chapter 1, the Prevent Review signals a step change by the British government, in that extremism, and not only violent extremism, is viewed problematically. Therefore, there is a danger that law enforcement approaches will increasingly reflect this problematization of identities rather than seek to work with groups and to develop initiatives that address violent behaviours, regardless of the religious and political identities of the groups concerned. This is not to say that law enforcement agencies should engage necessarily with all 'extreme' groups for counter-terrorism purposes, but, nonetheless, those deemed to be able to reduce threats from terrorism can and should be potentially engaged.

Faith awareness in policing

An interesting aspect of community-based counter-terrorism is the ways in which policing – a traditionally secular arena – has dealt with the shift towards recognizing and understanding religion, both within its ranks and the communities with which it interacts. This is particularly important given that, according to Kundnani (2009: 7), 'the main impact of Prevent work locally has been greater mistrust of the police. It's impacted all the wrong way. And there is more reluctance on the part of the Muslim community to engage at all'.

Along with the wider body of literature on the subject, the empirical data gathered by Spalek *et al.* (2009) has shown that counter-terrorism policing has changed rapidly since 2002. Understanding community values and religious commitments has helped non-Muslim police officers to interpret community members' behaviour that could not be otherwise comprehended or would be mistakenly interpreted as suspicious. The police authorities now issue guidance booklets that pay particular attention to religious customs in order to make members of the police service better equipped to deal with similar situations. Working with Muslim groups therefore brings religious values and spirituality into the normally secular police work environment, with non-Muslim police accommodating the religious needs of Muslim partners, for example, making time for prayers during/between meetings, providing clean and quiet spaces for prayers and including halal food in canteens. This suggests that the traditional separation of the secular from the sacred, as featured in Enlightenment values underpinning modern society in general and the modern criminal justice system specifically, is an artificial construct. If the position is taken that religious affiliation and spirituality may constitute important aspects of the self-identity of some individuals, it seems that the artificial separation between the secular and the sacred is no longer tenable within criminal justice and other contexts. Indeed, the next section specifically focuses upon the experiences of Muslim counter-terrorism officers, whose multiple identities raise interesting questions.

The experiences of Muslim police officers

Interviews with Muslim police officers who work within counter-terrorism reveal that sometimes Muslims can find joining the police service problematic: i) because of tensions with their communities as a result of their particular line of work; and ii) because they have had to resolve emotional and intellectual issues about the nature of their work, how it affects their close communities and the legitimacy of certain aspects of police work, i.e. the use of intelligence/spying as a method of gathering information in general, from an Islamic viewpoint. It is worth taking a closer look at the work of the MCU, a counter-terrorism unit that employed Muslim police officers. It appears that Muslim police officers have been instrumental in building bridges with members of mosques, developing trusting relationships with mosque communities and then extending these relationships to the non-Muslim police officers working on the MCU. They have also brought important cultural and religious understandings to the unit. The following is a quotation from an interview with a Muslim MCU police officer:

Well one critical factor in our success is having officers on the unit who are experienced Special Branch officers, working together hand in hand with Muslim officers who have an experience in policing community matters and live and work amongst that community with a certain degree of religious credibility and respect. Why? Because when you're dealing with people who are very passionate about their religion, who are prepared, in many cases, to die for their religion because Jihad or whatever, they feel very strongly ... You have to have religious sincerity and credibility, again community credibility and respect to be able to turn round and engage and help engage. There are people that we go and talk to where we open the doors for our colleagues to come and join us and talk to them. (Spalek, 2010: 807)

Interestingly, it appears that, within the context of 'new terrorism', Muslim police officers working within the MCU had to trust the role, focus and methodology of this policing unit, as the following quotation from a Muslim MCU officer illustrates:

> First of all I wasn't sure exactly where the so-called war on terror was going. If you recall back in 9/11 the way the Muslim community perceived it was not a war on terror, it was a war on Islam and I'm from the Muslim community, I'm not immune from those kind of things. And as I say being a police officer as well I know how certain things worked, I know how the police service as an institution worked, you know. I know how policy, public policy works and so on ... having first trusted what X and Y were doing, I think trust was a major issue. Once I was happy that I trusted both of them, we then started to ... I started to take them to mosques and things and people that I knew within the community and that's how we built it up. (Spalek, 2010: 807)

The above quotation appears suggests that for Muslim police officers to become involved in counter-terrorism policing, they first need to trust the aims and objectives of the counter-terrorism operations that they are being asked to engage in. It seems that their identities as Muslim police officers mean that they have a concern that counter-terrorism operations are conducted to prevent terrorism, not to act as part of a wider politicized regime of denigrating Islam. This serves to demonstrate the complexity to trust, whereby perhaps Muslim police officers working within counter-terrorism units will have concerns that are specific to them as Muslims in relation to developing trust towards the policing units in which they are working.

Another important factor to consider is the backlash that Muslim police officers who are openly involved in counter-terrorism community policing may face from within their own communities, which can have negative effects not only for them but also for their families. Such problems betray a relative lack of understanding of the nature of counter-terrorism work on the part of communities. They also reinforce the call for a renewed understanding of Islamic jurisprudence with regard, in this context, to the question of the legitimacy of using 'spying' as a method of information gathering by the police.

Muslims follow the broad Qur'anic directive that prohibits spying (*wa la tajassassu*):

> Believers, avoid making too many assumptions – some assumptions are sinful – and *do not spy on one another* or speak ill of people behind their backs: would any of you like to eat the flesh of your dead brother? (Q. 49:12)[10]

This directive is also strongly supported through a number of prophetic *hadith*s, such as Bukhari 6064 and Muslim 2563.

The question of legitimacy goes beyond a problematic aspect of jurisprudence to the more confusing political sphere. Even if police work did not directly involve the use of intelligence, Muslim police officers participating in the research study by Spalek *et al.* (2009) still felt the need to clarify the issue for themselves as well as their communities. It was considered important to understand that although the work is performed in the context of the 'War on Terror', counter-terrorism policing is not against Islam but against crime committed in the name of Islam, carried out for the sake of public safety and therefore under one of the main priorities in the ethos of Islamic law.[11] A number of Muslim police officers have had to endure difficulties relating to their work, ranging from personal tensions to fractions in the community, to death threats against them and their families for being 'spies on their own'. This reflects the experiences of some community members whose work and preaching of non-violence in mosques has resulted in them coming under similar pressures (Spalek *et al.*, 2009). Interestingly, the number of Muslim police officers engaged in community counter-terrorism work is extremely low. According to a report by the National Association of Muslim Police and Demos, there were only 27 Muslims working in counter-terrorism nationally, of whom two were women (NAMP and Demos, 2008: 8). This may point to there being a general absence of trust between Muslim community members/police officers and the police within the 'new terrorism' context, despite initiatives like the MCU.

The role of religion in counter-terrorism work

Religious motivations for countering terrorism

Religious convictions can provide strong motivations amongst community members to cooperate with the police's efforts to fight religious violence. Many research participants have stated in powerful words that their commitment to Islam provided a feeling of moral responsibility or a duty to help the authorities in counter-terrorism work, to form good relations with others and help people around them. They, as well as people in the community, 'want to do good, but want to contextualize this "Islamically" within the framework of their own religious values', to solve social justice problems and the issue of religious violence through an Islamic framework. While engaging proactively, such community members also scrutinize the messages of violent extremists, exposing the non-Islamic elements and rejecting the violent approach to political change altogether.[12] In doing so, they draw their answers from *within*, not without Islam (Spalek *et al.*, 2009). However, the approach remains engaged and critical, and it seems that both Muslim community members and Muslim police officers may not cooperate with or support policies that they see as unjust or unacceptable from an Islamic point of view.

Religious knowledge as essential in fighting violent ideology

Knowledge of and experience in the various ideologies of political Islam, particularly an indepth understanding of the *'takfiri* ideology' (which is central to political violence in the name of Islam), is an essential factor in winning the ideological battle and driving preachers who promoted this ideology out of influential mosques. The success of the earlier efforts by groups has now resulted in a number of more sophisticated and less conventional projects that are all based on preventing violent extremism by exposing the illegitimacy of its ideological bases.

Perceptions of religion hindering cooperation between community members and the police in counter-terrorism work

It must be noted that the lack of knowledge about the exact nature of the police's counter-terrorism work, a general feeling that Muslim communities are under suspicion and that their religion is blamed, and a fear of individual and collective punishment for implication in terrorist plots has caused and continues to cause reluctance to take a proactive role in counter-terrorism. The research study by Spalek *et al.* (2009) reveals that in some cases research participants recounted that within some Muslim communities, *fatwas* – juristic opinions – have been issued against any such cooperation, or 'collaboration' as it is framed. In addition, community members who recalled being happy to cooperate with the police prior to 9/11 described their growing scepticism of the security services' methods, particularly with regard to repeated interrogations and the tactical passing of information to other detainees, a method which in certain contexts has led to individuals and their families receiving death threats. This matter is not unrelated to the problems experienced by Muslim police officers before and during their engagement with counter-terrorism work.

Conclusion

This chapter has focused upon the question of the role and place of religion in counter-terrorism. In particular, counter-terrorism policing has been explored for its connections with religion. The chapter has highlighted how secularism has been the dominant norm within modern society and the criminal justice system. Therefore, religious groups and identities have tended to be overlooked in the policies and practices of state agencies. The police, like other state agencies, have engaged with communities predominantly on the basis of their race/ethnicity rather than religious identities. Nonetheless, in a post-9/11 era with threats from 'homegrown' terrorists in relation to 'new terrorism', police officers have been engaging with Muslim communities. Engagement between the police and Muslim communities is complex and in constant flux, consisting of individual and organizational engagement, at local and national levels, involving 'harder' and 'softer' approaches in multiple and complex ways. A further issue that this chapter has focused upon is the work of Muslim police officers working in counter-terrorism. It may be that in order for Muslim police officers to become involved in counter-terrorism policing, they first need to trust the aims and objectives of the counter-terrorism operations that they are being asked to engage in. It seems that their identities as Muslim police officers mean that they have a concern that counter-terrorism operations are conducted to prevent terrorism, not to act as part of a wider politicized regime of denigrating Islam. At the same time, Muslim police officers face certain risks such as being stigmatized by members of their own communities, for counter-terrorism has traditionally been about maintaining nation state security rather than community or individual security. As a result, Muslim counter-terrorism police officers face many challenges.

Case study

In 2009 the FBI Director in the USA defended the FBI's use of informants within US mosques, despite complaints from Muslim organizations that worshippers and clerics were being targeted instead of possible terrorists. Muslim organizations claim that the FBI has been asking them to spy on Islamic leaders and worshippers. Organizations also claim that they have been asked to monitor people coming to mosques and donations that they make. According to the FBI Director: 'We don't investigate places, we investigate individuals. To the extent that there may be evidence or other information of criminal wrongdoings, then we will ... undertake those investigations.' FBI agents and prosecutors say spying on mosques is one of the best weapons to uncover lurking terrorists or threats to national security. However, this has posed a politically and legally thorny issue with members of Muslim communities who see themselves as unjustly monitored.[13]

Notes

1. Examples of similar views are rife in printed and electronic sources – a Google search produces over four million references to 'Islam taking over'.
2. A police officer participating in this research recounted how the phrase 'communities defeat terrorism' was a familiar police maxim often used during the IRA bombing campaign on the 'mainland' by heads of the Anti-Terrorist Branch such as George Churchill-Coleman. In this context, it signified the need for public vigilance rather than a notion of required community intelligence as signified by Sir Ian Blair.
3. For Bush's public speeches immediately following the 9/11 attacks, see George W. Bush, 'Remarks upon Arrival at the White House', 16 September 2001, White House News Releases, www.whitehouse.gov/news/releases/2001/09/20010916-2.html# (date accessed 15 December 2011); and 'President Bush, Colombia President Uribe Discuss Terrorism', 25 September 2002, White House News Releases, http://www.whitehouse.gov/news/releases/2002/09/20020925-1.html (date accessed 15 December 2011).
4. George W. Bush, 'Remarks upon Arrival at the White House', 16 September 2001, White House News Releases, www.whitehouse.gov/news/releases/2001/09/20010916-2.html# (date accessed 15 December 2011).
5. E.g. 'More than 1/3 of US Muslims see War on Islam', *Washington Times*, 19 October 2004, http://www.washingtontimes.com/news/2004/oct/19/20041019-115241-3792r/ (date accessed 15 December 2011);

L. Evans, 'War on Terrorism Looks Too Much Like a War on Islam, Arab Scholar Warns', 27 January 2003, UCLA International Institute, www.international.ucla.edu/article.asp?parentid=3010 (date accessed 15 December 2011).

6. E.g. Tony Blair's speech to the Labour Party Annual Conference, 2 October 2001, www.guardian.co.uk/politics/2001/oct/02/labourconference.labour6 (date accessed 15 December 2011).

7. 'Fight in the way of God those who fight you and do not transgress for God do dislikes those who transgress' (Q. 2:190). For a detailed argument on the interpretation of this verse that is contrary to Al-Qaeda's approach, see Ibrahim and others, *Istratigiyyat al-Qa'ida: al-Akhta' wa al al-Akhtaar* (*Al-Qa'da's Strategy: Risks and Mistakes*). For more on Ibrahim, see: www.jamestown.org/single/?no_cache=1&tx_ttnews%5Btt_news%5D=900 (date accessed 15 December 2011).

8. Q. 2:179.

9. For a brief summary of this debate, see, for example: www.islamicthinkers.com/index/images/spying_haraam.pdf (date accessed 15 December 2011).

10. The use of these texts for the purpose of verifying the legitimacy of using intelligence needs to be contextualized by qualified scholars who can explain the verse's and the hadiths' specific contexts and compare them to the contexts of modern state systems, the particular nature of the crime in question (e.g. political crime affecting societies and states and causing collective damage as opposed to crimes that affect individuals) and the level of necessity and public interest involved. To the author's knowledge, such ijtihad is yet to be conducted and thus rulings on this matter have not been issued.

11. Five ultimate aims stand behind the rulings of Islamic law. For any given ruling/law to be tenable, it has to be designed so as to achieve one or more of the following aims: protection of the faith, protection of human life, protection of the intellect, protection of property and protection of humankind.

12. With the exception of defensive jihad, which is obligatory on Muslim people if they come under attack, according to the consensus of Muslim jurists.

13. Associated Press, 2009, www.msnbc.msn.com/id/31177049/ns/world_news-terrorism (date accessed 16 December 2011).

References

Beckford, J. (1996) 'Postmodernity, High Modernity and New Modernity: Three Concepts in Search of Religion', in K. Flanagan and P. Jupp (eds), *Postmodernity, Sociology and Religion*. Basingstoke: Macmillan, pp. 30–47.

Beckford, J. and Gilliat, S. (1998) *Religion in Prison: Equal Rites in a Multi-faith Society*. Cambridge University Press.

Berger, P. (ed.) (1999) *The Desecularization of the World: Resurgent Religion and World Politics*. Grand Rapids, MI: William B. Eerdmans Publishing.

Caraballo-Resto, J. (2006) 'The Rhetoric of Secularism among First Generation Muslim Migrants in Dundee', paper presented at the Ninth EASA Biennial Conference, Bristol University, September.

Garland, J., Spalek, B. and Chakraborti, N. (2006) 'Hearing Lost Voices: Issues in Researching "Hidden" Minority Ethnic Communities', *British Journal of Criminology* 46: 423–37.

Innes, M., Abbott, L., Lowe, T. and Roberts, C. (2007) *Hearts and Minds and Eyes and Ears: Reducing Radicalisation Risks through Reassurance-Oriented Policing.* London: ACPO.

Jürgensmeyer, M. (2003) *Terror in the Mind of God.* Berkeley, CA: University of California Press.

Kilcullen, D. (2007) 'Counter-Insurgency', *Survival* 48(4): 111–30.

Kundnani, A. (2009) *Spooked! How Not to Prevent Violent Extremism.* London: Institute of Race Relations, available at www.irr.org.uk/pdf2/spooked.pdf (date accessed 16 December 2011).

Lambert, R. (2008). Empowering Salafis and Islamists against Al-Qaida: A London Counter-Terrorism Case Study', *PS: Political Science and Politics* 41(1): 31–5.

NAMP and Demos. 2008. *Diversity in Modern Policing: A Survey Conducted by the National Association of Muslim Police (NAMP) and Demos, with Key Findings and Solutions.* London: NAMP.

Schmid, A. (2007) 'Terrorism and Democracy', *Terrorism and Political Violence* 10(3): 14–25.

Silvestri, S. (2007) 'Radical Islam: Threats and Opportunities', *Global Dialogue* 9(3–4): 118–26.

——. (2009) 'Moderate Islamist Groups in Europe: The Muslim Brothers', in K. Hroub (ed.), *Political Islam.* London: Saqi Books.

Spalek, B. (2008) *Communities, Identities and Crime.* Bristol: Policy Press.

——. (2010) 'Community Policing, Trust and Muslim Communities in Relation to "New Terrorism"', *Politics & Policy* 38(4): 789–815.

Spalek, B., El-Awa, S. and McDonald, L.Z. (2009) 'Engagement and Partnership Work in a Counter-Terrorism Context', University of Birmingham.

Spalek, B., Lambert, R. and Baker, A.H. (2009) 'Minority Muslim Communities and Criminal Justice: Stigmatized UK Faith Identities Post 9/11 and 7/7', in H.S. Bhui (ed.), *Race and Criminal Justice.* London: Sage, pp. 170–87.

Spalek, B. and McDonald, L.Z. (2011) 'Preventing Religio-Political Violent Extremism Amongst Muslim Youth: A Study Exploring Police-Community Partnership', University of Birmingham.

Whitfield, D. (1998) *Introduction to the Probation Service*, 2nd edn. Winchester: Waterside Press.

Woodward, K. (2002) 'Concepts of Identity and Difference', in K. Woodward (ed.), *Identity and Difference.* London, Sage, pp. 7–62.

8
Policing, Terrorism and the Conundrum of 'Community': A Northern Ireland Perspective

John Topping and Jonathon Byrne

Introduction

On an international scale, Northern Ireland has enjoyed a relatively 'elevated' position in terms of the political, economic and not least research attention which has been devoted to the resolution of what has been a protracted, internecine armed conflict lasting nearly four decades. With global 'lessons' relating to the successes (or otherwise) of the country's transition from conflict to relative peace, on a number of political and policing plains, this shift has been presented as a model to behold for other societies ravaged with internal division and strife (Campbell *et al.*, 2003; Ellison and O'Reilly, 2008). Most prominently, the reforms to policing in the country have both been central to, and have tended to act as a catalyst for, wider political progress in the country, which have most recently included all-party political support for the policing institutions, along with devolved policing and justice powers for the Northern Ireland Executive for the first time since 1972 (Ryder, 1997; O'Rawe, 2003; Mulcahy, 2006; Topping, 2008a).

However, beyond this largely positive, broad-brush picture relating to the politics of the peace process, it would appear that little academic attention has been paid to the contemporary parameters of *policing* the peace by the Police Service of Northern Ireland (PSNI) – especially in terms of their ability to balance the delivery of a more 'normalized', community-oriented service in the face of a substantial and continuing terrorist threat from (mainly) dissident Republican factions (Frampton, 2010; Topping and Byrne, 2012). Indeed, the rather disparate, empirical 'state' of this community and

157

counter-terrorism policing narrative has been captured by Ellison and Mulcahy (2001: 244–5), who note that:

> Northern Ireland has until relatively recently existed in a kind of criminological netherworld ... its *raison d'être* seemed to be to provide a plethora of 'terrorism' and counter-insurgency 'experts' with the raw material to feed their often fanciful imagination ... a pre-Enlightenment void where the rules of the criminological game, as they were considered in Britain, did not apply.

Added to this, through the haze of what Bayley has termed 'Northern Ireland fatigue' (2007), international interest in the country's policing and security affairs has also diminished – especially as counter-terrorism policing and states of permanent terrorist emergency, once characteristic of the Northern Ireland conflict, have been replaced with the dominant political narrative of the country as a peaceful and shared society to the wider world (Hillyard, 1988; Topping, 2008b).

Thus, the intention of this chapter is to re-examine the contemporary policing landscape in the country, with a particular focus on the juxtaposition of the PSNI's current attempts to deliver a community-centred policing service in the face of a terrorist threat currently assessed as 'severe' by MI5, the highest level in over 12 years (IMC, 2010; McDonald, 2011). Furthermore, it will also explore some of the key junctures between community and counter-terrorism policing in the country. Through drawing out the subtleties of the conflicted security landscape, it will provide a framework through which 'softer', enabling modes of policing may be conceived (or not) as potential alternatives to the lessons of 'hard-edged' counter-terrorism policing which for so long served merely to disenfranchise and damage relations between the state, the police and communities in Northern Ireland (McVeigh, 1994; Hillyard, 2009).

Background

It has been ten years since the PSNI took its first, tentative steps onto the streets of Northern Ireland as the final piece of the political 'jigsaw' and as a means of rebalancing the policing landscape in favour of serving the whole community. As O'Rawe (2003) contends, with policing having occupied a symbolic, central position as part of the conflict, there was always a feeling that if policing could somehow 'be got right', the foundations for a lasting peace could be laid. In this respect, from the introduction of various discriminatory and draconian 'emergency' legislative measures since 1921, through to police control and direction under successive partisan Unionist governments, the PSNI's forerunner, the Royal Ulster Constabulary (RUC), played a significant role in both precipitating *and* holding the 'green line' between the Unionist, Republican and British government triumvirate (Buckland, 1979; Scorer and Hewitt, 1981; Hillyard, 1988, 1994; McEldowney and Gunter, 2003). With over 3,500 conflict-related deaths (of which approximately 300 were members of the RUC), including 48,029 injuries, 37,034 shooting incidents, 16,360 bomb explosions and 19,666 people charged with terrorism offences from 1969 to 2002 alone, Northern Ireland has undoubtedly witnessed a bitter, armed conflict (Hayes and McAllister, 2005). Yet, whatever the conflicting accounts of opposing political factions in regard to policing issues, the RUC consistently viewed itself as the bulwark between anarchy and order (cf. Ni Aolain, 2000; Ryder, 1997).

But central to the wider peace negotiations in Northern Ireland was the recognition of a need for a 'new start' to policing. Indeed, key to the deliberations of the 175 recommendations for reform under the Independent Commission on Policing for Northern Ireland (ICP) was the wrestling of nearly 30 years of state monopoly on policing from the police and giving it back to the community (Topping, 2008a). However, it must be noted that the Patten Report was only the beginning of a process of policing change, which over the past decade has kept the PSNI firmly at the centre of political attention – both locally and internationally. With the issue of policing in the country having acted as 'meta-bargaining' as to the very nature of the conflict (Campbell *et al.*, 2003), the task of 'getting policing right' was (and still is) a function of the complex interplay between the social, cultural and political interfaces of the country's traditionally divided communities (Shirlow and Murtagh, 2006), each with their own particular perspective on the 'shape' and delivery of policing within the new and inclusive landscape, which is itself informed by the recent history of policing experiences.

At a cursory level, one of the former Patten commissioners, Clifford Shearing, noted that the reforms to policing in Northern Ireland may be conceived in two distinct 'streams' (Kempa and Shearing, 2005; Topping, 2008a). In terms of the first stream of reforms, they may be imagined as relating to some of the more physical and symbolic manifestations of policing change in the country, such as names, badges and the controversial nature of 50/50 recruitment. Looking to the second stream of reforms, they may be conceived as relating to broader issues around the governance of security or policing as more broadly conceived (Topping, 2008a: 378). On the one hand, the authors would argue that the first decade of change to the policing landscape in Northern Ireland has predominantly focused upon implementing the first stream of reforms as the physical foundations to a permanent, acceptable and inclusive change process for both Loyalist/Unionist and Republican/Nationalist communities across the country. But, on the other hand, it is the second stream, anchored in Patten recommendation 44 around community policing or the 'policing with the community' (under the rubric of the ICP), which is of importance – especially in relation to the PSNI's counter-terrorism capacity.

Indeed, the PSNI's predecessor, the RUC, was both feared and revered in terms of its ability to withstand and actively combat almost 30 years of violent conflict in Northern Ireland (Ryder, 1997; Weitzer, 1999; Ellison and Smyth, 2000). However, it should be noted that a key tenet of the Patten reform process was about engendering a shift within the police as an organization which would enable it to change from a reactive, hierarchical, militaristic and counterinsurgency *force* into a proactive, community-oriented *service* working with the grain of the communities in which it policed (O'Rawe, 2003; Brogden and Nijhar, 2005). However, interestingly, in terms of the weight of such expectations around policing change in the country at the operational, political and community levels, Mulcahy (1999: 278) notes that 'in the aftermath of a ... conflict, peace itself can constitute a crisis to the extent that it undermines the policies, practices and assumptions ingrained and institutionalised over the years'.

Therefore, within the post-conflict transitional space of Northern Ireland (as shall be discussed below), the authors would argue that a much greater degree of analysis and understanding is required to negotiate the complex dynamics of the PSNI's role as part of its shift from its historical counter-insurgency role to community policing, while trying to balance these policing imperatives as part of the new policing and political landscapes and to reduce disconnections with communities (both Protestant and Catholic) traditionally marginalized from the policing debate (Jarman, 2002; Byrne and Monaghan, 2008), while also dealing with the persistence of national terrorist threat (mainly) posed by the so-called dissident Republican paramilitaries (Frampton, 2010).

Considering the policing environment

At least from the perspective of the PSNI, it has long been held that it has struggled – at an organizational level – to fully realize the implementation of Patten recommendation 44 in relation to community policing in line with the core recommendation of the ICP (ICP, 1999; Byrne and Monaghan, 2008; Topping, 2008a, 2008b, 2009). With the PSNI as a relatively 'young' organization due to the changes in composition of the service as part of the reform process, this too has raised questions in respect of the experiential base underpinning its counter-terrorism capacity – once world-renowned in terms of the de facto commodification and export of such expertise on a global scale (Brogden, 2005; Ellison and O'Reilly, 2008; BBC News, 2010a; *Belfast Telegraph*, 2010a). The departure of many experienced, senior officers from the organization through generous severance packages has depleted the organization of both strategic and operational counter-terrorism capacity and knowledge. However, while recent criticism has been levelled at the PSNI's ability to deliver on both the community policing and counter-terrorism fronts, it is also important to note that the operational environment in which the PSNI polices is by no means conducive to the delivery of 'normal' policing within any Peelian conception of the term as part of the still conflicted and divided post-conflict society of Northern Ireland (Kelling, 2005; Topping, 2008b; Frampton, 2010; McDonald, 2010).

In reference to this environment – and specifically violent dissident Republicanism – while their terrorist capabilities are in no way comparable to the threat posed by mainstream Republican paramilitaries at the height of the conflict, it must be acknowledged that dissident factions are still engaged in an armed campaign, along with the delivery of 'civil policing', within certain areas of Northern Ireland. This has manifested itself through the planting of viable explosive devices and concerted efforts to kill members of the security forces across the country (*Belfast Telegraph*, 2008a, 2008b, 2008c,

2010a; *Irish News*, 2008, 2009), resulting in the deaths of British soldiers Patrick Azimkar and Mark Quinsey outside the Massereene Barracks in Co. Antrim on 8 March 2009 and the murders of Constable Stephen Carroll on 10 March 2009 and Constable Ronan Kerr on 12 April 2011 (McDonald and Townsend, 2011). Indeed, it is a continuing feature of the post-conflict landscape that the terrorist threat is now at its highest in 12 years, with PSNI annual statistics evidencing 78 recorded 'shooting and bombing' incidents in 2006/7, rising to 129 by 2009/10 (IMC, 2010; Kearney, 2010; Owen and Dutta, 2011; PSNI, 2011). It is also important to recognize that paramilitary activity has not been limited solely to those from a Republican background. Within a number of Loyalist working-class communities, paramilitary structures still remain in place to control communities and orchestrate widespread violence, as witnessed in East Belfast during June 2011, where approximately 500 people were involved in violence over three nights, which included gun battles between Loyalist and Republican paramilitary groupings along with the shooting of a Press Association photographer. It is fair to conclude that the presence of proscribed organizations at the community level along with their terrorist capacity is thus far from being consigned to the annals of Northern Irish history (McDonald, 2011).

Therefore, within this violent environment, along with the competing community policing and counter-terrorism agendas that existed (and still exist), there was significant disengagement and alienation of the Republican/Nationalist and, to a lesser extent, Unionist/Loyalist communities from any normal understanding of interaction with the police (Ellison and Mulcahy, 2001; Mulcahy, 2006; Topping, 2008a). When combined with lingering police legitimacy issues associated with the legacy of the conflict, along with the fact that a sizeable minority of the population in Northern Ireland remains at best ambivalent about engaging with the PSNI on what may be conceived as 'normal' policing issues (Byrne and Monaghan, 2008), one becomes aware of the conflicted policing landscape.

The operational boundaries of 'alternative' counter-terrorist policing

Beyond the practical operating environment which shapes the delivery of policing in Northern Ireland, one of the key starting points

from which to consider 'softer' counter-terrorism strategies is with
the organizational priorities attached to these seemingly antithetical
policing imperatives within the PSNI. As noted above, one of the
central issues for policing reform in the country was about the police
moving away from their militaristic, counter-insurgency roots and
placing community policing at the core of deliberations as part of
the ever-normalizing policing environment (Ryder, 1997; Topping,
2008a). However, somewhat ironically for the PSNI, this appears to
be at variance with its colleagues in the constabularies of England and
Wales as counter-terrorism policy continues to pervade and destabi-
lize its Peelian roots which for so long have underpinned values and
relations between the police and the policed (Emsley, 2009).

However, in specific reference to the PSNI and beyond the empirical
evidence which has questioned the operationalization of its shift to
becoming a community-oriented service, a more recent inquiry from
Her Majesty's Inspectorate of Constabulary (HMIC) (2007) has also
posed questions with regard to the suitability of the PSNI's 'shape'
in respect of this shift in the post-Patten era. It is thus interesting to
observe that HMIC has confirmed that the PSNI still retains a relatively militaristic structure to deliver Patten's community policing
vision, with its retention of public order and counter-insurgency
capabilities in comparison to 'most similar forces' in England and
Wales as a striking organizational feature.

Even six years after the implementation of the ICP reforms, only 35
per cent of District Commanders in Northern Ireland have claimed to
be carrying out policing under what might be conceived as 'normal'
conditions, as the persistence of a terrorist threat constrains the ability of the PSNI to freely walk the streets in many areas of the country
(HMIC, 2007). In addition, there are approximately six times as many
officers dedicated to public order policing duties, with four times as
many officers dedicated to intelligence duties, than 'most similar
forces', although a proportion of this capacity is undoubtedly due to
the lack of immediate mutual aid from police services in England, or
indeed An Garda Siochana. Moreover, the police-to-population ratio
in Northern Ireland, at approximately 1:230, still remains one of the
highest in the Western world. Thus, when combined with a total
of 86,073 overtime hours undertaken by PSNI officers to cope with
the extra public order demands (equivalent to an extra £7,266 per
officer per annum) in 2007 alone, it gives a clear indication of the

priority which has been attached to (and necessity to retain) public order and terrorist policing capabilities in Northern Ireland (HMIC, 2007). On the one hand, it must be remembered that such facts actually pre-date the now heightened 'severe' terrorist threat in 2011. On the other hand, these facts only serve to reinforce the paradox of attempting a 'community policing' approach within Northern Ireland's conflicted democracy, especially where:

> the threat of domestic terrorism is always present in Northern Ireland … because officers are now more visible in communities where historically they would not have patrolled on foot or on bicycle, they are more vulnerable to attack … the threat level is currently assessed as high. (Chief Constable Sir Hugh Orde, cited in Marchant, 2007: 5)

Furthermore, with an increase in the terrorist security budget of £245 million over the next four years (BBC News, 2011b), there has not been any equivalent funding or implementation of strategies for the delivery of community policing beyond the Chief Constable's broad policy development around personal, protective and professional policing and the publication of the set of policing commitments (PSNI, 2011).

Thus, from an objective viewpoint, what emerges from the evidence is significant disjuncture between the PSNI's counter-terrorism and community policing capacities in the country. First, once in place, counter-terrorism structures, mentalities and modes of police operation are not easily dismantled and cannot suddenly be removed where a terrorist threat remains in place (Moran, 2008). Secondly, within the PSNI there still remains a very distinct cultural and operational separation between officers involved in counter-terrorism policing and those involved in community-oriented policing (Topping, 2008b). In this respect, any attempts to reconcile the differences between the PSNI's intelligence-gathering capacities and its neighbourhood policing operations beyond the parameters of the National Intelligence Model have yet to become apparent.

On a third and related point, a problematic and controversial issue which still dominates the policing agenda in Northern Ireland is that of the use of informants (Moran, 2010). With the legacy of collusion between the state, the police and Republican/Loyalist communities still contaminating the discourse of counter-terrorism operations in Northern Ireland, alternative means of gathering information, such as low-level 'community intelligence' gathered by neighbourhood officers on the ground, are unlikely to take hold. This is especially so when current modes of counter-terrorism practice have also become a 'path dependent' means for the PSNI over the course of the conflict (Peters, 1999). This is particularly the case when: i) recent data suggests that only 10 per cent of the PSNI's organizational capacity is actually dedicated to what might broadly be defined as neighbourhood policing duties (HMIC, 2011); and ii) holistic, community-level contact between the PSNI and many working-class Loyalist and Republican communities in Northern Ireland has yet to move beyond 'critical engagement' where contact with police remains at best an option of last resort (Byrne and Monaghan, 2008; Topping and Byrne, 2012).

In addition, the legacy of the conflict in terms of police investigations and operations within Northern Ireland has yet to be formally addressed within an agreed framework, which is highlighted by the contested nature of investigations by the Office of the Police Ombudsman for Northern Ireland (OPONI) and the Historical Enquiries Team (HET) within the PSNI (Lundy, 2011). To date, there has been at best an ad hoc and inconsistent approach to examining the historical roles and responsibilities of the RUC in delivering counter-terrorist policing associated with the conflict. As a result, the PSNI continues to be distracted, both financially and politically, by events from recent history, while communities from both sides find it increasingly problematic to distinguish between the old and the new policing dispensations. In this regard, the spectre of policing tactics related to the conflict (such as stop and search and the employment of terrorist legislation) continues to contaminate the current drive towards the delivery of more normalized, community-oriented policing at a local level by the PSNI.

Finally, what cannot be discounted from thinking related to the parameters of alternative, softer styles of counter-terrorism policing in Northern Ireland is the role of the Security Service (MI5). Indeed, MI5 continues to exert a strong and significant influence on counter-terrorism operations, especially through covert operations (mainly) against Irish Republican Army (IRA) activity. However, the location of its second largest headquarters in the UK just outside Belfast is a testament to the priorities of wider national concerns of the British government with regard to counter-terrorism in Northern Ireland. The fact that an estimated 60 per cent of MI5's electronic intercepts relates solely to monitoring dissident Republican terrorist activity (McDonald, 2008) demonstrates the trajectory of the Security and Intelligence Services, along with the PSNI, to continue within their current, path-dependent counter-terrorism strategy and policy.

Therefore, to give an overview of the current operational boundaries constraining potential movements and thinking by the PSNI towards 'softer' counter-terrorism strategies, the evidence would suggest that significant changes within both the PSNI and the current policing environment will be required to effect practical steps towards the Chief Constable's rather contradictory notion that:

> it would be a mistake to say that policing can be separated into security policing and community policing when police officers rely upon community support to do their job, day-in and day-out. (BBC News, 2011a)

Although in a desirable operating environment, community policing and counter-terrorism strategies would compliment one another, the current evidence would point to the fact they *have* become mutually exclusive policing tasks for the PSNI, limiting the potential synergy between the two strategies as a means of 'squeezing' the operating space for dissident Republican activity.

Smoke and mirrors: grasping the nettle of Northern Irish terrorism

In regard to the wider issues of dealing with home-grown terrorism in Northern Ireland, the peace process more generally has served a dual purpose in respect of what it signifies about progress within the conflicted polity. On the one hand, it demarcates a significant watershed in the country's brief history as part of the wider public rejection of violence as a means to political ends (Cox *et al.*, 2006). Furthermore, in a Weberian sense the reforms to policing have acted as a referent for more egalitarian, consensual and legitimating shifts in the state's governance of its still-divided communities (Shirlow and Murtagh, 2006). However, such sweeping changes to the socio-political landscape in Northern Ireland have only served to obfuscate the reality of the nature of continuing terrorist activity at a local level, along with the embedded nature of both Loyalist and Republican paramilitary activity within communities, as shall be explored below.

Beyond the operational realities of counter-terrorism policing (as noted above), probably one of the most contested terrains with respect to the terrorism debate is through the 'framing' of the 'politics of peace'. Indeed, an obvious example is through the contest relating to the 'official' picture of terrorist activities in Northern Ireland. In spite of the officially graded 'severe' threat which currently exists, as detailed by HMIC:

> There is a source of contention amongst some officers and the Police Federation of Northern Ireland when information is provided to the media (and other government departments) by PSNI on bombings and shootings. If asked by the media how many 'terrorist attacks' (bombings or shootings) have taken place in Northern Ireland, or when presenting figures connected to terrorism, *PSNI respond with a figure around 25% of the absolute total.* This is because PSNI describes terrorism as an assault on national security. This does not include attacks on civilian targets or on relatives of members of the police service. (HMIC, 2011: 26, emphasis added)

In this regard, the de facto state of the security situation thus becomes a matter of interpretation by the police, an action which itself politicizes security affairs beyond their technical definition. Furthermore, with the Police Federation for Northern Ireland (PFNI) estimating that approximately 200 gun and bomb attacks have occurred against PSNI officers alone in 2010–11, a rather fractured picture emerges with regard to the very nature of the terrorist threat in the country (McDonald, 2011). Ultimately, the battle for interpreting the scale and extent of the terrorist threat then becomes a site of conflict itself, detracting from the realities and impacts of such activities on officers and communities alike.

It should also be noted that, through the lens of peace process, even the concept of 'terrorism' and paramilitary activity (along with responses to it) has been politically commodified, which has done little except to simplify and polemicize what is a complex and multi-faceted problem, shielding the issue from wider counter-terrorism responses or debate. A primary example of this may observed through the implementation of the CONTEST strategy in Northern Ireland. Indeed, the authors are aware that within the PSNI, while the CONTEST strategy exists at an official level, Republican politicians have been extremely resistant to the language surrounding the 'Pursue' strand because of the historical connotations relating to the use of informers and collusion in Northern Ireland (HM Government, 2011). The extent of this opposition has been such that the CONTEST strategy has all but disappeared from the official and political discourse of counter-terrorism in this country, regardless of knowledge relating to operational scope or delivery.

Furthermore, a key issue which has been consistently ignored as part of the polemic, politicized debates surrounding counter-terrorism policing in the country has been the nature of the terrorist activity being dealt with. A feature of the activities of proscribed organizations in Northern Ireland is their multi-faceted nature, where issues of sovereignty, dissent from the peace process and organized crime underpin the basis for that which falls under the banner of terrorism.

Thus, far from paramilitary groupings operating as 'single issue' or religiously motivated terrorist groups with clear targets and goals employing a single *modus operandi* (Martin, 2006), the boundaries of their activities on both the Republican and to a lesser extent the Loyalist sides are somewhat blurred in respect of their operating capacities. In addition to their ability to plant viable explosive devices and kill members of the security forces, activities under the 'terrorist' umbrella also include: disruptive campaigns to transport and commerce through 'hoax' security alerts; intra-community paramilitary policing and 'punishment' attacks; inter-community attacks between Loyalist and Republican areas; the perpetration of organized crime; and the orchestration of mass public order violence. However, as noted by Topping and Byrne, such differentiation:

> continues to remain largely hidden from the policing and political discourse. This has tended to be deliberately crafted through a 'new' security discourse propagated by Government and the media – with those involved in paramilitary activity painted as 'conflict junkies' and 'Neanderthals'. Furthermore, attacks have

also been levied on the coherence of their political ideologies, with notions of politics replaced by a narrative of paramilitarism as a form of personal pursuit and gain through drugs, criminality and organized crime ... a difficulty with this over-simplistic political frame of assessment is that localized paramilitary policing tends to be conflated with the national terrorist threat posed by dissident Republicans; and packaged as an isolated aberration of the peace-time landscape. (Topping and Byrne, 2012: 51)

Thus, without sufficient acknowledgement of the 'layered' nature of activities involving proscribed organizations in Northern Ireland, recourse to potential alternative modes of counter-terrorism policing are dashed on the Leviathan of overarching 'security objectives', which trump softer strategies as first-line modes of protection of communities and the state.

Set against this macro-frame, policing tactics and operations used as part of counter-terrorism approaches are analysed and perceived in equally blunt terms, regardless of the purpose served or outcomes achieved. A primary example may be observed through recent debates concerning the use of 'stop and search' tactics by the PSNI under s. 44 of the Terrorism Act 2000. First, the occurrence of over 10,000 stop and searches recorded by the PSNI (prior to the European Court of Human Rights ruling it illegal in January 2010) and just 365 arrests is a clear example of what HMIC has noted as a lack of 'quality assurance processes in place to test claims of success in disrupting terrorist activity' (HMIC, 2011: 25), in spite of the PSNI's claims that the use of stop and search 'remains an essential tool in countering the terrorist threat' (BBC News, 2010b). Even at the political and community levels, unqualified, ritual conflagration between Unionist and Republican political parties over the necessity (or otherwise) of stop and search tactics by the PSNI does little except to recirculate historical discourse relating to debates on emergency powers (Hillyard, 2009; *Belfast Telegraph*, 2010c).

Ultimately, the overall effect of such blunt understandings relating to the nature of the terrorist threat, paramilitary activity and counter-terrorism responses by the state in Northern Ireland is to stagnate rather than enable community-focused debates relating to potential new ways to grasp the 'old nettle' of counter-terrorism policing in the country.

Considering 'community' in the counter-terrorism debate

A central but seldom explored question related to 'softer', community-oriented approaches to counter-terrorism is precisely *how* communities can be brought on board to both influence and improve the police capacity to deal with the terrorist threat. And certainly, while issues of social cohesion, 'soft power' and community intelligence all feed into wider debate, the practical outworking of such laudable ideas is somewhat less clear (Innes, 2006; Spalek and Imtoual, 2007; Pickering *et al.*, 2008; Weisburd *et al.*, 2009). Due to the transitional character of Northern Ireland's policing and security landscape, such a task is further complicated for the PSNI as it attempts to find a balance between its counter-insurgency and community policing roles (Ellison, 2007). However, it is important to note that at least in some areas, local policing initiatives *are* continuing to be delivered on the ground as a means of circumventing overt, 'hard-edged' counter-insurgency tactics with a softer, bottom-up approach which conducts policing *through* the community as a means of 'squeezing' the space in which the dissident terrorist campaign still operates (*Belfast Telegraph*, 2009; IMC, 2010; McDonald, 2011).

One such innovative scheme currently operating with success in the 'G' District area of Derry and Strabane in Northern Ireland is that of a 'cultural intelligence' programme targeted at the PSNI's response officers that is designed specifically to overcome the historical distance and distrust between Republican (and to a lesser extent Loyalist) communities and the police, to instill within PSNI officers a greater sense of operational and political sensitivity to their operations, and specifically to help the Republican communities of Derry (where dissident paramilitary activity tends to be concentrated outside of Belfast) move beyond politically 'cognitive' to wholehearted community support for the PSNI.

With an implicit recognition that the majority of PSNI response officers in the area were often either young, inexperienced or had limited contextual knowledge of the Republican and Loyalist working-class neighbourhoods in which they policed, the scheme draws parallels with Skogan's 'asymmetrical encounters' thesis (2006). With legacy issues around counter-insurgency policing during the conflict and past experiences of policing by community members at the hands of the RUC, combined with perceived limitations to the PSNI's community policing in a contemporary context, it was recognized that a significant, extra 'cultural value' could be attached to each and every 'contact' between the PSNI and the local community. Thus, at the heart of the scheme lay the importance of getting policing 'right' at the individual officer and organizational level within the area (Hillyard, 1985; Mulcahy, 2006; Byrne and Monaghan, 2008). This is because, as contemporary research has indicated, where officers are failing to engage fully with such hard-to-reach communities, it can aid in the creation of a 'social space' in which the dissident paramilitary groups may operate more freely to garner support through dealing with the germane concerns of local residents (*Belfast Telegraph*, 2010b; Topping and Byrne, 2012).

In this regard, the 'cultural intelligence' training model is about bringing together local police officers and community activists within G District to discuss not just contemporary concerns over the delivery of policing in the area, but also *cultural concerns* over counter-terrorism policing in regard to how the potential antagonisms of current, 'hard-edged' policing tactics (often reminiscent of the conflict) can best be mitigated – as a means of limiting damage to the tentative police–community relations which exist, while simultaneously enhancing community attitudes towards procedural justice (Sunshine and Tyler, 2003; Byrne and Monaghan, 2008; Topping, 2008b; *Belfast Telegraph*, 2010c). Indeed, a key proposition of the model is that dissident Republican paramilitarism is not a separate social 'entity' that operates at some peripheral community level; rather, such terrorist activity is bound up *within* the social fabric of Republican communities because of the political, cultural and segregation issues in the area which provide the 'space' in which the dissident terror groups can operate. Therefore, a security response alone will only succeed alongside the withdrawal of public support for dissident Republican activities.

Thus, beyond merely acting as a 'sounding board' for the grievances of local communities, the programme is designed to act as an educational tool for both the PSNI *and* individuals in the community to better understand the parameters of the fragile social chains which are ultimately necessary to facilitate information flows and networks relating to terrorist activity. Moreover, the selection of key, trusted community individuals to participate in the programme provides a means for those with a level of community influence and association to have a direct (if holistic) operational input into the policing of the locale – itself bridging the counter-terrorism and community policing agendas.

On a more fundamental level, another outcome of the programme has been that PSNI officers take *personal responsibility* for their conduct and tactics by incorporating and applying the community-based learning and awareness into the everyday (counter-terrorism) operational life of the area. With the historical antecedents of police–community interaction (as noted above) demanding much more than merely 'satisfactory' service to ameliorate experiences of the past, each and every contact was to be observed as either a 'stepping stone' or a 'stumbling block'. Thus, returning to the fragile chain of social contact conception, the programme aids officers in acquiring a distinct form of 'operational awareness' as a means of bridging the community/counter-terror policing divides.

First, it must be noted that the issue of community 'identity' has for a long time been a key contention within (mainly) Republican/ Nationalist communities during the conflict and post-conflict periods of Northern Irish history in terms of the 'targeting' of police opera- tions (Hillyard, 1994; *Belfast Telegraph*, 2010c). Thus, the programme is about increasing officer awareness of previously hidden social attitudes and variations in identity even within 'hard-to-reach' communities where threats to officer safety are high – beyond the desocializing and blanket approaches of counter-terrorism tactics of the past, so often the fait accompli of blunt and damaging police operations in the country. Secondly, through such a *community-focused* rather than *community-targeted* approach to policing, a distinct shift from a *control* to an *enabling* police agenda may also be observed. With officers better able to negotiate the community 'topology' of the area beyond a purely security lens, counter-terror strategy then moved beyond 'all or nothing' operations towards a more sophisticated and integrated form of counter-terrorism polic- ing to avoid whole sections of the community being 'punished' for the activities of a minority.

In this respect, the lesson of the 'G District' model concerns the need to create an enabling 'space' for a 'softer' policing discourse within an overarching counter-terrorism context and to help communities appreciate PSNI efforts at preventing dissident Republican terrorist activity beyond the controlling and narrow parameters of terrorist legislation and policy – itself acting as an ever-expanding focus of, and referent for, distrust and dislocation between police organizations and the communities they are meant to serve (Hillyard, 2009).

Conclusion

In exploring the 'conundrum of the community' as part of that which may be conceived as 'softer' approaches to counter-terrorism policing in Northern Ireland, it is clear that the juxtaposition between the PSNI's community-oriented and counter-terrorism roles remains somewhat strained. Even a decade after the reforms under the ICP (1999), the evolving and transitional nature of the policing landscape in the country has restricted the extent to which policing can both break from its (counter-terrorism) past and move forward into (community policing for) the future.

A key contention of the chapter has been the *limited* extent to which the PSNI has been able to deliver upon the community policing foundations as a central focus of the ICP (1999). However, this must also be set against the *limiting* security context in which policing is delivered, restricting the delivery of 'normal', Peelian conceptions of a police service to all but a limited selection of communities in Northern Ireland. Thus, in taking a step back from the evidence, there is somewhat of a mixed narrative of 'success' pervading contemporary policing debates in the country. On the one hand, political and police rhetoric is dominated by contentions of peace, normality and the need for communities previously dissociated from the state and the police to move into a 'new' beginning for policing. Yet, on the other hand, it is precisely those communities – mainly urban, working-class Protestant and Catholic communities – that are absorbing the cost of such 'colourful' accounts of 'peace'. With a heavily militarized police presence still dominating the style of policing received at a local level, it is still an apt contention that:

> while the PSNI have been radically transformed in the post-Patten era, the change to policing on the ground has been largely unaffected, and in many areas ... policing largely mirrors the reactive style of policing characteristic of the Troubles, albeit in a relative peace-time context. (Topping, 2008a: 391)

Ultimately, there is little evidence to suggest that 'softer' styles of policing by the PSNI, in view of the current climate, would have any discernable effect upon the macro-level terrorist threat posed by dissident Republican factions at present. At a local level, examples of good practice – as with the 'G District' model noted above – are yielding benefits in terms of enabling PSNI officers to consider more fully the environment in which they deliver policing. However, this is but one localized solution within the complex, dynamic and deep-rooted 'Northern Ireland problem', which demands 'normal' policing yet the operationalization of which is tainted by the political legacy of counter-terrorism measures of the past. Thus, in terms of looking to the future and considering 'alterative' means of dealing with terrorism in the country, until the omnipresent 'abnormalities' associated with policing can be drawn out of the 'wound' of its transitional landscape, engaging communities on counter-terrorism issues will remain a conundrum beyond the tried-and-tested policing tactics which, the evidence suggests, have become so ingrained within the PSNI at a strategic and operational level – not least because that conundrum is itself a source of the continuing terrorist threat to the PSNI and communities alike.

Case study: the PSNI's G District Cultural Intelligence Model

The PSNI's 'G District' covers the north-west corner of Northern Ireland, encompassing the council areas of Strabane, Limavady, Foyle and Magherafelt. The District has a population of approximately 145,000, with almost 67 per cent defining themselves as Catholic, although this demographic balance is not spread evenly in geographical terms. The main focus of G District is the City of (London) Derry, the name of which provides the focus for social and political tension itself in regard to Catholic (Derry) or Protestant (Londonderry) identification and nomenclature. More recently, the City of Derry has been awarded the title of UK City of Culture for 2013, cementing the significant strides for the city as it has shifted out of conflict and into an era of relative peace.

However, below the surface, G District still suffers from a host of conflict-related issues which impact upon the delivery of 'normal' policing by the PSNI. With much of the area, and particularly the centre of Derry, still affected by the recent memory of the conflict (epitomized by 'Bloody Sunday'), riven by sectarian division, the continued presence of dissident republican paramilitaries and their archaic policing tactics, and a series of bomb attacks in the city, the task for the PSNI to deliver community policing in any form has been at best challenging. While local neighbourhood officers on the ground have been making progress in terms of interacting with Republican/Nationalist communities, the overarching 'severe' dissident Republican terrorist threat has entrenched the dominance of counter-terrorism over community policing approaches in much of the area. Indeed, beyond the operational conundrum of attempting 'normal' policing in the area, at a political level there is also pressure on the PSNI to depart from counter-insurgency policing that is reminiscent of the conflict.

A key issue for policing in the area, outside that of the locally based neighbourhood policing teams, has been the use of response officers in dealing with day-to-day policing issues. With response officers used to cover large geographical areas within G District, it is perceived that they lack key contextual and local knowledge of neighbourhood teams in the delivery of policing operations. In this regard, beyond the need to deliver merely 'satisfactory' policing in the area, at a social and political level the PSNI must also attempt to provide a service which can ameliorate the recent experiences of the local population in terms of previous experiences of policing in the locality, which was dominated by counter-insurgency tactics during the conflict. As a means of circumventing this gap between neighbourhood and response officers, G District implemented 'cultural intelligence' training in order to provide response officers with a broader contextual and historical knowledge of the area and its residents. Designed specifically to overcome the historical distance and distrust between Republican (and to a lesser extent Loyalist) communities and the police, the training was also about instilling within PSNI officers a greater sense of operational and political sensitivity to their policing delivery and specifically to help the Republican/Nationalist communities of Derry move beyond politically 'cognitive' to wholehearted community support for the PSNI.

In this respect, it was recognized that a significant, extra 'cultural value' could be attached to each and every 'contact' between the PSNI and the local community. Thus, at the heart of the scheme lay the importance of getting policing 'right' at the individual officer and organizational levels within the area.

References

Bayley, D.H. (2007) 'Police Reform on Your Doorstep: Northern Ireland and the World', seminar held at the Transitional Justice Institute, University of Ulster, Jordanstown, 19 February.

BBC News (2010a) 'Number of PSNI Officers Fell Too Quickly – Matt Baggott', 4 December, www.bbc.co.uk/news/uk-northern-ireland-11919158 (date accessed 16 December 2011).

——. (2010b) 'Police Random Stop-and-Search Powers Halted, 8 July, www.bbc.co.uk/news/10548112 (date accessed 16 December 2011).

——. (2011a) '50–50 Police Recruitment "Achieved a Lot" – Baggott', 18 April, www.bbc.co.uk/news/uk-northern-ireland-13112723 (date accessed 16 December 2011).

——. (2011b) 'Matt Baggott Welcomes Extra £245m for Police', 18 February, www.bbc.co.uk/news/uk-northern-ireland-12500020 (date accessed 16 December 2011).

Belfast Telegraph (2008a) 'Civilians Targeted by Dissident Republicans', www.belfasttelegraph.co.uk/news/local-national/civilians-targeted-by-dissident-republicans-14016763.html (date accessed 16 December 2011).

——. (2008b) 'Dissident Republicans Blamed for Gun Attack on Police', www.belfasttelegraph.co.uk/breaking-news/ireland/dissident-republicans-blamed-for-gun-attack-on-police-13954291.html (date accessed 16 December 2011).

——. (2008c) 'Dissidents Vowed to Kill Catholic Officer after McGuinness Visit', www.belfasttelegraph.co.uk/entertainment/film-tv/news/dissidents-vowed-to-kill-catholic-officer-after-mcguinness-visit-14079612.html (date accessed 16 December 2011).

——. (2009) 'Boy was "Shot to Curry Favour with Community"', 8 June, www.belfasttelegraph.co.uk/news/local-national/boy-was-lsquoshot-to-curry-favour-with-communityrsquo-14330308.html (date accessed 16 December 2011).

——. (2010a) 'Dissident Republican Threat Severe after MI5 Attack', 13 April, www.belfasttelegraph.co.uk/news/local-national/dissident/republican-threat-severe-after-mi5-attack-14764876.html (date accessed 16 December 2011).

——. (2010b) 'Editor's Viewpoint: Police in Battle to Regain Upper Hand', 30 April, www.belfasttelegraph.co.uk/opinion/viewpoint/editors-viewpoint-police-in-battle-to-regain-upper-hand-14787976.html (date accessed 16 December 2011).

——. (2010c) 'Increase in Stop and Search Use "Justified"', 17 December, www.belfasttelegraph.co.uk/news/local-national/northern-ireland/increase-in-stop-and-search-use-lsquojustifiedrsquo-15032472.html (date accessed 16 December 2011).

Brogden, M. (2005) '"Horses for Courses" and "Thin Blue Lines": Community Policing in Transitional Societies', *Police Quarterly* 8(1): 64–98.

Brogden, M. and Nijhar, P. (2005) *Community Policing: National and International Approaches*. Cullompton: Willan.

Buckland, P. (1979) *The Factory of Grievances*. Dublin: Gill & Macmillan.

Byrne, J. and Monaghan, L. (2008). *Policing Loyalist and Republican Communities*. Belfast: Institute for Conflict Research.

Campbell, C., Ni Aolain, F. and Harvey, C. (2003). 'The Frontiers of Legal Analysis: Reframing the Transition in Northern Ireland', *Modern Law Review* 66(3): 317–45.

Cox, M., Guelke, A. and Stephen, F. (2006). *A Farewell to Arms? Beyond the Good Friday Agreement*, 2nd edn. Manchester University Press.

Ellison, G. (2007). 'A Blueprint for Democratic Policing Anywhere in the World: Police Reform, Political Transition and Conflict Resolution in Northern Ireland', *Police Quarterly* 10(3): 243–69.

Ellison, G. and Mulcahy, A. (2001). 'Policing and Social conflict in Northern Ireland', *Policing and Society* 11: 243–58.

Ellison, G. and O'Reilly, C. (2008). 'From Empire to Iraq and the "War on Terror": The Transplantation and Commodification of the (Northern) Irish Policing Experience', *Police Quarterly* 11(4): 395–426.

Ellison, G. and Shirlow, P. (2008). 'Community Attitudes to Crime, Anti-social Behaviour and Policing in the Greater New Lodge', unpublished report.

Ellison, G. and Smyth, J. (2000). *The Crowned Hard: Policing Northern Ireland*. London: Pluto Press.

Emsley, C. (2009) *The Great British Bobby: A History of British Policing from the 18th Century to the Present*. London: Quercus.

Frampton, M. (2010) *The Return of the Militants: Violent Dissident Republicanism*. London: ICSR, www.icsr.info/publications/papers/1289498383ICSR_TheRet urnoftheMilitantsReport.pdf (date accessed 16 December 2011).

Hayes, B. and McAllister, I. (2005) 'Public Support for Political Violence and Paramilitarism in Northern Ireland and the Republic of Ireland', *Terrorism and Political Violence* 17: 599–617.

HM Government (2011) *CONTEST: The United Kingdom's Strategy for Countering Terrorism*. London: The Stationery Office.

HMIC (Her Majesty's Inspectorate of Constabulary) (2007) *Baseline Assessment Police Service of Northern Ireland*. London: HMIC.

——. (2011) *Police Service of Northern Ireland, Inspection Findings*. London: HMIC, www.hmic.gov.uk/SiteCollectionDocuments/Specialist/S13_20110221.pdf (date accessed 16 December 2011).

Hillyard, P. (1985). 'Popular Justice in Northern Ireland: Continuities and Change', *Research in Law, Deviance and Social Control* 7: 247–67.

——. (1988) 'Political and Social Dimensions of Emergency Law in Northern Ireland', in A. Jennings (ed.), *Justice under Fire: The Abuse of Civil Liberties in Northern Ireland*. London: Pluto Press, pp. 191–212.

——. (1994) 'Irish People and the British Justice System', *Journal of Law and Society* 21: 39–56.

——. (2009) 'The Exceptional State', in R. Coleman, J. Sim, S. Tombs and D. Whyte (eds), *State, Power, Crime*. London: Sage, pp. 129–44.

Holen, T. and Eide, E. (2000) *Peace Building and Police Reform*. London: Frank Cass.

IMC (Independent Monitoring Commission) (2010). *Twenty-third Report of the Independent Monitoring Commission*. London: The Stationery Office.

Independent Commission on Policing for Northern Ireland (ICP) (1999) *A New Beginning: Policing in Northern Ireland*. Belfast: HMSO (the Patten Report).

Innes, M. (2006) 'Policing Uncertainty: Countering Terror through Community Intelligence and Democratic Policing', *Annals of the American Academy of Political and Social Science* 605: 222–41.

Irish News (2008). 'Bombers Trying to Kill Officers: Detective', 11 September, p. 11.

——. (2009) 'Real IRA Determined to Murder PSNI Officers', 5 January, p. 8.

Jarman, N. (2002) *Managing Disorder: Responding to Interface Violence in North Belfast*. Belfast: Community Development Centre/Office of the First and Deputy First Minister.

Kearney, V. (2010) 'Dissident Threat Level Increases', http://news.bbc.co.uk/1/hi/northern_ireland/8638255.stm?ad=1 (date accessed 16 December 2011).

Kelling, G. (2005) 'Community Crime Reduction: Activating Formal and Informal Control', in N. Tilley (ed.), *Handbook of Crime Prevention and Community Safety*. Cullompton: Willan, pp. 107–42.

Kempa, M. and Shearing, C. (2005) 'Post-Patten Reflections on Patten', public lecture, 8 June, Queen's University of Belfast.

Lundy, P. (2011) 'Paradoxes and Challenges of Transitional Justice at the "Local" Level: Historical Enquiries in Northern Ireland', *Contemporary Social Science* 6(1): 89–106.

Marchant, C. (2007) 'Threat Level to Visible PSNI Officers is High, Says its Chief', *Police Review*, 22 June, p. 5.

Martin, G. (2006) *Understanding Terrorism: Challenges, Perspectives and Issues*, 2nd edn. London: Sage.

McDonald, H. (2008) 'MI5 Targets Dissidents as Irish Terrorist Threat Grows', *The Guardian*, 28 July, www.guardian.co.uk/uk/2008/jul/28/northern ireland.uksecurity (date accessed 16 December 2011).

——. (2010) 'One in Seven Northern Ireland Nationalists Sympathise with Dissident Terrorists', *The Guardian*, 6 October, www.guardian.co.uk/uk/2010/oct/06/one-in-seven-nationalists-support-terrorists (date accessed 16 December 2011).

——. (2011) 'The Truth about Belfast's Riots', *The Guardian*, 27 June, www.guardian.co.uk/politics/2011/jun/27/the-truth-about-belfasts-riots (date accessed 16 December 2011).

McDonald, H. and Townsend, M. (2011) 'For Ireland's Hardcore Dissidents "the Queen is a Legitimate Target"', *The Observer*, 24 April, www.guardian.co.uk/uk/2011/apr/23/ireland-dissidents-queen-legitimate-target (date accessed 16 December 2011).

McEldowney, J. and Gunter, W. (2003) *Human Rights in Transition*. Frankfurt: Peter Lang.

McVeigh, R. (1994) *It's Part of Life Here: The Security Forces and Harassment in Northern Ireland*. Belfast: Northern Ireland: Committee on the Administration of Justice.

Moran, J. (2008) *Policing the Peace in Northern Ireland: Politics, Crime and Security after the Belfast Agreement*. Manchester University Press.

——. (2010) 'Evaluating Special Branch and Informant Intelligence in Northern Ireland', *Intelligence and National Security* 25(1): 1–23.

Mulcahy, A. (1999) 'Visions of Normality: Peace and the Reconstruction of Policing in Northern Ireland', *Social and Legal Studies* 8(2): 277–95.

——. (2006) *Policing in Northern Ireland: Conflict, Legitimacy and Reform*. Cullompton: Willan.

Ni Aolain, F. (2000) *The Politics of Force: Conflict Management and State Violence in Northern Ireland*. Belfast: Blackstaff Press.

Northern Ireland Policing Board (2010) *Perceptions of the Police, The DPPs, and the Northern Ireland Policing Board*. Belfast: Northern Ireland Policing Board.

O'Rawe, M. (2003) 'Transitional Policing Arrangements in Northern Ireland: The Can't and Won't of Change Dialect', *Fordham International Law Journal* 22: 1015–73.

Owen, J. and Dutta, K. (2011) 'More People Go Armed as Ulster Dissident Threat Grows', *The Independent*, 5 June, www.independent.co.uk/news/uk/crime/more-people-go-armed-as-ulster-dissident-threat-grows-2293183.html (date accessed 16 December 2011).

Peters, B.G. (1999) *Institutional Theory: The New Institutionalism in Political Science*. London: Cassell.

Pickering, S., McCullough, J. and Wright-Neville, D. (2008) *Counter-Terrorism Policing: Community, Cohesion and Security*. New York: Springer.

PSNI (Police Service of Northern Ireland) (2011) 'Personal, Protective, Professional Policing – What Do You Want from Your Police Service?', www.psni.police.uk/psni_commitments_mailer.pdf (date accessed 16 December 2011).

Ryder, C. (1997) *The RUC 1922–1997: A Force under Fire*. London: Mandarin Paperbacks.

Scorer, C. and Hewitt, P. (1981) *The Prevention of Terrorism Act: The Case for Repeal*. London: National Council for Civil Liberties.

Shirlow, P. and Murtagh, B. (2006) *Belfast: Segregation, Violence and the City*. London: Pluto Press.

Skogan, W. (2006a) 'Asymmetry in the Impact of Encounters with Police', *Policing and Society* 16(2): 99–126.

Spalek, B. and Imtoual, A. (2007) '"Hard" Approaches to Community Engagement in the UK and Australia: Muslim Communities and Counter-Terror Responses', *Journal of Muslim Minority Affairs* 27(2): 185–202.

Sunshine, J. and Tyler, T. (2003) 'The Role of Procedural Justice and Legitimacy in Shaping Public Support for Policing', *Law and Society Review* 37(3): 513–48.

Topping, J.R. (2008a) 'Community Policing in Northern Ireland: A Resistance Narrative', *Policing and Society* 18(4): 377–98.

——. (2008b) 'Diversifying from Within: Community Policing and the Governance of Security in Northern Ireland', *British Journal of Criminology* 48(6): 778–97.

——. (2009) 'Beyond the Patten Report: The Governance of Security in Policing with the Community', doctoral thesis, University of Ulster, Northern Ireland.

Topping, J.R. and Byrne, J. (2012) 'Paramilitary Punishments in Belfast: Policing Beneath the Peace', *Behavioral Sciences of Terrorism and Political Aggression* 4(1): 41–59.

Weisburd, D., Feucht, T., Hakimi, I., Felson Mock, L. and Perry, S. (2009) *To Protect and Service: Policing in an Age of Terrorism*. New York: Springer.

Weitzer, R. (1999) 'Policing and Security', in P. Mitchell and R. Wilford (eds), *Politics in Northern Ireland*. Boulder, CO: Westview Press, pp. 170–94.

9

Communities and Counter-Terrorism: Some Final Reflections

Basia Spalek

Introduction

The notion that 'communities can defeat terrorism' has generated and continues to provoke much controversy and debate. The chapters in this book have illustrated that community as a notion is important to consider when examining terrorism and counter-terrorism, even though it raises many ethical, social, political and other questions. This chapter aims to reiterate some of the key themes that have emerged from the chapters in this book. In particular, 'top-down' and 'bottom-up' approaches to counter-terrorism are discussed in relation to community-focused and community-targeted perspectives. Questions of governance and citizenship are also discussed here. Community policing in relation to counter-terrorism is then discussed, as this is an emerging field of policy and practice. Mentoring in relation to counter-terrorism is also highlighted as this is another emerging area of policy and practice. Questions of gender, age and religion are then discussed in relation to the notion that 'communities can defeat terrorism'. Finally, community-based approaches to counter-terrorism are explored through the notion of transnationalism, for terrorism can be a transnational phenomenon and, as such, community-based approaches are likely to be influenced by transnational, as well as national and international, dynamics. This chapter highlights some key future questions that researchers might address.

'Top-down' approaches to counter-terrorism

Traditionally, counter-terrorism policy and practice has been very 'top-down', being driven by nation-state and geopolitical power plays, thereby marginalizing and even potentially stigmatizing communities. 'New terrorism' discourse illustrates this, for 'new terrorism' policies and practices have largely been driven by political, social and media elites targeting specifically Muslim communities (Pantazis and Pemberton, 2009, 2011). 'New terrorism' policies are likely to have eroded trust between the police and Muslim communities, as the broader research literature suggests that trust in the police can be seriously undermined in situations where communities feel that they are being over-policed (Hall *et al.*, 1978; Sivanandan, 1981; Bridges and Gilroy, 1982; Smith and Gray, 1985; Jefferson *et al.*, 1992; Macpherson Inquiry, 1999; Jones and Newburn, 2001; Waddington *et al.*, 2004; Thacher, 2005; Sharp and Atherton, 2007; and Bowling and Phillips, 2007). Moreover, the use of police undercover work to gather human intelligence, officially sanctioned state deception can further erode trust between communities and the police. The erosion of trust is particularly significant given that a number of research studies highlight the importance of trust in obtaining community intelligence. The erosion of trust is a significant issue because, according to Loader (2006), security is not only about the levels of material threat that individuals face but also about the degree of trust that individuals have in institutional arrangements, and so where hard and covert policing strategies decrease individuals' trust, this also impacts more broadly upon individuals' perceptions and feelings of security and therefore their sense of belongingness. According to Thacher (2005), who draws upon a case study of the US city of Dearborn, surveillance and information gathering can detrimentally affect a city's social life by undermining trust and cooperation with police. At the same time, through targeting a particular social group for intrusive policing rather than targeting a general and abstract class of suspected criminals, police officers can stigmatize an entire social grouping, thereby potentially damaging the honour of individuals (Thacher, 2005). Traditionally, 'hard' policing tactics have been used for intelligence gathering, investigations and arrests consisting of the use of informants, surveillance and the utilization of police powers like stop and search (Hewitt, 2010). At the same time, 'hard' policing strategies in relation to countering terrorism also feature 'counter-subversion' strategies which aim to target and stigmatize those groupings deemed subversive in the same way that terrorists would be targeted. Counter-terrorism policing has therefore traditionally been top-down, prioritizing nation-state security over the security of individuals and communities.

It is important to highlight that counter-terrorism is a highly politicized arena in which debates around broader, normative issues in relation to questions of citizenship, multiculturalism and integration seem to impact significantly on counter-terrorism policies and practices, making the work of practitioners and community members particularly challenging. Wider questions about community and social cohesion and integration, alongside discussions about Britishness, profoundly influence counter-terrorism arenas. This means that rather than making a rational assessment according to which community groups can help best combat terrorism, policy makers instead allow themselves to be influenced by these wider questions of community and social cohesion and integration. For example, in relation to 'new terrorism' post-9/11, it appears that government projects in the UK aimed at fostering dialogue and community participation tend to be underpinned by broader questions and debates around what sorts of Muslim identities should be encouraged in the UK and what kinds of Muslim identities should be actively discouraged and/or suppressed. This can serve to detract from putting together the most effective strategies to counter terrorism. According to Modood (2007: 23), 'the upheavals and wars that characterise the Reformation are present in the Muslim world today but non-Muslim powers, especially the US, are major players'. It appears that UK government policy regarding the involvement of Muslim communities in helping to combat extremism is being influenced by international geopolitical power plays, so that within government rhetoric, those Muslims and community organizations that are viewed as being 'moderate' are seen to be allies in the prevention of terrorism (Spalek and Imtoual, 2007). Muslim identities that appear to value the Ummah[1] over feelings of Britishness or that appear to isolate themselves from wider society are negatively judged and seen as a threat to social cohesion. Engagement in this context is often led by the imperatives of the government, with only certain sections of Muslim communities being included. This can create an untenable situation for many Muslims (see Spalek and Imtoual, 2007).

Because counter-terrorism policing has been dominated by top-down 'hard' global and national policing strategies, as discussed above, the emergence of community policing models aimed at fostering dialogue, engagement and partnerships between police and communities is particularly interesting. Might these community policing-based models of counter-terrorism challenge and indeed subvert the dominance of top-down 'new terrorism' governmentality? Many questions are raised. If we draw upon Virta's (2008) conceptualization of community policing as promoting community-based problem-solving strategies to address the underlying causes of crime and building police legitimacy, then within a counter-terrorism context, the question of what this means needs to be raised. For instance, within a counter-terrorism context, the promotion of community-based strategies to address the underlying causes of terrorism raises the question of which communities and which community groups are best placed to work with police. Moreover, if those groups best placed to counter terrorism are deemed 'suspect' by policy makers and influential commentators (top-down global and nation-state approaches), then how does this impact upon any attempts at engagement and partnership made by police officers? What does building police legitimacy look like within local spaces within a counter-terrorism context? If community empowerment is an important aspect to building police legitimacy, then what does empowerment mean within a counter-terrorism context and can this challenge top-down approaches? Partnership means equality and transparency, but within a counter-terrorism context what are the challenges here? It may be, for example, that communities want to hold on to information, they may want to govern crime themselves, whereas the police may want control over information and over crime control. As illustrated in Chapter 3, since 9/11 in some local contexts around the world, community policing models have been drawn on and utilized for the purposes of tackling 'new terrorism'. In the USA, whereas counter-terrorism has traditionally relied on the analysis of domestic and friendly foreign government intelligence information rather than the engagement of communities and the development of partnerships between communities and local law enforcement agencies, more recently there has been a movement towards the utilization of community policing within a counter-terrorism context, with partnerships being developed between Muslim, Arab, Sikh and South Asian American communities and the police (Ramirez, 2008).

Similarly, in Canada, the Royal Canadian Mountain Police (RCMP) has established a National Security Community Outreach Program (NSCOP). This has adopted community-based policing within its remit of national security policing (Hanniman, 2008). Community policing within counter-terrorism has a number of important strands. For example, community policing enables trust to be built between the police and communities, particularly those minority communities that are most affected by national security measures (see Hanniman, 2008; Spalek, 2010). Partnerships between police and communities are also said to provide the police with important cultural and linguistic insights, vital information and cooperation, and informed observations that can become part of a productive strategy for terror crime prevention. At the same time, these partnerships are said to help to ensure the mitigation of damage to communities that results from 'hard' policing strategies, and they also purportedly make it possible for hate crimes to be effectively investigated and prosecuted (Ramirez, 2008).

'Bottom-up' approaches to counter-terrorism

'New terrorism' has generated substantial critique amongst critical scholars keen to make visible and explore the ways that 'new terrorism' has influenced the ways in which we govern and are governed, in particular the impact of 'new terrorism' upon the erosion of civil liberties within liberal democracies and the impacts upon those communities deemed 'suspect' (Mythen and Walklate, 2006; Kundnani, 2009; Pantazis and Pemberton, 2009). Nonetheless, what is missing from the vast majority of accounts of 'new terrorism' in particular, but in accounts of terrorism regarding communities generally, is the importance of bottom-up approaches that may arise. Therefore, despite the abuse of human rights by traditional, 'top-down' approaches and the corrosive impact of counter-terrorism legislation and practices upon liberal democratic freedoms, locally driven, 'bottom-up' initiatives may comprise sites at which dominant policies and practices associated with 'top-down' governance may be challenged and subverted. Bottom-up approaches also mean the increasing involvement of civil society in government in terms of playing a role in decision-making processes and holding decision makers to account (Brennan *et al.*, 2007).

This shift from government to governance is perhaps indicative of broader socio-politico-cultural changes within liberal democratic societies, which many commentators have argued are reflexive societies. When conceptualizing the notion of reflexivity, Lash (1994: 200) draws upon the work of Beck (1992) to suggest that this might be viewed as consisting of the ways in which the side-effects, dangers or 'bads' arising out of modernity's production of goods are dealt with in order to minimize insecurities associated with the social changes here. Importantly, reflexivity can include reflection, where reflection might be thought of in terms of individuals, collective groups and/or institutions intentionally and rationally reflecting upon the part that they play in the perpetuation of identified social problems as well as reflecting upon ways in which they can intervene and act so as to minimize harms (Lash, 1994; McGhee, 2005). Reflection might also be thought of as comprising a participative democracy, whereby state institutions open themselves up to the communities that they serve, with the lay public engaging with, as well as critiquing, rival forms of expertise (Spalek and Lambert, 2008).

Bottom-up approaches are those that stress community involvement, whereby any partnerships and engagement that take place between communities and state agencies are influenced by communities' concerns and experiences. The involvement of communities in relation to countering threats from 'new terrorism' reflects the involvement of communities in tackling other social problems such as anti-social behaviour, unemployment, etc. Similar to traditional forms of crime, the governance of 'new terrorism' reflects broader developments in governance, whereby responsibility and accountability for preventing terror crime is increasingly focused towards local levels, whilst at the same time centralized control in terms of resources and target setting is maintained. In addition, formal responsibilities for policy implementation and service delivery are progressively being shared across statutory, voluntary agencies and community groups in the form of partnership work. A further aspect to the governance of 'new terrorism' which might be linked to bottom-up approaches is reflectivity. Here, the greater visibility of security intelligence in the public domain has led to an increased awareness, scrutiny and critique by politicians, media commentators, non-governmental organizations (NGOs), communities and the general public.

The post-9/11 period has seen annual growth in the funding of security intelligence. This has facilitated a more extensive nation-wide security intelligence presence via regionalization, increased surveillance of targets (both by depth and range) and improved liaison between security intelligence and police agencies. This changed security situation has afforded security intelligence a greater visibility and has brought intelligence strategies into the public domain in ways that have increased awareness, scrutiny and critique by politicians, media commentators, NGOs and the general public. Criticism of 'new terrorism' governmentality has come from a variety of different Muslim groupings. In relation to criticisms coming from Muslim communities, police stop and search statistics under counter-terrorism legislation have generated concern. For example, according to the Muslim Council of Britain (MCB):

> The police are misusing their new powers ... We think that the institutional racism highlighted by the Macpherson Report is morphing into institutional prejudice against Muslims. We are worried a generation of young Muslim men is being criminalised. (Cowan, 2004: 8, in Garland et al., 2006)

More recently, the Prevent strand within CONTEST and CONTEST 2 has been criticized, with the following being a quotation taken from a Muslim activist, as presented in the report by Kudnani (2009: 27), *Spooked!*:

> The main impact of Prevent work locally has been greater mistrust of the police. It's impacted all the wrong way. And there is more reluctance on the part of the Muslim community to engage at all.

Therefore, a key aspect of bottom-up approaches to 'new terrorism' has been a scrutiny of counter-terrorism policies and practices by wide-ranging non-state actors. The involvement of communities in counter-terrorism can therefore lead to a greater scrutiny of policies and practices and a greater openness by statutory agencies in relation to the information they hold and the basis of the kinds of work that they carry out. However, this is not necessarily always the case, depending upon how strong a network of organizations and community groups a society has. Within many societies, activists, members of civil liberties organizations and others are regularly arrested, detained in prison and deemed 'suspect', and so it is only perhaps in liberal democratic states that enough freedoms are afforded in order for community groups and others to question and challenge counter-terrorism legislation, policies and practices. The question that arises here is whether local contexts, involving 'bottom-up' approaches to counter-terrorism, can sufficiently challenge and even transform 'top-down' approaches to counter-terrorism. For instance, the top-down, nation-state perspective may be that all Salafi and Islamist groups, and indeed all 'extreme' groups, are dangerous and should be the target of counter-terrorism rather than the solution. Nonetheless, in some local contexts it may be that counter-terrorism practices involve partnering and/or engaging with Salafi and other groups, thereby directly challenging national, state-led perspectives. It may be that in creating partnerships between community members and state actors like the police, there is less reliance upon the use of informants, an issue that generates much suspicion and concern within communities. It may also be that community policing models potentially offer accountability, openness and community involvement in decision making regarding counter-terrorism, a process of political communication in which both governors and governed can negotiate a way forward. Again, there may be possibilities and opportunities here to challenge 'top-down' approaches. Furthermore, it may be the case that some local contexts are impenetrable to state authorities and so can only be governed through community members. Within these contexts it may be that 'top-down' approaches are transformed into 'bottom-up', community-led approaches due to the reliance upon credible community members in any initiatives that are undertaken. Police engaging with and partnering minority communities and groups may be viewed as being part of a broader multicultural dynamic, for in the process of engagement work, both state institutions and communities are involved in mutual interaction and dialogue, with there of course being points of contestation. Ongoing engagement work can be seen as constituting part of a pluralistic process whereby community groups can help shape government policies and the practices of state agencies, as well as being shaped by these themselves (see Modood, 2007). Ongoing engagement work can be viewed as influencing the very cultures of those groups involved in partnership. Therefore, an aspect of partnership work is that those groups involved in engagement are mutually influencing each other's cultures, where cultures are seen as constructed by 'crossover, by hybridization and by innovation' (Young, 1999: 89). Drawing upon the work of Castells (2004), engagement work constitutes a process through which resistance identities (viewed as generated by those individuals who occupy devalued or stigmatized positions within society, who build trenches of resistance and survival on the basis of principles different from, or opposed to, those permeating the institutions of society) become project identities, seeking to transform society (as can be seen in what have been called 'new social movements' based on, for example, 'race', gender or sexual orientation), perhaps even eventually becoming dominant in the institutions of society, thus becoming legitimizing identities. Similarly, the identities of those professionals involved in engagement work may be influenced by partnership work, this being an under-researched area.

Community-focused and community-targeted counter-terrorism

Whilst Lowndes and Thorp (2010: 123–4) stress that 'tensions between a locally driven, community-focused approach and a nationally led, security-oriented agenda have been ongoing', it is important to make a distinction between community-focused and community-targeted approaches, as there appears to be an assumption that all bottom-up approaches are necessarily community-focused, when in fact they may not necessarily be so. At the same time, both top-down and bottom-up approaches to countering terrorism may involve both state and non-state actors and organizations, and so the often-used distinction between top-down and bottom-up approaches perhaps over-generalizes through assuming that bottom-up involves communities when both approaches can involve communities. Indeed, the idea that communities can defeat terrorism features in both top-down and bottom-up approaches, with the notion of 'community' predominantly viewed through the lens of 'problem' within top-down approaches, whilst in bottom-up approaches 'community' is viewed largely as 'solution'. Where 'community' is viewed as 'problem', counter-terrorism strategies can be used which target those communities deemed to be problematic. Where 'community' is viewed as 'solution', counter-terrorism strategies can be used that involve community members and may also involve partnerships between communities and statutory agencies. It is likely that within the notion that 'communities can defeat terrorism', 'community' is viewed as both 'problem' and 'solution'. Interestingly, different state and other agencies and groupings may view community organizations differentially, and so whilst one state agency or individual working within the agency or one governmental body may view a particular community group as 'problem', other agencies and individuals may view the same group through the lens of 'solution'. Tensions are therefore perhaps inevitable. Moreover, wider public opinion may also view particular community groups through the lens of 'problem', perhaps for being religious fundamentalists, for example, and so state actors involved in engaging and developing long-term partnerships with members of 'problem' communities are likely to attract criticism.

As highlighted in Chapter 2, a community-targeted approach might be characterized as one that ignores the issue of gaining the consent of those communities that are being targeted, with the well-being of targeted communities often being compromised through striving to achieve the broader goal of maintaining nation-state security. At the same time, a community-targeted approach is characterized by distrust between communities and security officials and practitioners. Community-focused approaches, on the other hand, can perhaps be characterized by partnership between communities and state officials, by community consent and participation in the actual governance of the various strategies and approaches that are applied, and by trust existing between state officials and security practitioners and community members (Spalek *et al.*, 2009). At the same time, a community-focused approach embraces communities for their complexities in relation to ethnicity, religion, politics, emotions, grievances, locales, histories, etc. This approach seeks to work with rather than to manipulate communities. Future research might therefore look into examining a range of initiatives taking place within a particular local context in order to try and ascertain to what extent these initiatives by themselves and collectively comprise community-focused or community-targeted approaches and the implications of these. This links to broader issues of governance. According to Brennan *et al.* (2007: 13), 'the world of governing has seen a revolution expressed in a shift from government to governance'. For them, the notion of governance is to be understood as that which includes both government and civil society, with the state and the civic engaging in decision making and other processes, through the interaction of top-down, state-led imperatives and bottom-up approaches which include networks, groups, communities and others that are part of what might be deemed civil society. It would appear that the notion of governance is key in relation to exploring and understanding community-based approaches to counter-terrorism. Future research might address the following key questions:

• How might governance be understood in relation to counter-terrorism?
• What tensions are there between 'top-down' and 'bottom-up' approaches?
• How might state and non-state actors influence each other's cultures in the process of counter-terrorism work?
• To what extent is self-governance a key notion in counter-terrorism? To what extent are state imperatives such as security bound to the management of the self? To what extent are governmental modes in everyday life individualized in relation to counter-terrorism?
• What are the intersections between government–self relations and self–community relations?

As demonstrated in Chapter 3, community policing in relation to counter-terrorism is another, related future research area, as will now be discussed below.

Counter-terrorism policing and communities

One area that is likely to generate growing research and policy focus is that of counter-terrorism policing vis-à-vis communities. Policing has been undergoing a significant learning curve due to the intro-duction of community policing models within the counter-terrorism arena. In the UK, since the introduction of the Prevent strategy, counter-terrorism policing has increasingly drawn upon overt models of engagement with communities and it is important to highlight that there are different models of overt engagement that the police utilize. In the Northern Ireland context too, following on from the Independent Commission on Policing (ICP) report (1999) and the subsequent major police reform process undertaken, communities are, in theory at least, increasingly being seen as key partners in building broad-based security. Thus, the steep learning curve experienced by communities and police and other practitioners in relation to community-based efforts to counter Al-Qaeda-linked or influenced terrorism is increasingly of interest to communities and practitioners in Northern Ireland in relation to 'domestic terrorism' and vice versa.

It is probably fair to say that the most widespread model of overt counter-terrorism policing in the UK is one linked to the neighbourhood policing model. Under this model, police officers include within their remit a focus upon preventing violent extremism, and so alongside their everyday work in relation to preventing ordinary crime there is also a focus upon countering terrorism. The foundational basis of this model has been the work of Professor Innes, who has argued that in responding to individuals' routine security concerns around issues such as anti-social behaviour or crime, police officers will be more likely to persuade community members of the benefits of assisting them in relation to counter-terrorism (Innes, 2006). A slight variation on this model is that of overt counter-terrorism officers who largely operate in uniform, who are based in neighbourhood police stations and who are called Security and Partnership Officers. Nonetheless, when it is deemed inappropriate to wear uniform (for example, when community members may tell these police officers that their presence in uniform is not welcome), these police officers will wear civilian clothes (see the report by Silk, 2009). Within this model, police officers tell community members that they are counter-terrorism police officers. The Muslim Contact Unit (MCU) is another model of overt counter-terrorism policing. The MCU has developed perhaps a unique model of partnership of engagement with key members of those communities that are encountering issues with violent extremism. It differs from the more generic neighbourhood policing model in that partnership with communities is actively pursued, where 'partnership' might be defined as involving equality, transparency and legitimate cooperation between partners, which may involve participants with different interests forming a partnership to carry out work that they collectively decide to do (Spalek *et al.*, 2009).

Overt counter-terrorism policing raises many questions for future research to explore. Police accountability towards communities is increasingly a feature or indeed a problematic of initiatives, for if community policing is to involve problem-oriented policing that requires police to be responsive to citizens' demands, then if police officers are working within areas that are deemed to be vulnerable to terrorism, they will need to be accountable to the communities that reside in those areas. Future research will need to examine what comprises accountability and how police officers working in relation to counter-terrorism can be accountable to communities, particularly when a lot of intelligence is likely to be sensitive so that not all of it can be shared with communities. Police officers are grappling with what information to release to communities regarding terrorism and counter-terrorism-related issues, how to go about sharing this and to whom this should be made available. The extent to which overt counter-terrorism police officers attempt to change the traditionally secretive culture of counter-terrorism policing is an interesting area to explore further. Overt counter-terrorism policing models can be used to gain information from communities that may have traditionally been obtained through covert policing strategies. Future research will need to examine the value of an open approach by the police, the extent to which information has been obtained through overt rather than covert approaches and where the balance between overt and covert approaches should lie. There also needs to be further discussion and analysis of the links between overt and covert approaches, and the information that is shared between them. Moreover, in those geographical areas deemed to be vulnerable to violent extremism, it is likely that both overt and covert policing is taking place and so further research needs to explore the links between the two and the impacts of these upon communities. Future research also needs to explore what role (if any) community members can play in helping to risk assess those individuals who have come to the attention of the police or other agencies for a perceived vulnerability to violent extremism, for there may be aspects to individuals' lives that only community members can witness and understand. Future research also needs to address the notion of risk, for there may be a danger that statutory agencies enter into relationships and agreements with community members that may prioritize the risk and other needs of those agencies rather than the risks and the needs of community members themselves. Moreover, who should identify risk, how is this to be managed and ultimately who decides whether a set of vulnerabilities constitutes risk of violent extremism are questions that research needs to increasingly address in the future. Furthermore, in a situation where risk is being assessed by different agencies, whose voice carries most weight and is there a potential that the voices of communities in particular are marginalized? In relation to the notion of partnership, is there equality, transparency and legitimate cooperation between partners when cases that fall between prevent and pursue are apparent? The notion of trust also requires further consideration. Thus, it may be the case that distrust is a good thing, for communities' distrust of police officers is not necessarily something negative, as this may prevent the penetration of civilians to be used as spying networks. A more realistic position, therefore, may be that there needs to be sufficient trust in order for engagement and partnership work to take place between community members and police officers, but for there also to be an element of ongoing scrutiny. What such scrutiny comprises requires further research. Future research should also consider the extent to which any sensitivities in relation to police–community engagement and counter-terrorism are the result of community and socio-cultural dynamics or whether these sensitivities are inherent to the counter-terrorism arena. Also, to what extent is counter-terrorism policing similar to policing crimes like gang violence and organized crime, and to what extent does it differ from this? There also needs to be some focus upon the notion of partnership. Partnership models that exploit trust for intelligence are intelligence-gathering mechanisms rather than true partnerships. It would appear that building implicit trust between police officers and key members of communities who can help prevent terrorism is key to establishing long-term partnerships. Implicit trust might be considered to be found in committed, stable relationships and is less focused upon short-term outcomes (Spalek, 2010). Trust is an issue that requires future exploration.

Future research might also address the following set of questions:

- To what extent can community policing models, based on the principle that the police at all times should maintain a relationship with the public that gives reality to the historic tradition that the police are the public and the public are the police, be utilized in efforts to counter terrorism?

- What is effective overt community-based counter-terrorism policing? Can police and community perspectives differ as to what comprises effectiveness and, if so, is it possible to bridge gaps between perceptions?
- What is effective covert counter-terrorism policing? Can police and community perspectives differ as to what comprises effectiveness and, if so, is it possible to bridge gaps between perceptions?
- What is an effective balance between covert and overt counter-terrorism policing? What might the impact of the split between overt and covert counter-terrorism policing be for intra- and inter-community tensions and social cohesion?
- Is the reliance on covert counter-terrorism policing an operational necessity or an embedded set of cultural practices which are no longer an appropriate response to the modern terrorist threat?
- Do the benefits of covert and overt approaches differ depending on the nature of the violent political ideology being tackled, i.e. Irish-related, Al-Qaeda-influenced, animal rights-related, etc?

Communities and counter-terrorism

As demonstrated in all the chapters in this book, community in relation to counter-terrorism raises many questions that future research will need to explore. Within security policies and strategies tackling terrorism, there are likely to be significant tensions between approaches that emphasize community cohesion and those that emphasize liberal freedoms associated with liberal democracy. The former problematize particular sets of identities for their perceived lack of integration into mainstream society. For example, in relation to Al-Qaeda-linked terrorism, Muslim identities have been problematized, for Islamic ideology here is portrayed as dangerous and in conflict with 'Western values', and so Muslims are viewed as not integrating with wider British society. At the same time, particular political, religious and ethnic identities associated with being a Muslim and with a perceived propensity/risk to commit acts of violence are securitized, and so are responded to by the state above and beyond established rules and frameworks that exist within what might be termed 'normal politics', that might be viewed as comprising counter-subversion. Approaches that emphasize liberal freedoms, on the other hand, seek not to problematize or securitize particular identities, but rather seek to enable individuals to draw upon the liberal freedoms associated with liberal democracy in order for a wider range of actions to be considered legitimate, so that individuals no longer see violence as a means to pursue their aims. This work includes wide-ranging activities like encouraging political participation from within communities, enhancing education and supporting social and political activism. This work also seeks to draw upon individuals formerly and/or currently practising 'securitized identities' as mentors in order to attempt to rehabilitate those deemed at risk of committing acts of violence so that they are no longer at risk of pursuing violent action. The following list consists of a set of questions that should help generate future research:

- How and in what ways is the notion of 'community' to be understood in relation to counter-terrorism? How has the notion of 'community' in relation to counter-terrorism changed according to different historical, social, political and other contexts?
- What are the cultural, political, social and other factors that may help assist terrorist activities in local areas, how may these be linked nationally and internationally, and what can the police, other statutory agencies and communities do to address these?
- To what extent are communities with broad support for particular political and/or religious ideologies exploited by terrorists as a recruiting ground or as safe havens and how can the police work with these communities without stigmatizing them or without creating inter- and/or intra-community tensions?
- How can counter-terrorism policing manage the challenges related to protecting the broader population from a terrorist threat posed by specific minority elements of particular communities and still maintain the trust of both?
- How might community-based interventions in relation to counter-terrorism be made more effective?
- What are the tensions and potential overlaps between security approaches that emphasize community cohesion and those that emphasize liberal freedoms?
- To what extent have all Muslim identities been problematized as a result of the demise of multiculturalism as a model and the

increased focus on integration? To what extent have particular Muslim identities been securitized and what are the implications of securitization upon those carrying and practising these identities?

- What state and non-state actors are involved in community cohesion strategies that are linked to security policy? How are these strategies experienced and are there forms of resistance? How are community cohesion policies influencing the relationship between police officers and local communities, and what does this mean for police accountability?
- What state and non-state actors are involved in security strategies that place considerable value upon liberal freedoms? How are these experienced and what is the relationship of these to those strategies that emphasize community cohesion? What is the role of the police and security services?
- To what extent do security strategies that place value on liberal freedoms pursue disengagement from terrorism rather than deradicalization? Disengagement means desisting from violence but that an individual may continue to engage with broader terrorist and other movements, and may be committed to subversion.

Mentoring in relation to preventing terrorism

Mentoring might be viewed as a community-focused approach to counter-terrorism because it can involve drawing upon the skills of community members in order to help try and dissuade individuals from committing acts of terrorism. Mentoring in relation to counter-terrorism is an under-researched and under-explored area. Whilst there is considerable, and growing, research examining various programmes and initiatives aimed at the deradicalization and rehabilitation of terrorist and other extremist offenders in the EU, North America and the Middle East, the vast majority of this research does not give much attention to the notion of mentoring. Research examining why terrorists walk away from terrorism does not sufficiently examine the mentoring process itself and its significance for questions regarding the rehabilitation of terrorist and other extremist offenders, and the prevention of violence within vulnerable individuals, even though it would appear that mentoring is a central aspect to the process of rehabilitation (Garfinkel, 2007; Horgan, 2009). Systematic research on mentoring effects generally is seen as thin (Dubois *et al.*, 2006). A study by Spalek, Davies and McDonald (2010) found that mentors use both a befriending and an interventionist approach, that mentoring should represent a safe space to discuss issues which includes a consideration of ethics, empathy and trust between mentor and client, and that it is important for there to be a diverse range of mentors so as to match wide-ranging clients with appropriate mentors. However, the study also highlights a number of possible challenges to the mentoring process. For example, there are a wide range of views on how success might be measured and conceptualized; on whether mentoring styles should be hard and confrontational or soft and empathetic, and when which is appropriate and for whom; whether with Al-Qaeda extremists this is a purely theological concern which can be solved with theological arguments; and the extent of supervision and support of mentors. At the same time, because mentoring is something that in the UK has traditionally taken place informally on an ad hoc basis, often involving community members responding to the needs of individuals they encounter in their daily lives, the current policy movement towards the expansion and professionalization of mentoring in relation to violent extremism presents a number of key challenges. For example, there is the potential for mentoring schemes to become part of broader net-widening law enforcement strategies which comprise the over-zealous and ill-informed flagging of individuals for 'vulnerability', ensuring the unnecessary collection of personal data. Future research will need to examine these and other questions.

A related issue here concerns prisoners who have been convicted of terrorism-related offences. This is a growing issue due to increasing numbers of individuals being imprisoned for terrorism-related offences who are increasingly likely to be released from prison back into communities. Thus, since 2000 in the UK, there have been 20 significant jihadist terror plots, resulting in the imprisonment of 235 people, with more awaiting trial (Clarke and Soria, 2010: 24). The transition from the prison to the community is notoriously fraught with challenges, but also presents an opportunity for crime prevention. Research on how individuals 'desist from crime' has been influential in the development of interventions for ex-prisoner reintegration. However, the reintegration of individuals convicted under terrorism legislation such as the Terrorism Act 2006 in the UK may present unique challenges in this regard as traditional risk-assessment and risk-management strategies may not be appropriate. Ex-prisoners being released are opening a potential new 'frontline' in counter-terrorism work involving offender managers. If done wrongly, offender manager strategies in prison and in the community might increase the radicalization of vulnerable individuals and their communities by breeding grievances, triggering processes of social exclusion, labelling or defiance. Done correctly, the offender management process provides an ideal opportunity for reintegration and deradicalization for vulnerable individuals and their communities. Future research therefore needs to address the following questions:

- What factors contribute to successful disengagement versus alienation and defiance?
- What role might imprisonment experiences play in radicalizing (or deradicalizing) individuals and their communities?
- What role can risk-assessment and risk-management strategies utilized in the community play?

Gender and counter-terrorism

As illustrated in Chapter 5, while gender and security has become an area of increasing academic interest, the normative position has been one of disinterest. More specifically, the male-dominated arenas of terrorism and counter-terrorism may be viewed as having an embedded and invisible assumption that security is the business of men: where women are included in discourse or practice, it is usually as an interesting aside or an aberration to the security context. According to McDonald in Chapter 5, for a group so problematized within British society, inclusion and recognition in the state's security programme presents a great potential for Muslim women to participate, contribute to and even shape the ways in which acts of terror crime are prevented. Thus, the Prevent strand between 2005 and 2010 included a very broad understanding of 'preventative work', from hard-ended interventions with individuals considered vulnerable to violent extremism to cohesion-related community projects, including the funding of Muslim women's groups and networks. This blurring of state security with community development thus opened up a space for individuals and groups willing to be categorized under their gender and religious identities as 'Muslim women' to raise issues and lead community projects within the security framework. Future research can further explore the role of women in relation to community and nation-state security and the links between the two.

Young people and counter-terrorism strategies

As highlighted in Chapter 6, young people have been identified as an 'at risk' group in relation to issues of violent extremism. Potential sites of radicalization include universities, cafes, youth centres and other places frequented by young people. Youth work has increasingly been alerted to the risks that young people are potentially faced with in terms of radicalization. Turning more specifically to the issue of Muslim youth work, this is a growing area in the UK, whether formalized into local Youth Inclusion Projects or carried out within third sector and informal voluntary groups, and this work relies on an inherent understanding of young people's perspectives and their multiple identities and experiences, including elements of faith. For Muslim youth work, not only is faith – in the broadest sense – acknowledged, but it is viewed as being central as each young person declares it to be, from active interest in theological issues to identity-led expressions of Islam, in which religious practice plays little part but identification as Muslims and with Muslims is paramount. Young people are not viewed as homogeneous and religion is not 'preached' – the case of each young person is approached individually. Innovative and religiously or culturally appropriate projects are developed, according to the needs of young clients, for example, forms of conflict resolution to tackle gang tensions in Birmingham, where loyalty and identities are sometimes expressed through affiliations to tiny localities – a few streets in a neighbourhood between Muslim youth from different ethnic or even intra-ethnic groupings – such as the use of Punjabi *Panchayat*-style mediation.

The trust and ability to communicate at a street level is also fundamental, involving an inclusive approach that seeks to work with young people in their own spaces and environments. As highlighted in Chapter 6, successful youth work as defined by youth workers highlights the importance of communicating with young people on their own terms and allowing individuals to express their views, discuss their problems and work towards solutions in a safe space. In a context where other spaces – community and state – may be deemed hostile or judgemental, Muslim youth work provides opportunities to discuss, debate and challenge. This is the point at which one may locate the first tension: for those youth workers involved with young people at the very margins of our communities, the most pertinent issues are often those most problematic in relation to the state and the law. Where young people are involved in forms of criminality, such as drug dealing or gang activity, youth workers rely on their professional judgement to help their clients, allowing them space to discuss and deal with problems while conforming to legal requirements. However, this challenge has become more difficult in the context of security and the catch-all character of current British counter-terrorism laws. For those youth workers equipped to deal with issues of violent extremism, allowing young people space to discuss their views or, in some cases, to raise concerns about the behaviour of their peers becomes a potentially dangerous activity in which knowledge of potential – and ill-defined – radicalization may be deemed of state interest, yet is necessary in order to work through issues with individuals, maintain trust and challenge views to avoid an escalation of a situation and the involvement of the authorities. This is an area of risk taking and managing that may not only mean the difference between failure and success regarding interventions, but may also have a direct impact on the safety of youth workers in relation to the law and state perceptions of their work.

In particular, future research needs to include the voices and perspectives of young people themselves, for they may be the subjects of counter-terrorism initiatives and yet their experiences are often overlooked in research and policy literature. Future research needs to address the following key questions:

- To what extent is there a relationship between the occurrence of violence in young people's lives and factors that place young people at high risk of violent extremism?
- What kinds of relationships do young people have with police officers and what are the potential impacts of these relationships for counter-terrorism?
- To what extent do young people feel that they are targeted by policing strategies and how does this impact on community-focused efforts to counter-terrorism?

- To what extent do young people feel that they are targeted by police as a result of particular identities that they may hold?
- How do young people connect with their peers, their communities and wider society, and what are the implications of this for counter-terrorism? For example, the use of technology like mobile phones, Facebook and YouTube has significantly influenced young people's connectivity and so what challenges does this pose for counter-terrorism?

Religion and counter-terrorism

As highlighted in Chapter 7, the events of 9/11 and 7/7 brought religion, and Islam in particular, abruptly and forcefully to the forefront of security and policing issues. This chapter further reveals that, contrary to the common assumption that commitment to Islamic values and religious doctrines is a root cause of terrorism, religion can provide a stronger commitment and a feeling of moral responsibility – a duty or a religious obligation – to help solve the problem of violence committed in the name of Islam, build bridges and form positive relations with other UK communities. Thus, religious convictions can provide strong motivations amongst community members to cooperate with the efforts of the police to fight religious violence. A commitment to Islam can provide a feeling of moral responsibility or a duty to help the authorities in counter-terrorism work, to form good relations with others and help people around them. A recent study has found that of particular interest to the subject of violent extremism and its prevention is the importance of jihad as a concept to uphold and openly discuss within communities (Spalek and McDonald, 2011). Conscious of the misuse and abuse of jihad as an Islamic principle by violent extremists and proponents of the new terror discourse, youth workers and community organizations can help to reclaim jihad, including its meaning in relation to physical struggle, as a positive and legitimate concept and action. It is also viewed as one of the central theological debates in challenging violent radical ideology and thus is a key tool in the process of 'deradicalization'.

At the same time, however, it is important to note that Chapter 7 also highlights how religious and religio-political perceptions can hinder cooperation with the police. A general feeling that Muslim communities are under suspicion and that their religion is blamed, along with a fear of individual and collective punishment for implication in terrorist plots, has caused, and continues to cause, reluctance to take a proactive role in counter-terrorism. At the same time, in some cases research participants recounted that within some Muslim communities *fatwas* – juristic opinions – have been issued against any such cooperation, or 'collaboration' as it is framed.

In this respect, future research could address the following key questions:

- How is the notion of jihad being reclaimed by communities and what implications does this have for counter-terrorism? Are there other examples of the relevance of religious knowledge to counter-terrorism?
- How are traditionally secular agencies like the police increasingly including religious minorities and identities in their work in relation to counter-terrorism?
- To what extent does increasing religious knowledge within those deemed at risk of violent extremism reduce the risk of violence?
- Are young people actively involved in religious institutions like mosques or do they feel alienated from them? How does this impact upon and influence prevention work that involves religious institutions?
- How important and how effective is religion, religious text and knowledge in work aiming to prevent violent extremism? How is it used? How important are religious institutions?

Counter-terrorism and transnationalism

So far, research in relation to community-based approaches to counter-terrorism has tended to be locally focused, so that any connections between local initiatives and broader transnational dynamics have been given little attention. Nonetheless, it might be argued that for international forms of terrorism, local counter-terrorism initiatives can only be understood in relation to socio-political dynamics taking place transnationally. Future research therefore needs to examine community-based initiatives aimed at countering Al-Qaeda- and Islamist-linked terrorism across a series of geographical locations in order to explore questions in relation to the role that transnational dynamics may play and the implications for programmes of intervention involving communities. For example, the Arab Spring has multiple implications for community-based approaches to Al-Qaeda-linked or influenced counter-terrorism, because as Islamists regain their freedom of speech and activity, this will impact upon their activities and ideology, and hence their perception locally and internationally will, in turn, impact upon the community, the state and international security. These dynamics will impact upon Muslim diasporas across the world, so that community-based counter-terrorism programmes currently taking place in many contexts across the world will need to take these revolutionary changes into account. Future research might explore the following questions:

- How does a focus upon transnationalism enable us to think more critically about the Arab Spring and its implications for community-based counter-terrorism interventions internationally?
- What implications of the Arab Spring are there for community-based programmes in the UK, the EU, the USA and other locations, and to what extent might these implications also matter for other countries involved in countering Al-Qaeda- and Islamist-linked terrorism?
- How are the political and social changes taking place in Egypt, Syria and other Arab countries affecting Islamists there and Muslim communities in the West, and what are the implications of these changes for community-based counter-terrorism programmes?
- How do communities, and those statutory agencies working with communities, draw upon broader global political, social and cultural dynamics in the counter-terrorism work that they undertake?

Conclusion

This chapter highlights some of the key areas that policy and research in relation to communities and counter-terrorism will need to increasingly address in the future. These areas straddle across wide-ranging disciplines like politics, sociology, sociology of religion, theology, criminology, international relations and social policy, illustrating the inter-disciplinarity of work broadly related to security. Empirical data addressing the set of questions highlighted in this chapter is essential for policy and practice to be evidence-based. This in itself is a significant undertaking, for counter-terrorism is an arena marked by distrust, thereby making data gathering more difficult, particularly when some communities may feel that they have been over-researched or over-scrutinized. It is important for researchers to engage in trust-building activities themselves in order to generate the kind of trust that is necessary to gain access to community members, police officers, policy makers and others. This is likely to be time-consuming work. Nonetheless, it is essential that a space for critical, rigorous and applied academic work is carved out because security is too important an issue to be left to policy makers, politicians and the media. Community-based approaches to counter-terrorism herald potentially innovative and exciting approaches to preventing terror crime. Nonetheless, significant tensions are likely to continue in relation to experiences and perceptions as to whether community-based approaches are community-focused or community-targeted and links here with 'top-down' and 'bottom-up' forms of governance. This book is the beginning of a long conversation and journey.

Note

1. The concept of 'ummah' might be thought of as comprising a global Islamic community that supersedes national or ethnic identities.

References

Beck, U. (1992) *Risk Society: Towards a New Modernity*. London: Sage.

Bowling, B. and Phillips, C. (2007) 'Disproportionate and Discriminatory: Reviewing the Evidence on Police Stop and Search', *Modern Law Review* 70(6): 936–61.

Brennan, T., John, P. and Stoker, G. (2007) 'Re-Energising Citizenship: What, Why and How?', in T. Brennan, P. John and G. Stoker (eds), *Re-Energising Citizenship: Strategies for Civil Renewal*. Basingstoke: Palgrave Macmillan, pp. 8–25.

Bridges, L. and Gilroy, P. (1982) 'Striking Back', *Marxism Today* (June): 34–5, www.amielandmelburn.org.uk/collections/mt/pdf/82-06-34.pdf (date accessed 10 June 2010).

Castells, M. (2004) *The Power of Identity*, 2nd edn. Oxford: Blackwell.

Clarke, M. and Soria, V. (2010) 'Terrorism: The New Wave', *RUSI Journal* 155(4): 24–31.

Cowan, R. (2004), 'Young Muslims "Made Scapegoats" in Stop and Search', *The Guardian*, 3 July, p. 8.

Dubois, D., Doolittle, F., Yates, B., Silverthorn, N. and Tebes, J. (2006) 'Research Methodology and Youth Mentoring', *Journal of Community Psychology* 34(6): 657–76.

Garfinkel, R. (2007) 'Personal Transformations: Moving from Violence to Peace', *United States Institute of Peace Special Report* 186, April.

Garland, J., Spalek, B. and Chakraborti, N. (2006) 'Hearing Lost Voices: Issues in Researching Hidden Minority Ethnic Communities', *British Journal of Criminology* 46: 423–37.

Hall, S., Critcher, C., Jefferson, T., Clarke, J.N. and Roberts, B. (1978) *Policing the Crisis: Mugging, the State, and Law and Order*. London: Macmillan.

Hanniman, W. (2008) 'Canadian Muslims, Islamophobia and National Security Royal Canadian Mounted Police', *International Journal of Law, Crime and Justice* 36(4): 271–85.

Hewitt, S. (2010) *Snitch! A History of the Modern Intelligence Informer*. London: Continuum.

Horgan, J. (2009) *Walking Away from Terrorism*. London: Routledge.

Innes, M. (2006) 'Policing Uncertainty: Countering Terror through Community Intelligence and Democratic Policing', *Annals of APSS* 605 (May): 1–20.

Jefferson, T., Walker, M. and Seneviratne, M. (1992) 'Ethnic Minorities, Crime and Criminal Justice: A Study in a Provincial City', in D. Downes (ed.), *Unravelling Criminal Justice*. London: Macmillan, pp. 138–64.

Jones, T. and Newburn, T. (2001) 'Widening Access: Improving Police Relations with Hard to Reach Groups', Policing and Reducing Crime Unit: Police Research Series Paper 138, http://rds.homeoffice.gov.uk/rds/prgpdfs/prs138.pdf (date accessed 16 December 2011).

Kundnani, A. (2009) *Spooked! How Not to Prevent Violent Extremism*. London: Institute of Race Relations, available at www.irr.org.uk/pdf2/spooked.pdf (date accessed 16 December 2011).

Lash, S. (1994) 'Reflexivity and its Doubles: Structure, Aesthetics, Community', in U. Beck, A. Giddens and S. Lash (eds), *Reflexive Modernization: Politics, Tradition and Aesthetics in the Modern Social Order*. Cambridge: Polity Press, pp. 110–73.

Loader, I. (2006) 'Policing, Recognition and Belonging', *Annals of the American Academy of Political and Social Science* 605(1): 201–21.

Lowndes, V. and Thorp, L. (2010) 'Preventing Violent Extremism – Why Local Context Matters', in R. Eatwell and M. Goodwin (eds), *The New Extremism in 21st Century Britain*. London: Routledge, pp. 123–42.

Macpherson Inquiry (1999) *The Stephen Lawrence Inquiry, Report of an Inquiry by Sir William Macpherson of Cluny*, Cm 4262-I. London: The Stationery Office.

McGhee, D. (2005) *Intolerant Britain? Hate, Citizenship and Difference*. Maidenhead: Open University Press.

Modood, T. (2007) *Multiculturalism*. Cambridge: Polity Press.

Mythen, G. and Walklate, S. (2006) 'Criminology and Terrorism', *British Journal of Criminology* 46(3): 379–98.

Pantazis, C. and Pemberton, S. (2009) 'From the "Old" to the "New Suspect" Community: Examining the Impacts of Recent UK Counter-Terrorist Legislation', *British Journal of Criminology* 49(5): 646–66.

Ramirez, D. (2008) 'Partnering for Prevention', www.northeastern.edu/law/academics/institutes/pfp/index.html (date accessed 16 December 2011).

Sharp, D. and Atherton, S. (2007) 'To Serve and Protect? The Experiences of Policing in the Community of Young People from Black and Other Ethnic Minority Groups', *British Journal of Criminology* 47(5): 746–63.

Silk, D. (2009) 'Outreach between Muslim Communities and Police in the UK: Preliminary Report'. See www.fulbright.co.uk/about-fulbright/meet-our-scholars/past-fulbrighters-case-studies/daniel-silk (date accessed 16 January 2012).

Sivanandan, A. (1981) 'From Resistance to Rebellion: Asian and Afro-Caribbean Struggles in Britain', *Race and Class* 23(2–3): 111–52.

Smith, D.J. and Gray, J. (1985) *Police and People in London. The PSI Report.* Aldershot: Gower.

Spalek, B. (2010) 'Community Policing, Trust and Muslim Communities in Relation to "New Terrorism"', *Politics & Policy* 38(4): 789–815.

Spalek, B., Davies, L. and McDonald, L.Z. (2010) 'Key Evaluation Findings of the West Midlands (WM) 1-2-1 Mentoring Scheme', www.birmingham.ac.uk/Documents/college-social-sciences/social-policy/IASS/news-events/west-midlands-1-2-1-evaluation-findings.pdf (date accessed 16 December 2011).

Spalek, B., El-Awa, S. and McDonald, L.Z. (2009) 'Engagement and Partnership Work in a Counter-Terrorism Context', University of Birmingham.

Spalek, B. and Imtoual, A. (2007) '"Hard" Approaches to Community Engagement in the UK and Australia: Muslim Communities and Counter-Terror Responses', *Journal of Muslim Minority Affairs* 27(2): 185–202.

Spalek, B. and Lambert, B. (2008) 'Muslim Communities, Counter-Terrorism and De-Radicalisation: A Reflective Approach to Engagement', *International Journal of Law, Crime and Justice* 36(4): 257–70.

Spalek, B. and McDonald, L.Z. (2011) 'A Study Exploring Questions Relating to Partnership between Police and Muslim Communities in the Prevention of Violent Religio-political Extremism amongst Muslim Youth', University of Birmingham.

Thacher, D. (2005) 'The Local Role in Homeland Security', *Law & Society Review* 39(3): 635–75.

Virta, S. (2008) 'Community Policing Meets New Challenges', in S. Virta (ed.), *Policing Meets New Challenges: Preventing Radicalization and Recruitment.* Tampere, Finland: University of Tampere, Department of Management Studies, CEPOL. pp. 15–41.

Waddington, P.A.J., Stenson, K. and Don, D. (2004) 'In Proportion: Race, and Police Stop and Search', *British Journal of Criminology* 44(6): 889–914.

Young, J. (1999) *The Exclusive Society.* London: Sage.

Index

CPSIA information can be obtained
at www.ICGtesting.com
Printed in the USA
LVOW13s2048170817
545395LV00019B/307/P